Swift to Battle

Swift to Battle

No. 72 Squadron RAF in Action
Volume 1: 1937–1942

Tom Docherty

Pen & Sword
AVIATION

First published in Great Britain in 2009 by
Pen & Sword Aviation
An imprint of
Pen & Sword Books Ltd
47 Church Street
Barnsley
South Yorkshire
S70 2AS

ISBN 978 1 84415 829 4

A CIP catalogue record for this book is
available from the British Library

Typeset in 10pt Palatino by Mac Style, Beverley, East Yorkshire
Printed and bound in the UK by the MPG Books Group

Pen & Sword Books Ltd incorporates the Imprints of Pen & Sword
Aviation, Pen & Sword Maritime, Pen & Sword Military, Wharncliffe
Local History, Pen & Sword Select, Pen & Sword Military Classics, Leo
Cooper, Remember When, Seaforth Publishing and Frontline Publishing

For a complete list of Pen & Sword titles please contact
PEN & SWORD BOOKS LIMITED
47 Church Street, Barnsley, South Yorkshire, S70 2AS, England
E-mail: enquiries@pen-and-sword.co.uk
Website: www.pen-and-sword.co.uk

Contents

Acknowledgements

I cannot stress enough how grateful I am to the following people for their contributions to this book. A large number of them served with 72 Sqn, and many are staunch supporters of the No. 72 Squadron Association. Those of you already familiar with the squadron will note several names in these acknowledgements of persons who are now deceased. I have included them in the list in grateful thanks for their contributions, which otherwise would be lost to history.

Matt Adams
A.E. Allen
A. Allsopp
Roy Anderson
John Augoustis
Mick Bajcar
Jim Barton
Jeff Bird
Ted Boakes
Eric Boddice
Brian Bond
Ken Boyd
Paul Bradley
Steve Brew
Darryl Briggs
Jack Browne Jr
Ernie Burton
Mrs Casey
Chris Charland
A. Chater
Matt Clague
Malcolm Clarke
John Clegg
Jim Corbett

Jimmy Corbin
Joe Dade
C. Davis
Keith Deary
Patrick Downer
R.D. Elliot
T.A.F. Elsdon
Greggs Farish
Richard Ferriere
Vic Flintham
Diana Foster-Williams
Laurie Frampton
Michael J Freer
Graeme Gillard
Richard Gledhill
Fergal Goodman
Des Gorham
Ernie Graveney
Eric Gray
R.H. Gregory
Betty Gridley
Hugh Halliday
Ian Haskell
Robert Hawkins

Ben Hitt
Tom Hughes
Angela Jobson
Jack Lancaster
David Lane
Bruno Lecaplain
K. Lindsay
R. Lindsay
P.D. Lodge
Alan Lowe
Donald MacLean
Erik Mannings
Angus Mansfield
P. McMillan
Ross McNeill
John Meddows
Ron Mitchell
G.M. Monahan
D.C. Nichols
Roy Norfolk
Cyril Nugent
Tony Peacey
M.A. Pocock
D.E. Pool
Peter Pool

Harold Powell
Glyn Ramsden
Mark Ray
R. Rayner
Bill Rolls
Robbie Robertson
Rodney Scrase
Wallace Shackleton
M.J. Shaw
Desmond Sheen
Cedric Stone
Bert Sweetman
Ken Summers
John Sydes
Tom Thackray
Simon Thomas
Piet Van Schalkywyk
Sean Waller
K.C. Weller
Henk Welting
Jerry Wilkinson
Steve Williams
Ray Woods
Keith Worrall
Irvine Wright

Preface

Ifirst considered writing the history of No. 72 Squadron in its entirety when I joined the squadron in 1993 and became the deputy squadron historian. At the time the squadron was in the early stages of forming a squadron association for both ex-air and ex-ground crew, from every period of its existence, as well as for serving members who wished to join. Since then I have been actively involved with the association as membership secretary, a post I still fill today.

Having collated a vast amount of information over this period and spoken to members of the association ranging in service from 1937 to the present, I realized that to cover the history in one book would not do it justice. The cost of such a book would put it out of reach of most buyers! Another reason I decided to limit the scope of the book was that from the late 1960s to 2002 No. 72 Squadron was actively involved in operations in Northern Ireland and much of its activities are still classified. It seemed logical, therefore, to look for natural breaks in the squadron's existence and cover that period in detail. Following a brief existence in World War I, and preceding its period as a support helicopter squadron, No. 72 Squadron existed as a fighter unit, both day and night, for a period of twenty-five years from 1937 to 1961.

This volume is a humble effort to record the history of the squadron during the period 1917–42 using official records and the reminiscences and recollections of those who lived and breathed No. 72 Squadron through this period of its life. Volume 2 will cover 1942–61. I hope that fellow historians will find it a useful reference and that the reader will enjoy the story of a famous squadron and its men.

T.G. Docherty
Forres
2008

CHAPTER ONE

World War I and Re-formation

W hen the First World War commenced in 1914 the Royal Flying Corps (RFC) was a very small part of the British Army and was equipped with a wide variety of flimsy biplanes, used in the main for artillery spotting and reconnaissance. By 1917 the RFC was a very different organization and had grown from the original small number of squadrons to over 100 operating some of the most advanced aircraft of the period.

It was in this expanded and still expanding RFC that No. 72 Squadron was formed on 28 June 1917. Commanded by Capt H.W. Von Poellnitz, the squadron was based at Upavon in Wiltshire and was equipped with Avro 504 trainers that it had brought with its nucleus of men and equipment from 'A' Flight of the Central Flying School. The squadron had a training role at this point, and soon added the highly regarded Sopwith Pup to its inventory, training scout pilots for the Western Front. The squadron moved to Netheravon and then to Sedgeford in Norfolk, where it began preparations to move to Mesopotamia for operations against the Turks.

After a long journey by land and sea the squadron arrived in Basra and was joined by seventeen flying officers from Egypt. The squadron received two types of aircraft as its equipment – the monoplane Bristol M1C, which despite official prejudice proved itself to be a very successful fighter type, and the Martinsyde G.100 Elephant, a slow but forgiving fighter/reconnaissance type. It was with these two types that the squadron fought a successful campaign in support of the Army.

With the formation of the Royal Air Force (RAF), 72 Sqn continued to serve in Persia, Mirjana and Samarra, before being recalled to Baghdad, where it was reduced to a cadre in February 1919. By September 1919 the rapid run-down of the RAF was in full swing, and among those to disband was 72 Squadron on 22 September 1919.

Maj H.W. Von Poellnitz. (72 Sqn)

Ground crew enjoying mounted wrestling during squadron sports, Christmas 1918. (72 Sqn)

Pilots looking on as the ground crew do battle, Christmas 1918. (72 Sqn)

The RAF was to suffer many lean years throughout the 1920s and early 1930s, but the possibility of another war was looming: with the blatant rearmament of the German armed forces following Adolf Hitler's Nazi Party's rise to power, all that was to change. The RAF began a planned series of expansions, each one being rapidly overtaken by events, and finally, on 22 February 1937, 72 Squadron was re-formed. The story that follows is the history of No. 72 Squadron and its

The squadron observes the arrival of the first Handley Page 0400 bomber in Mesopotamia in 1918. (72 Sqn)

Lt Leech and Lt Carrol in Mesopotamia on 1 April 1919. (72 Sqn)

Sgt H.L. Howard photographed in Baghdad in 1919. (72 Sqn)

'C' Flt 72 Sqn Bristol M1Cs at Baghdad in 1918. At the time the flight were attached to 3rd Corps. (72 Sqn)

72 Sqn Bristol M1C viewed from the rear. (72 Sqn)

72 Squadron camp at Baghdad in 1918. (72 Sqn)

72 Sqn aircraft in captured Turkish hangars, Baghdad 1918.

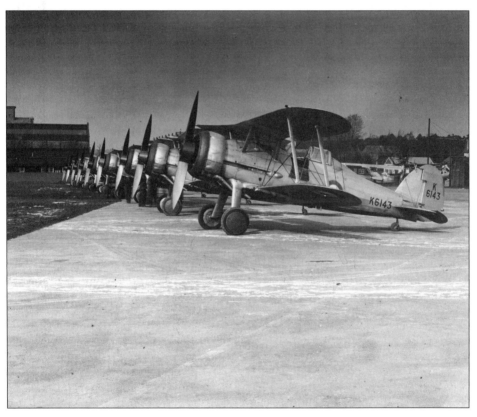

72 Squadron's new Gladiators, K6143 to the fore. (72 Sqn)

Another view of the new Gladiators. (72 Sqn)

72 Squadron Gladiators at Tangmere in 1937. (L. Henstock via 72 Sqn)

The Gladiators paraded outside the squadron hangar at Tangmere in 1937. (L. Henstock via 72 Sqn)

Spitfire prototype K5054 at Tangmere in 1937. A portent of things to come. (L. Henstock via 72 Sqn)

twenty-five years of unbroken service as one of the premier fighter units of the RAF.

As with most squadrons which were re-formed during this expansion period, the nucleus would be provided by air and ground crews from established squadrons; 72 Sqn was no exception. The squadron destined to provide that nucleus was No. 1 Squadron, which at that time was equipped with the last of the line of sleek Hawker biplanes, the Fury. The pilots of 'B' Flt, 1 Sqn, were initially not very keen to leave as it was rumoured that the squadron was to be shortly re-equipped with the new Hawker Hurricane. Nevertheless, the flight commander, Flt Lt E.M. Donaldson, took his pilots to Gloster's factory to collect the first Gladiator biplane fighters to join Fighter Command. Donaldson returned to 1 Sqn after four months with 72 Sqn. Over the

Plt Off L. Henstock. (L. Henstock via 72 Sqn)

following months the pilots became used to their new mounts and the ground crew became familiar with the servicing requirements.

Just one month before the squadron re-formed, Hitler had renounced the Treaty of Versailles, which had stood since 1919, and thus began the inevitable descent into war. By May 1937 Britain had a new Prime Minister in Neville Chamberlain, but he would prove to be ineffective in dealing with Hitler, and easily duped into believing Hitler's lies and posturing.

No. 72 Sqn shared Tangmere with three other fighter squadrons – 1, 43 and 87. On Empire Air Day, 29 May 1937, all four squadron took part in a four-hour flying display during which the crowds were thrilled by demonstrations of fighter interceptions, aerobatics, air drills and ground attacks.

Finally, in June 1937, now commanded by Sqn Ldr E.J. Hope, 72 Sqn moved to its permanent station at RAF Church Fenton in Yorkshire. Here the squadron shared the airfield with 213 Sqn, which was still operating the Gladiator's predecessor from the Gloster stable, the Gauntlet. During this period the squadron was presented with its badge,

The cockpit of Gladiator 'R' of 72 Sqn. (L. Henstock via 72 Sqn)

Gladiator K6138 at Tangmere in 1937. (L. Henstock via 72 Sqn)

K 6140 F.O. HENSTOCK
K 6142 F.O. HUMPHERSO
K 6143 F.O. SHEEN

Gladiators K6140, K6142 and K6143 flown by Flg Off Henstock, Flg Off Humpherson and Flg Off Sheen respectively, Tangmere 1937. (L. Henstock via 72 Sqn)

The tail of a Gladiator marked with the 72 Sqn Swift inside the standard 'fighter squadron arrowhead'. (72 Sqn)

Flight mechanic LAC Jimmy Hess in the cockpit of Gladiator K6138 at Tangmere. (A. Allsopp)

Gladiators K6135, K6134 and K6130 at Church Fenton in 1937. (72 Sqn)

Gladiator K6140 at Church Fenton in October 1937. (72 Sqn)

signed by King George VI, by Air Marshal Sir Hugh Dowding. Dowding and 72 Sqn would be linked again during the Battle of Britain.

Les 'Ginge' Dwyer was among the first ground crew posted to 72 Sqn at Tangmere. and recalls the early days with the Gladiator:

After training as a fitter's mate at RAF Manston and then as a flight rigger at RAF Henlow I was posted to 43(F) Sqn at Tangmere, and prior to helping form 72(F) Sqn was a flight rigger on Hawker Fury K1932, Sgt 'Tich' Carey's kite. [Carey fought with distinction in the Battle of Britain and later became a group captain].

Having collected our quota of Gloster Gladiators we followed a Gauntlet squadron to open up the new station – RAF Church Fenton, where I was a flight rigger on K1940 of 'B' Flt. It was Flt Lt Edwards', our flight commander's kite, until I was posted onto a fitter IIa course at Hednesford. VC holder Nicholson was a pilot officer in 'A' Flt, a very tall lad. A very popular officer in 'B' Flt was an 'Aussie', Flg Off Des Sheen. He borrowed a Hawker Hart from somewhere and took a lot of the ground staff up for their first flip, and I was lucky to be one of them.

72 Sqn adorned its shiny new Gladiators with gaudy bands of red and blue atop the upper wing and along the fuselage sides, and took them to Farnborough in Hampshire for the 1937 Air Exercises. In addition to the red/blue markings the Gladiators were also adorned with fin and wheel hubs painted variously red, yellow or blue to denote each flight commander's aircraft. Following this, the squadron adopted the RAF peacetime routine and carried out training in individual pilot skills, formation flying and air gunnery from its base at Church Fenton. The squadron lost one Gladiator on 23 July 1937 when it crashed near

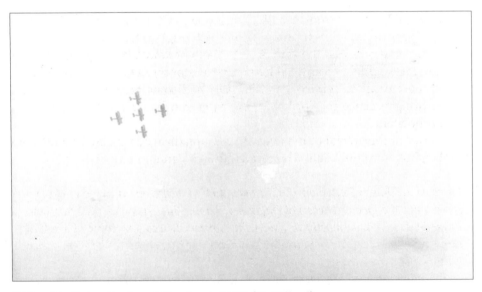

72 Sqn Gladiator display at Elmdon in 1937. (G. Gillard)

Ground crew with Gladiator K6143 at Church Fenton in October 1937, including Hess and Bluyer. (G. Gillard)

Barnsley, killing the pilot, Plt Off Philip Hughes Crompton. The Gladiator was an improvement on the earlier biplane types in RAF service, though the enclosed cockpit was not universally popular with pilots brought up in the days of open-cockpit flying, though they soon came to appreciate the protection the canopy provided from the elements.

Sqn Ldr J.B.H. Rogers replaced Sqn Ldr Hope as CO on 15 January 1938, and the squadron continued its training regime. Although a stable aircraft to fly, the Gladiator could bite, and the squadron lost another aircraft and pilot when Plt Off Alfred Alexander Devany crashed his Gladiator on 7 February near Brough. Like all new types to service, the Gladiator had some teething troubles, and during firing practice in April 1938 the squadron had a few problems with holed propellers.

Just prior to the arrival of the new CO the squadron had a new ground crew member, Bob 'Lupino' Lane, who recalls Church Fenton in those days:

I arrived at Church Fenton on 13 December 1937. I looked out at the acres of soggy snow amid the gloom. I was not impressed, having just spent the last two years in the Fleet Air Arm, mostly in the Mediterranean. It was something of a culture shock going into the 72 Sqn billet – bright lights, highly polished wood floor, central heating and spring beds!

The following morning found me in the hangar, where, amazingly, I didn't know a soul. My previous four postings had all been among folk I'd met, and here I found

I was in the new, expanded Air Force. We had either airframe mechs or engine mechs, whereas I was a metal rigger and it looked as though I would end up in the workshops until they found I could kick a football!

So began what to me – until 8 May 1939 – was the most friendly posting of my service. Everyone seemed to have a spare hand to help with and there was a lot of laughter. We had resident comics, like Wakefield and 'Perry' Como (who dived off a freight train that didn't slow enough at 4 a.m. wearing my new roll-neck sweater). Spud Murphy, an older guy, played football for Bootle JOC and had a chronic 'indigestion' problem which he relieved with his bottle of McLean's and a request for a 'spare ciggy'. He got posted to Leconfield later and achieved fame as Cheshire's rigger.

Other good mates were Willy Hughes, who worked for the Brabazon after the war, Graeme Gillard and Reg Eady. Spud Murphy always wanted a broom house with a blue-tiled bathroom, which he achieved after the war by marrying a greengrocer's daughter. Reg 'Ozzy' Osram ran the 'fag swindle and loan club' and saw we were never short. 'Griff' Griffiths, a married man with an Austin 7, ferried us back and forth at weekends and never failed us once. Then there were Dick Strickland; Reg Hanniset, whose uncle was 'Cassandra' of the Daily Mirror; Richardson, the orderly room clerk, who took many a 30 shillings (£1.50) from me for a weekend standby guard (last heard of he was a squadron leader), and his little mate, the runner, who was always there to put the aircraft away at night; Colin Jones, the 'Kid Glove Rigger' who always wore white gloves. He was an ex-Brighton Public School boy and cricketer, who sadly went down with a Sunderland in the Bay of Biscay just after the war started.

We had a big party when our badge was approved (I, incidentally, painted the first Swift on a fin, and was most surprised to find I could only paint the bird flying

Laurie Henstock and Des Sheen at Church Fenton in 1938. (T.A.F. Elsdon)

Three Gladiator pilots at Church Fenton in 1938. (D. Foster-Williams)

one way, and the starboard side would face backwards). All the old-timers back from the 1914–18 war were invited, and many brought trophies, scarves, silk stocking and crests like 'U bend 'em. We mend 'em'. There was much debate over the motto, and the first effort of 'Swiftly we come' was hooted out by the officers' ladies.

Monthly crew room parties were a feature, with beer donated by the pilots, and Nicholson frequently ended up wearing only pants, playing 'Scissor, stones, paper'. When I arrived the CO was sick and did not return. Sheen was adjutant before moving on to higher things. Flt Sgt Greenhaugh used to let me fly the Hart and Magister. Our new CO used to parade us at lunchtime throughout 1938 and interpret the news of war from The Times *and the* Telegraph, *and when Germany annexed Austria how we might have to go over as part of a League of Nations force. Our monthly flying hours were higher than any bomber squadron at that time.*

Fine as the Gladiator was, it was a product of a bygone era, and the pilots of 72 Sqn could only look on in envy as other squadrons were re-equipped with modern Hurricanes, Spitfires and Blenheims. They watched and waited as Hitler's troops marched into Austria in March 1938, ostensibly to quell 'public disorder', annexing this state the following day. While the country waited, some semblance of normality was maintained, and on 20 May 72 Sqn and 64 Sqn, which had replaced 213 at Church Fenton, put on a spirited air display at the station's first Open Day. Sadly, 29 June 1938 brought another loss to the squadron when Flt Lt William Forster Pharazyn was killed in a mid-air collision with another Gladiator. The delusion of normality, so fervently believed by many in the country, was rudely shattered in September 1938. On 23 September Hitler demanded that the Czechs evacuate the Sudetenland region. This demand brought about the period known as the 'Munich Crisis'. A week after Hitler had made his demand, the heads of state of Germany, Italy, France and Great Britain met in Munich and the RAF prepared to go to war.

No. 72 Squadron's shiny Gladiators soon lost their sparkle under a coat of camouflage paint and toned-down roundels. The overall silver was replaced with a dark green and dark earth disruptive camouflage pattern on the upper surfaces, and the under surfaces split into equal halves of black and white. The country held its collective breath as the politicians talked. Czechoslovakia was divided up and Chamberlain returned with a worthless piece of paper, the Munich Agreement, declaring that Hitler had no more territorial ambitions and that he held in his hand 'peace in our time'. The people of Britain breathed a sigh of relief, but the RAF and 72 Sqn continued to prepare for war as Hitler's army marched into the Sudetenland.

On 14 December 1938 Sqn Ldr Rogers was replaced by the airman who would ultimately lead 72 Sqn to war, Sqn Ldr R.B. Lees. By January 1939 Hitler was calling for the return of Danzig to Germany, while 72 Sqn busied itself with further training, including a visit to Aldergrove in Northern Ireland for an armament training camp at No. 2 ATS, utilizing the extensive range

H.M. DOWDING C in C PRESENTING NO 72 SQDN. WITH THE SQDN CREST SIGNED BY H.M. THE KING.

CHURCH FENTON 1937

The squadron on parade and receiving the squadron badge from MRAF Lord Dowding. (72 Sqn)

K8004

K 8004

72 Sqn Gladiator K8004 at Hooton Park on 9 September 1938. (72 Sqn)

Gladiator K6136 at Hooton Park in September 1938. (72 Sqn)

The squadron badge approved by the King in February 1938. (72 Sqn)

The NCOs of 'A' Flt with a Gladiator in 1938. (A. Allsopp)

72 Sqn in 1938. (G. Gillard)

facilities on the shores of Lough Neagh. Les Dwyer went with the Gladiators to Aldergrove:

> At Aldergrove with 72 Sqn on Gladiators we had a few props splintered until the armourers got their act together. We had our six weeks' practice camp there and enjoyed it very much, betting on who would finish on top of the daily target practice board.
>
> Four of us rowed across Lough Neagh (out of bounds) and came ashore at the 'Castle' [Shane's Castle], where the very old caretaker showed us around his greenhouses which were full of perfume-scented geraniums. We took snaps of the

row of cannon, but decided against an invitation to visit some dungeons. The café at Antrim hung out over the river and did teas with many varieties of super bread. Feasts to remember!

The only evidence of troubles when we were there was some bullet marks on the canteen, where some keen 'bod' years before had driven through the camp one Easter and sprayed a few shots as he went through.

Flg Off D.F.B. Sheen of 'A' Flt in Gladiator K6143 in formation with K6140 and K6142 during the summer of 1938. (72 Sqn)

Red Section of 'A' Flt, comprising K6140, K6142 and K6143. (72 Sqn)

Another view of K6140, K6142 and K6143 in formation. (72 Sqn)

A photo of the same formation. (T.A.F. Elsdon)

Formation of four Gladiators, K6130, K6131, K6142 and K6144, showing off the red and blue squadron bar marking on fuselage and wings. (A. Allsopp)

72 Sqn Gladiator formation: K6130, K6142, K6144, K6131 and K6134 show off the squadron red/blue upper wing and fuselage marking to good effect. (72 Sqn)

L to R: L. Henstock, unknown, unknown, Des Sheen, unknown. (T.A.F. Elsdon)

Flg Off L. Henstock with his ground crew. (72 Sqn)

Watercolour painting of Gladiator K6143, commissioned by Desmond Sheen in 1939. (D. Foster-Williams)

Desmond Sheen in mess dress pre-war. (T.A.F. Elsdon)

Desmond Sheen in civilian clothes pre-war. (T.A.F. Elsdon)

Gladiator K6131 in flight.

In March the German Army marched into Prague, and Czechoslovakia ceased to exist. The Poles continued to argue Germany's right to Danzig and the 'Danzig Corridor', and Hitler annexed German-speaking Memel. By the end of the month of March, Britain and France had declared their intention to jointly defend Poland against any aggressor. The battle lines were being drawn.

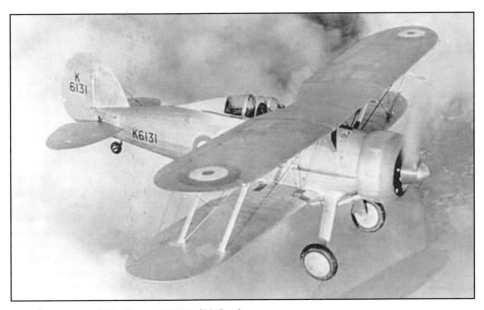

Another view of Gladiator K6131. (72 Sqn)

72 Sqn Gladiator K6132 in flight.

72 Sqn Gladiators, including K6135, lined up at Church Fenton. (72 Sqn)

Gladiators outside the 72 Sqn hangar at Church Fenton. (72 Sqn)

72 Sqn Gladiators lined up outside the squadron hangar at Church Fenton in 1938. (72 Sqn)

Gladiator K6133:F of 72 Sqn taxiing. (Glyn Ramsden)

72 Sqn Gladiators 'attacking' a Whitley bomber during an Air Defence of Great Britain (ADGB) exercise in 1938. (G. Gillard)

Three Gladiators attack the Whitley. (G. Gillard)

The Whitley involved in the ADGB exercise at Church Fenton in 1938. (G. Gillard)

The Munich Crisis brought about a hasty change of markings for the RAF, and aircraft began to lose the white part of the roundel and don dull camouflage colours. K7922 is not yet camouflaged but has the modified roundel. (72 Sqn)

Lysander K9646 following an unfortunate landing incident involving Flg Off Desmond Sheen. (72 Sqn)

Gladiator K6144 was abandoned in a spin and crashed at Monk Fryston, Yorkshire, on 1 December 1938. (72 Sqn)

Ground crew servicing Gladiator K9878, seen here with a mixture of pre- and post-Munich Crisis markings. (72 Sqn)

Two 72 Sqn Gladiators with different stages of camouflage and marking application. (72 Sqn)

The sun sets on the Gladiators at Church Fenton in 1939. (72 Sqn)

A fully camouflaged Gladiator at Church Fenton in 1939. (72 Sqn)

72 Sqn Gladiator RN-D showing the use of the RN codes for the first time in 1939. (72 Sqn)

Gladiator RN-S flown by Flg Off Nicholson, who would later be awarded the Victoria Cross. (72 Sqn)

Twelve-Spitfire flypast by 72 Sqn at the opening of Derby Airport in 1939. (T.A.F. Elsdon)

SD-coded Spitfire of 72 Sqn, by Ken Summers. (via L.J. Barton)

In April 1939, while the government began planning the 'call up' (compulsory military service), 72 Sqn at long last began to re-equip with modern aircraft in the form of the soon-to-be world-famous Supermarine Spitfire. The squadron immediately began working up to operational readiness, while keeping one eye on Hitler's moves.

Bob Lane recalls the arrival of the Spitfire:

The Spitfires began to arrive, ending up in the mud on their noses. Church Fenton is four feet below sea level. Peterborough of the Telegraph *boobed when he talked of 'Scorpion's Corner', with all the twisted props – ours didn't bend, they broke!*

Jimmy Elsdon with Spitfire Mk I SD-M (R.D. Elliot)

The squadron discipline corporal poses with a newly delivered Spitfire Mk I. (A. Allsopp)

Cyril Nugent also joined the Squadron around this period:

Passing out from Electrical Training School at Cranwell, my posting notice read 72(F) Squadron Church Fenton, and I arrived on 27 April 1939, coincidentally the CO's birthday, not much of a present. The hangar was full of aircraft, Gladiators, Spitfires and one Magister. The squadron was being re-equipped, and throughout April Spitfires had been delivered.

BRADFORD TELEGRAPH & ARGUS 9 JUNE 1939

R.A.F. Spitfire Bombers Thrill 50,000 Bradford Crowd With Mock Attack

Peel Park housed one of its largest-ever crowds last night, between 40,000 and 50,000 people attending the A.R.P. demonstrations held there in connection with the city's "Defence Week", which comes to an end to-morrow with a parade of mechanised forces.

The outstanding feature of last night's programme was a realistic mock bomb attack by three Spitfire bombers.

The proceedings began with a parade by the Bradford Air Cadet Squadron, at which the Lord Mayor (Alderman T.J. Robinson), accompanied by the Lady Mayoress, took the salute. The Lord Mayor afterwards complimented the cadets on their extreme smartness and efficiency and they certainly presented a striking spectacle in their neat uniforms as they marched four deep around the roped-off enclosure in which the whole of last night's events were staged.

AERO DISPLAY

Then came the high spot of the night – the aero display by five Supermarine Spitfire machines from Church Fenton. They were piloted by the men of the 72nd Squadron R.A.F., which is affiliated to Bradford, and they gave the crowd a thrilling impression of an actual air raid – without the bombs, of course.

Capable of a speed approaching 400 miles an hour, the 'planes gave ten different demonstrations of formation flying, beginning with the "arrow head " formation, then the "inverted U" and concluding their display with "W", "X" and "Y" flights.

The speed at which they travelled, their daring swoops and turns, held the crowd spellbound.

Two machines returned to Church Fenton, leaving three to give the city its first taste of "aerial warfare" – a mock bomb attack.

"INCENDIARY BOMBS" DROPPED

In the middle of the enclosure a "house" of wood and canvas structure had been erected. On it was piled highly inflammable material, and as the 'planes swooped down and over flames leaped from the windows.

An imaginary incendiary bomb had been dropped. (Actually the "house" had been lighted by someone on the ground). Then, when the flames had reached a fair height, the "alarm" was given, and on rushed a detachment of the Auxiliary Fire Brigade.

Hose was laid and the fire put out. Finally, in darkness, the 49th Anti-Aircraft Battalion R.E. (Bradford) put on a searchlight exercise, "spotting" and illuminating "enemy" aircraft as it flew over the park.

Between items of music was provided by the band of the 49th A.A. Battalion, and another interesting feature of the programme was the commentary from an R.A.F. van loudspeaker, this keeping the crowd in touch with the movements of the 'planes. The van, incidentally, contained wireless apparatus, by which the formation flights were directed.

The Lord Mayor, who was highly pleased with the demonstrations, made a short speech in which he appealed for more volunteers for National Service in Bradford. He said enrolments in the past few months had not been satisfactory and the city still needed something like 5,000 more volunteers. He hoped this week's events would have the happy effect of filling the gap in the city's defence forces.

Over 2,000 air wardens were required (450 of them women), nearly 1,100 men for first-aid parties, and 1,000 men and women as ambulance and motor drivers.

In addition there were still serious deficiencies in the strength of the auxiliary fire service. The auxiliary police service was now fully manned, but the police war reserve had 400 vacancies.

Members of Bradford National Service Committee also watched the display.

On 20 August Hitler announced to his generals his intention to attack Poland, and on the 29th he gave Poland an ultimatum on Danzig and the Corridor. On the penultimate day of the month the government began the evacuation of civilians from London.

On 1 September the Germans began the invasion of Poland and the RAF went onto a war footing. The government demanded the withdrawal of German forces from Poland, and when the deadline for acceptance of the demand was reached on 3 September Britain and France declared war on Germany. No. 72 Sqn was ready and waiting.

SD-coded Spitfire of 72 Sqn at Sydenham, Belfast, in 1939. (via Eric Gray)

Corporals Griffiths and Stark with Spitfire SD-F. (72 Sqn)

A massed assembly of Spitfires at Digby, including 72 Squadron's, in 1939. (72 Sqn)

CHAPTER TWO

Phoney War

No. 72 Squadron's war may rightly be said to have commenced on 24 August 1939, when the CO, Sqn Ldr Lees, received a secret cypher giving preliminary warning of orders for a dispersal of the squadron's Spitfires around the airfield. The order for mobilization followed on 1 September, giving the 2nd as Mobilization Day.

As part of this dispersal of aircraft, Sqn Ldr Lees, flying a Spitfire, and Flt Lt Graham, in the squadron's Magister, flew over to Church Fenton's satellite airfield to ascertain its suitability for Spitfire operations. Later that evening Lees was airborne again in an unsuccessful 1½-hour sortie in an attempt to locate a breakaway barrage balloon near Hull. This was to be the last peacetime sortie for the

Flt Lt E. 'Ted' Graham.

squadron. On the next day, 3 September, war was declared, and the squadron was ordered to prepare to move to its dispersal airfield at short notice. Desmond Sheen recalls the mood at Church Fenton on that fateful day:

Flt Lt E. Graham. (72 Sqn)

On 3 September at Church Fenton we were all listening to the radio, and learned that we were at war. The general reaction was that the waiting was over and that we should get on with it. It was then back to preparing aircraft shelters and getting to readiness states.

In the early hours of 4 September the squadron was ordered to prepare to take off and intercept enemy bombers in the first of many such alerts. The bombers, however, turned out to be friendly, and the pilots were stood down, with one section remaining on standby until relieved by 64 Sqn. For the remainder of the month the squadron waited vainly for action, while its strength increased daily with an influx of pilots, electricians, fitters, armourers, instrument repairers and flight riggers. Among the pilots posted in were Flg Off R.A. Thompson from 73 Sqn at Digby and Sgt M. Gray. While the squadron waited for the *Luftwaffe* the Germans rapidly crushed the brave, but outnumbered and poorly equipped Poles. By the end of the month the Polish government-in-exile was established in Paris and Hitler was planning his next conquest.

No. 72 Squadron's first 'victory' of the war was neither armed nor enemy – At 1205 hrs Flt Lt F.M. 'Hiram' Smith lifted his Spitfire from the Church Fenton grass to intercept a barrage balloon, which had broken away from its moorings. Forty minutes later he located the balloon and brought it down near Pateley Bridge.

Flg Off R.A. Thompson, who had been posted in on 4 September, found himself on the move again on 10 October, when he was detached to Northolt for an Air Fighting course. He was not the only one on the move, as the squadron was warned of a change of station on the 14th to Leconfield, beginning the move there the following day. By the 17th the whole squadron was established at Leconfield, and 'B' Flt was placed on standby that morning, beginning patrols and convoy escorts the same day.

The morning of 21 October dawned hazily, with the cloud base down to 800 ft. By early afternoon a convoy was making its way past Spurn Head and a plot was building in the control room, showing an enemy raid approaching the ships. Red and Yellow Sections of 'A' Flt were brought to readiness at 1410 hrs, and five minutes later they were scrambled to intercept the raid off Spurn Head. As soon as 'A' Flt was airborne, Blue Section of 'B' Flt weas brought to readiness. At 1430 hrs Green Section was scrambled, but only two Spitfires took off, flown by Flg Off Desmond Sheen (K9959) and Flg Off T.A.F. 'Jimmie' Elsdon (K9940). The third Spitfire had failed to start. Sheen and Elsdon were ordered to proceed toward Spurn Head, and were then turned to a position ten miles east of the convoy; meanwhile 'A' Flt had failed to find the enemy raid and returned to Church Fenton.

Sheen and Elsdon soon sighted a loose formation of bombers, identified as Heinkel He 115s, and turned towards them. The bombers, on sighting the approaching Spitfires, immediately turned north, and the Spitfires fell upon

Building a sandbagged dispersal. A: Flt Sgt Steere, B: Flg Off Pigg, C: Sgt Sam Staples, D: Sgt Winter. (72 Sqn)

Graeme Gillard and Calaghan at Church Fenton on 1 September 1939. (G. Gillard)

Plt Off O. St J. Pigg. (72 Sqn)

At readiness: Sgt Staples, Flt Lt Smith, Plt Off Robson, Plt Off Viller and Sgt Winter. (72 Sqn)

L to R: M. Smith, J.B. Nicholson, J.B. Humpherson, D. Sheen, O. St J. Pigg, R.A. Thompson, T.A.F. Elsdon. (T.A.F. Elsdon)

Sgt Hamlyn, Flt Sgt Plummer and Flt Sgt McKenna. (72 Sqn)

the rear formation of three bombers. The Heinkels gave up any semblance of a cohesive defence almost immediately, and scattered. Sheen and Elsdon made numerous attacks on the bombers, concentrating on four of them and shooting down two before they ran out of ammunition. Sheen only claimed his He 115 as probably destroyed, but it was subsequently confirmed that it had been destroyed. At this point a section of 46 Sqn appeared and continued the fight while Green Section returned to base. The bombers were from 1/KuFlGr406, seven of which were shot down by 72 and 46 Squadrons. Within minutes of landing, Green Section was rearmed and refuelled, and just over an hour later was on standby once more. Blue Section was scrambled again at 1700 hrs to patrol Flamborough Head, but this time without result. Desmond Sheen recorded the action in his logbook thus:

Ops. Green Leader – 12 Heinkel 115 intercepted. 2 damaged, 1 confirmed shot down.

Some time later Sheen was interviewed for the radio programme *In England Now* for the Empire Services. He told the listeners:

A bunch of 12 to 14 Heinkel 115 seaplanes were bombing a convoy. There were three of us on patrol. We attacked them, and got two of the Germans down. Then six Hurricanes came around and shot down another five. That was seven German aircraft and crews lost and nothing to show for it all. They didn't hit a single ship.

The following days were taken up with patrols and convoy escorts with no contact with the enemy; then, on 28 October 'A' and 'B' Flts were moved to Drem, near the Firth of Forth, leaving HQ Flt behind at Leconfield.

The first week of November saw 'A' and 'B' Flts operating from Drem, with HQ Flt and the ground crew remaining at Leconfield. HQ Flt was ordered to return to Church Fenton on the 7th, but the order was quickly rescinded and it remained at Leconfield. Over the coming weeks the pilots flew numerous patrols from Drem over the Firth of Forth and its coastline without result until the 22nd, when action appeared imminent. Red Section, Flg Off Nicolson (K9942), Sgt Hamlyn (K9925) and Sgt Winter (K9928), was scrambled to intercept a plot. The aircraft turned out to be friendly and they returned to Drem. Cyril Winter was born in South Shields and joined the RAF as an engine fitter in 1932, then applied for pilot training and was accepted. He joined 72 Sqn at Church Fenton and was commissioned in April 1940.

T.A.F. Elsdon. (T.A.F. Elsdon)

A group of 72 Sqn SNCOs, with Sgt Pocock on the left and Sgt Winter on the right. (72 Sqn)

The following day it was the turn of Yellow Section, once again led by Flg Off Nicolson (K9942) to intercept yet another friendly aircraft. That night an interception was attempted by Flg Off Henstock (L1056:RN-K) while patrolling over Drem at 5,000 ft. Despite the attempts of searchlight batteries to illuminate the raider, Henstock was unable to spot the enemy aircraft and was forced to return to base. Night interceptions were extremely difficult during this early part of the war. The intercepting aircraft lacked later refinements such as radar, and in the case of the Spitfire the pilots suffered greatly from degradation of their night vision from the glare of the engine exhausts.

On the third patrol carried out on 24th November, Red Section, led by Sqn Ldr Lees (K9958), was over May Island at 4000 ft when it was ordered to intercept an aircraft. Once again it turned out to be friendly, as was the case again on the 26th, 27th and 28th, when among other types a Hudson was intercepted. Enemy aircraft were hard to find, it seems, and the remainder of the month was taken up with unrewarded patrols.

HQ Flt finally relocated to Drem over the first three days of December, and the squadron began standing patrols in the Turnhouse sector, covering the Firth of Forth and Edinburgh. On 5 December Blue Section patrolled over Dunbar, and on the return to Drem Blue 3, Sgt Norfolk (L1078), had a very lucky escape while descending through cloud. Roy Norfolk recalled the incident:

Jack Steere and I were scrambled to intercept a bandit, but after spending some time above a thick layer of cloud and seeing nothing we were told to return to Drem. A female voice gave us a course to steer and notified us to descend. She did not tell us there was a hill of some 2,000 ft between us and the aerodrome. As we descended the conditions got blacker and blacker, and I told Jack I did not like it and was climbing and flying east to descend over the sea. Jack reached the same conclusion some seconds later, but as he altered the attitude of the aircraft to climb he made contact with the ground.

When I landed at Drem Jack had not returned, which worried me, but about ten minutes later he approached the aerodrome with his aircraft in a very sorry state, but it landed safely.

Desmond Sheen also recalled this incident:

In early December we moved to Drem, which was a good grass airfield in East Lothian, Scotland. Facilities were not particularly good at that time. Night operations were conducted from a caravan, and I think it was Roy Norfolk who was on duty one night and reported the weather to control as 'foggy', when it was in fact condensation on the windows!

Jack Steere, after being above cloud for some time, asked control if it was safe to come down. Being assured that he was over the sea, he let down, but on breaking cloud found himself heading into a hill. Pulling the stick back he climbed up the hill, taking quite a bit of undergrowth with him. Going over the top he returned to base, where it was found that both wings were so bent up I don't believe the aircraft flew again.

During this period friendly aircraft appeared to be the favourite types for interception, the *Luftwaffe* being conspicuously absent. On the 7th, Yellow Section intercepted a Hudson and the following day Blue Section encountered a Spitfire and Gladiator in the morning. By the afternoon the situation had changed and the *Luftwaffe* was on its way. Just after midday 'B' Flt was scrambled to patrol over Montrose, leaving Blue 3 behind when his engine failed to start. They were informed that seven enemy aircraft were flying south along the coast near Montrose, and they sped to meet them. Just north of Arbroath two formations of Heinkel He 111s, one of four, the other of three, were sighted. As the Spitfires approached, the Heinkels closed formation and descended to sea level. 'B' Flt split into sections, and Green Section, Flg Off Henstock (K9935), Flg Off Jimmie Elsdon (K9940) and Sgt Roy Norfolk (K9938), went after the leading element of the enemy formation. Flg Off Desmond Sheen (K9959) and Flt Sgt Steere (L1078) of Blue Section attacked the rear element of bombers. After the initial section attacks it quickly became a free-for-all, with the whole flight concentrating on the rear formation of Heinkels. The only exception to this was Flg Off Elsdon, who continued to take on the leading formation single-handedly. He continued to attack until he ran out of ammunition.

The rear formation of bombers put up a strong defence, and Desmond Sheen was wounded twice in the leg and narrowly avoided being killed when a bullet smashed through the sliding canopy of his Spitfire, hit the earphone of his helmet, smashing it completely, and left the aircraft through the same side of the canopy. Sheen was determined to continue the attack, but fumes from a holed

'RN'-coded 72 Sqn Spitfire in winter 1939. (72 Sqn)

fuel tank were so bad he was forced to break away. Sheen put down at Leuchars and was quickly speeded away by ambulance to hospital in Edinburgh. The remainder of the flight returned to Drem, where they compared notes. None of the Heinkels were seen to go down, and it appeared that 72 Sqn had come off worse, with Sheen wounded and Henstock and Elsdon returning with damaged aircraft. It was subsequently discovered that two of the bombers had failed to return. The formation of He 111s was from *1/KG26* and had been attacked by 72 Sqn and 603 Sqn. The two bombers lost were shared between both squadrons and Flg Off Elsdon was credited with a share in both. Sheen was awarded a one-third share. Desmond Sheen noted the action in his logbook:

Ops. Blue Leader. 7 Heinkel 111 intercepted. Wounded ear & thigh. FCC LDD [force landed] Leuchars. 2 Heinkels shot down.

Once again Desmond Sheen was heard on the radio relating the events of the dogfight:

It was in early December, five of us in Spitfires were patrolling off the east coast of Scotland. Suddenly we saw seven Heinkel 111s coming towards us. They were almost dead ahead, flying south, and very low towards the Firth of Forth. It was a hazy day, visibility was by no means perfect and it was rather cold. The time was about midday. The enemy bombers, as I told you, were already flying low, but as soon as they saw us they dived even lower, to sea level, which means about 50 ft. The reason for this is that if they got near enough the sea we wouldn't have been able to get underneath to attack them from below. As soon as they got down they turned east, for home. We went after them, and after the first attack one of the Heinkels dropped his undercarriage, a sure sign of distress. He began to lose height and we turned our attention to the other three. We circled to come at them again, and during our sweep around we were below the top of a lighthouse which is on a rock about fifteen miles out to sea. That lighthouse keeper certainly had a grandstand view of the fight. We finished the turn and attacked the Germans again. I once more went for the Heinkel on the extreme right, but the other three turned their guns to attack me. My victim had ceased firing, and was losing formation, but I was caught in the enemy's crossfire, and stopped a couple of bullets. One of them went through my earphones, and the other got me in the thigh, though it wasn't much of an injury. The first one cut my ear and made it sing for quite a time, but it seems all right now. The most serious of all was a bullet in my fuel tank. The petrol began to stream into the cockpit, and I couldn't see very clearly. I went in again to attack, but I was dizzy now and decided to turn for home. I was then only thirty to forty feet above the sea, and I was told later that the fight had finished only fifteen feet above the water.

Desmond Sheen spent a month in hospital before rejoining the squadron. Roy Norfolk recalled the attacks:

Although we expended all our ammunition, only two aircraft were destroyed. This did not please 13 Group so they instigated an inquiry, which was taken by the CO of 111 Sqn, Sqn Ldr Harry Broadhurst, who was also at Drem. He concluded that we did not do very well but put down our failure to the very dispersed bullet group in use at the time, which covered about 20 ft wide and 3 ft high. He recommended that the eight guns should be focused at 300 yd, and this was accepted. From then on I think all Spitfire and Hurricane guns were re-focused, and I am sure this had a great influence on the success of these aircraft in the Battle of Britain.

After the combat an unnamed He 111 gunner wrote of his part in the running battle (recorded here verbatim):

Fly over North Sea, Scotland, Firth of Forth to see if battleships there. Also this day, as we were lacking experience, we were flying low – 500–600 m [1,600–2,000 ft]. All quiet over Scotland as usual. Came down from the north over Aberdeen. As we did so I received code message, three letters only, meaning 'Careful, you have been detected by the defence.' Don't know how they knew this. I passed message to Staffel Kapitan in my own aircraft. Staffel Kapitan said, 'Oh, rubbish! The English defences are no good.' This, because it was always quiet over Scotland. But just to be on the safe side he went up to 1,200 m to approach Firth of Forth. Staffel Kapitan said, 'We won't go back – we haven't fulfilled our mission – we will go on to the Firth of Forth.' However, he took the precaution of flying higher.

Then as we came to Firth of Forth, I was sitting in the rear cockpit and I saw a Staffel [8 or 9] Spitfires high above us, I passed this to Staffel Kapitan: 'Behind us fighters!' Staffel Kapitan said, 'All right, we turn away to North Sea, because we can fly for a long time, they can't. We'll have to shake them off.'

I passed this message to the two other aircraft of our Kette [the Kettenhunde – chained dogs] to close in on us. The moment we were closing, the Spitfires dived down almost vertically on them. Stern attack. The Spitfires let fly what they had – it was a hell of a lot – and I let fly with what I'd got. One of the Spitfires I fired at, I noticed, I had in gun sight and really let him have it – something came out of him, smoke, or something – he went down and made for the coast..

No, nervous I was not. Only the first time – the attack on ships in Skagerrak in September. I've always been an excellent shot. But it came as a complete surprise to me to see they had cannon. It was my first close combat with Spitfires. Now what we did at that time was this – we never put on our parachute, but simply sat on it. Rather fall into the sea than fall into the hands of the English. Partly it was propaganda, what we had been told, partly it was because when you are a POW you are out of it all, can't fly again; I'd rather be drowned.

The other Spitfires closed in on both beams. I couldn't pay much attention to the other He 111s. Spitfires came from above and rear – fired – dived past – climbed up – and attacked again in the same way. Just for a fraction of a second I looked back at the two **Kettenhunde**, left and right, and noticed that in the rear cockpit of the aircraft on the right side, the machine-gun was just wobbling up and down, and no fire. Assumed gunner was wounded or dead. A few seconds later the aircraft crashed – it turned away, diving slowly, then in increasing steepness until it went into the sea.

The aircraft on the left: rear gunner was a very young man, very inexperienced, slack and slow, and he hardly shot at all, so of course the Spitfires had great fun with him; they literally hung on to his tail before they tuned away – and only then would he shoot.

This machine was going slowly, due to all the hits, and as the battle progressed they were gradually pushing down closer and closer to the sea until they were almost touching the waves. Then it ditched, and we were all so low that we got the spray from the other machine as it ditched.

The crew baled out, but they didn't have a dinghy, but went in their Mae Wests, and the last I saw of them was their heads swimming in the water.

While this was going on, we were being attacked too, but the machine with the slow gunner attracted most attention from the Spitfires. I was practically out of ammunition. So I turned round and shouted to the **Staffel Kapitan**: 'All the ammo you have, back at once to me.' Rising excitement, jumping with excitement – all of us.

So the **Staffel Kapitan** got down on hands and knees and crawled along the catwalk between the bomb racks, carrying the ammo. Spits attacking all the time; no ammo at all now at the rear gun.

I took the ammo of the **Staffel Kapitan**, whipped drum on, fired; and as I was firing, cried out to **Staffel Kapitan**: 'More – quick!' So he crept back as fast as he could and brought more. You've no idea – the tension, absolutely nerve wracking!

This went on – firing, shooting, creeping – until I eventually hit the Spitfire. Spit turned away – don't know if it crashed in sea or reached the land, but it was smoking. This was the last attack; all Spitfires broke off and went home.

We relaxed, wiping sweat from our brows; the trousers of **Staffel Kapitan's** best uniform were worn through at the knees from crawling.

After the Spitfires turned away, we surveyed the damage in our aircraft – it looked like a robbers' cave. All the bits and pieces from ammo and drums, flying anyhow, were in the 'tub' [the lower gunner's position]. Aircraft itself also cluttered with it. The aluminium inside of the aircraft ripped and torn by bullets from the Spitfires. One of my fur boots felt a bit uncomfortable, so I took it off, tipped it upside down and an odd assortment of bullets from the enemy and my own cartridge cases fell out onto the floor with a clatter. But I had not been hit. (Boots very wide and floppy at the top; bits had fallen in). So I put my boots on again, calmly.

Now we were set, and turned back to the place where the other plane had ditched. They were still swimming, with their heads popping up and down. The He 111 had sunk. Crew swimming without their aircraft. We dived low and started to circle these chaps. I opened the floor hatch – and, of course, all the ammo drums, etc., came clattering out and sprayed into the sea. Then I stood with legs spread over the open hatch and dropped them out a dinghy, food, etc., also our own Mae Wests. Floatable food boxes too. Then we circled once more, waved the chaps goodbye and they waved back. We went home. Same day Air-Sea Rescue went out, but they were never found.

We ditched our bombs in the sea. During the return flight, low down, obviously bad hit, aircraft would not go up at all. I wanted to pass messages:

a) We have been in battle.
b) Two Spitfire hit.
c) One He 111 ditched, crew in water.

Give position of crew in water – for we might never get home ourselves.

The wireless didn't work at all. The D/F apparatus was our last chance to get home – no idea where we were or what course to fly. At that moment one motor stopped. Now, we thought, any moment we'll have to ditch. We were dragging along only 30–50 m above the sea. But with D/F got our position and direction to go. Expected any moment the machine to give out. Nearest airfield was Westerland, Sylt. We headed for it and reached it, making a belly landing. Counted holes in aircraft – 350 bullet holes.

Flt Lt 'Hiram' Smith's Spitfire
on its nose. (72 Sqn)

A second view of the same Spitfire with the ground crew working out how to get it back on an even keel. (72 Sqn)

Problem solved with a large number of ground crew and a series of ropes. (72 Sqn)

Acting Pilot Officer R. Deacon Elliot arrived at Church Fenton to join the squadron in December 1939 and found they were not there:

On 12 December I reported to the station adjutant RAF Church Fenton, the home base of No. 72(F) Squadron, only to find the squadron had moved to RAF Drem in Scotland. The next day I headed north over snow-covered roads in my 1936 Austin 7, eventually arriving intact but almost frozen. My room was in a long wooden hut and I soon had a fire going, which was most rewarding.

I felt rather lonely, a complete stranger in this entirely changed environment. A few weeks earlier from being just another fellow flying with the Royal Air Force Volunteer Reserve (RAFVR) and now an Acting Pilot Officer in a regular unit – a member of 72(F) Squadron. However, I was soon to discover I was not alone in this new venture; another VR acting pilot officer, 'Dutch' Holland, came in the following day. The next day we met the CO, an Australian by birth, who welcomed us to the squadron and made us feel very much at home.

Deacon Elliot recalled the extremely harsh conditions during the winter of 1939/40 and the difficulty in keeping the aircraft serviceable and ready to scramble at a moment's notice:

Plt Off Elliot DFC. (72 Sqn)

The winter of 1939/40 was particularly cold, and Drem, I am quite sure, was the coldest spot on earth. The aircraft, always in the open, were frequently covered by a film of ice, which to remove, using lead-weighted wire-bristled brooms, kept both pilots and the untiring ground crews constantly busy, especially in the early morning. Looking back and re-living some of the scrambles literally fills me with horror. Everyone alert, pilots in the dispersal trying to keep warm by an antiquated iron stove and playing 'Uckers' [a form of Ludo]. Ground crews who, always on their toes, were able to distinguish the familiar tone of the 'ops' phone, for a scramble, from the admin line. Then it would happen – Ucker board sent flying, pilots grabbing helmets, followed by a mad rush to their respective aircraft. Ground crews already there standing by battery starters. Engines bursting into life – not all; flat batteries meant starting by hand, a most exhausting operation. Now, aircraft starting to move with temperature gauges at minimum readings for take-off – full throttle straight out from dispersal – no runways to consider, ice on wings, temperatures still dangerously low, how they became airborne will remain a miracle to this day.

The squadron was often required to provide aircraft on night readiness to intercept incoming night raiders. Deacon Elliot was acting as aerodrome control officer on one such night when he almost came to grief at the hands of one of his fellow pilots:

Ground crew wrapped up against the winter cold, and aircraft hangared for protection from the elements, in the harsh winter of 1939. (72 Sqn)

The CO, together with Flg Off Oswald Pigg and one other, were scrambled just before dark. I immediately started to prepare the flare path for their return. I had just put the totem poles in position when I heard the aircraft back in the circuit and was requested to light the flare path without delay. As I was up that end I lit the head of the 'T' first, and just about to work down the main flare path, finally to switch on the Chance Light, there was an almighty crash behind me. Oswald Pigg, running short of fuel, thinking the first three lighted goosenecks were part of the main flare path, landed as usual to their right and completely smashed the totem poles, but fortunately with only comparatively minor damage to the aircraft.

Oswald St J. Pigg was the son of the vicar at Chatton, Northumberland, and had joined 72 Sqn on 27 November 1937.

The next possibility of action for 72 came on the 18th, when a formation of six bombers was reported approaching the Fife coast near Crail. Red Section, led by Sqn Ldr Lees (K9958), scrambled into a cloud base of only 200 ft to attempt to intercept the enemy formation. Before it could reach the enemy position the formation turned tail and fled eastwards. The remainder of the month was taken up with standing patrols and interceptions of friendly bombers.

The early days of the New Year were dank and foggy, and the squadron had been ordered to return to Church Fenton at the earliest opportunity. On the 7th a cannon-armed Spitfire arrived on attachment for experimental testing by Flt Lt Proudman. The fog persisted at Drem, however, and the squadron remained frustratingly inactive.

By the 10th the weather had improved and the squadron recommenced standing patrols and convoy escorts. Two days later the weather had cleared sufficiently for the Spitfires to depart for Leconfield, as Church Fenton was still fogbound. The road convoy left immediately, spending the night at Newcastle before proceeding directly to Church Fenton. The air party, comprising fourteen Spitfires, two Handley-Page Hannibals and a Magister, took off in the afternoon, leaving Proudman and his cannon Spitfire behind at Drem, and by mid-afternoon the squadron was at readiness at Leconfield. The following day all returned to Church Fenton. The remainder of the month was taken up with uneventful patrols.

The weather in February was little better than the preceding month, and the squadron continued to carry out inconclusive patrols, with no enemy aircraft in the area to enliven the days. Finally, on the 15th, it appeared that some action was looming. Green Section was airborne at 0840 hrs, ordered to patrol over Filey on the Yorkshire coast at 10,000 ft to intercept an unidentified raid. It was unable to intercept and returned to base. Later in the afternoon it was the turn of Red Section, which was patrolling at 18,000 ft when it was ordered to intercept and identify three aircraft. A few minutes later Green Section was airborne to lend support, but the three aircraft turned out to be Hurricanes.

Flg Off Henstock and Flg Off Hobson were posted to 64 Sqn on the 17th, and on the 20th the *London Gazette* carried the notice of the award of a Mention in Dispatches to Flg Off T.A.F. Elsdon. The preceding two months had been very quiet for the squadron. In contrast to foggy Yorkshire, Finland was putting up a brave fight against the Russians, while Russia and Germany were agreeing to supply each other with raw materials and military equipment, and HMS *Cossack* had carried out a daring raid on the prison ship *Altmark*, freeing 299 British prisoners. For 72 Sqn this period was truly the 'Phoney War'.

On 1 March there was a little more excitement when Yellow Section, led by Flg Off Nicolson, took off to investigate unidentified aircraft. They was to be disappointed again as they turned out to be friendly. The following day the squadron moved from Church Fenton to Acklington. Desmond Sheen recalls Acklington at that time:

> I was with 72 Squadron when they arrived at Acklington on 2 March 1940. The grass airfield was waterlogged and we had difficulty parking our aircraft. Subsequent movement was only possible with somebody hanging on the tail to stop the aircraft from tipping over. Jimmy Elsdon did on one occasion do a circuit of the airfield with Tom King on the tail. The CO, Sqn Ldr Ronnie Lees, managed to get hold of a few Gladiators, which we used for pre-dawn take-offs for convoy patrols. The take-offs in the dark were quite interesting.

Harold Powell was a member of the squadron ground crew in 1940 at Acklington, and recalls the incident involving Tom King:

> Tom King was taken aloft on the tail of a Spitfire (K9940:RN-Q); George Coggle was also with him at the time but decided to 'bale out' before it left the ground. George and I arrived late back from leave once, after missing a connection at Leeds station, and earned ourselves seven days confined to barracks. At the time the squadron was providing night-fighter cover over Newcastle and a detachment was flown to Newcastle airport (Woolsington) at dusk every day, so George and I volunteered to go. This got us out of camp and we also missed 'jankers' [defaulters] parade late at night and early morning.

Tom Thackray was an 18-year-old ground crew member with the squadron at this time, and recalls many of the events of the period:

> The squadron at that time was equipped with half Gladiators and half Spitfires, mainly with two-bladed propellers. We soon moved to Acklington and fitted the Spitfires with three-bladed de Havilland propellers (not constant speed but only fine or coarse pitch). I was with the major maintenance echelon in the hangar, not on the flights. Our flight sergeant in charge was called Harrap, which of course said quickly sounded like Arab, so naturally he was labelled 'Abdul', not within his earshot you understand. He had two sergeant assistants called Sgt Nelson and Sgt Rayment, who had his wings, but had been grounded, so he was now a fitter.

Before the Battle of Britain started we had to carry out a modification to the Spitfires, the fitting of armour plating onto the rear of the pilot's seat and headrest. Another modification we carried out was fitting fully constant-speed propellers; this made quite a difference to the power on ground runs of the engines. So much so that the tail of the Spitfire used to lift off the ground. This resulted in us fitters having to lie across the tailplanes to hold the aircraft down.

Due to the grass airfield at Acklington, two men had to lie on the tailplanes during taxiing into position for take-off. One day the pilot swung straight round into wind and took off. With the tremendous noise and dust, the poor 'erks' on the tailplane didn't realise for a second or two what was happening. Eventually, before the aircraft became airborne, one 'erk' dropped off, but the other clung on and suddenly found himself airborne lying across the tailplane of a Spitfire. The pilot did one circuit and on finding the tail heavy decided to come back in and land. After landing and coming to a halt an airman appeared and said, 'I've just done a circuit with you, sitting on the tailplane.' The pilot was dumbfounded to say the least. The airman's name was Tom King, ever after known as 'Ace' King. The 'erk' who dropped off the tailplane was more hurt than the one who stayed on.

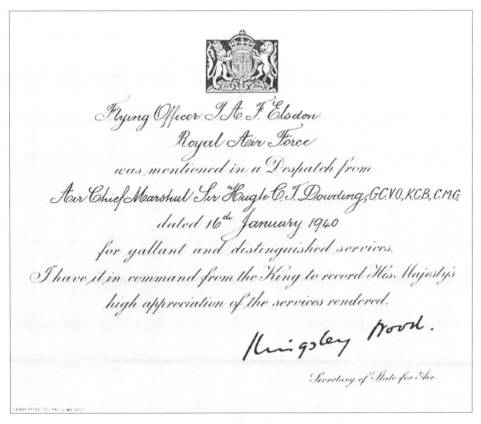

Flg Off T.A.F. Elsdon's Mention in Dispatches. (T.A.F. Elsdon)

Flt Sgt Law, Cpl Howden, George Coggle, Jimmie Garvie, Jimmie Spiers, George Price, Joe Garrett, Gillespie, Unknown, Harold Powell. (H. Powell)

A moment of relaxation at Acklington in 1940. Plt Off Winter, Flt Lt Smith, Plt Off Robson, Plt Off Villa and Plt Off Hogben (intelligence officer). (72 Sqn)

Spitfires RN-A and RN-M at Acklington. (72 Sqn)

Flg Off Pigg at readiness, Acklington, 1940. (72 Sqn)

Harold Powell and George Coggle with Spitfire RN-Q at Acklington. (H. Powell)

Flt Sgt Laws of 'B' Flt with Spitfire 'P'. (72 Sqn)

Pilots playing table tennis at readiness. (72 Sqn)

The pilots react to the 'Scramble' call. L to R, Sgt Winter, Flt Lt Smith, Flt Lt Graham and Sgt Norfolk. (72 Sqn)

The dash to the aircraft. (72 Sqn)

Flt Lt Graham climbs onto his Spitfire as the ground crew wait to strap him in. (72 Sqn)

Flt Lt Graham steps into the 'office'. (72 Sqn)

Ground crew hold onto the wingtips as the Spitfires taxi out from dispersal. (72 Sqn)

Spitfires taxi to the runway during a scramble. (72 Sqn)

Graeme Gillard was a corporal airframe fitter at Acklington with 72 Sqn during this period, and recalls several incidents there:

I was a regular airman and I joined 72 Sqn at Church Fenton in 1937, where we were still stationed when war broke out. Being a fully day and night operational squadron we were soon on the move to any danger areas, mainly on the east coast. We did a couple of tours at Acklington, by this time I was promoted as an airframe fitter to corporal. Being a regular, nearly all my worldly goods were with me, including my Brownie box camera. Cameras were forbidden, of course. I foolishly finished the film at Acklington and took it into a chemist at Ashington for processing. The proprietor must have been suspicious when he saw the photographs, and he took them to the authorities. This resulted in me being carpeted, but I was not dealt with too harshly as I explained that the camera was no longer on camp. I was allowed to keep the photographs.

During our stay at Acklington we had a reasonable amount of 'off-duty' periods and enjoyed the pleasant surrounding area and people. My favourite place was Ashington, where we were made to feel at home; trips to the pictures, the Princess Ballroom, skating rink and the working men's clubs, where we could get beer and a Drambuie for 7d (3p). If our transport back to camp had left, leaving us stranded, we were always welcome to stay at some miner's house for bed and breakfast.

Graeme Gillard was another witness to the tail-borne flight of Tom King:

My job as corporal fitter at this time, after the daily aeroplane servicing, was to supervise the take-offs. An air test was required on one Spitfire and two airmen were detailed to strap the pilot in and then to hold the tail down while the pilot checked his 'revs'. Normally the ground crew would have been waved away. In this instance the pilot, Flg Off Jimmy Elsdon, started to move, not realizing that the two men were still in

Sqn Ldr Lees tries to relax with a book while on readiness at Acklington in 1940. (72 Sqn)

Flt Lt 'Hiram' Smith rests in the flight hut while on readiness at Acklington in 1940. (72 Sqn)

position on the tail. George Coggle, the flight comedian, jumped or fell off after a few yards and suffered a bruised back. I looked on in disbelief at the sight of Tom King still wrapped around th · fin and tailplane as the aircraft took off. The worst thought was in my mind and I really expected him to fall off.

Fortunately the situation had been seen from the control tower and the pilot was told to return to the airfield, which he did, making a perfect landing. Tom seemed quite unruffled. He was taken away in the ambulance for a check-up, and was soon back at work saying that he couldn't have fallen off and would do it again for a fiver [£5]. He got all sorts of nicknames afterwards, mainly 'Ace' King or 'Clem John' (the man who was trying to free fly at that time). He was, of course, much sought after by local girls.

Joe Garrett, another ground crew member, witnessed Tom King's predicament and tried to avert the potential disaster:

I had got my kite scrambled, and seeing what was happening ran like hell to another aircraft nearby on readiness, grabbed the helmet, depressed the transmit button and called the pilot about to take off to alert him of the situation. But to no avail – the jack plug was not inserted into the socket. I then received a severe reprimand and threat of 252 [charge] action for making unauthorized use of R/T equipment AND then got a commendation for showing great initiative.

After a series of patrols and convoy escorts over the next few days it fell to Green Section, on the 7th, led by Desmond Sheen, to intercept two aircraft plotted sixteen miles east of the Farne Islands, off the Northumberland coast.

Pilots at readiness, Acklington 1940. L to R: Unknown, Flg Off Pigg, Sqn Ldr Lees, Sgt Gray, Plt Off Robson. (72 Sqn)

The two aircraft were identified as friendly Whitley bombers. Later in the day Yellow Section had an equal lack of success when it was ordered to intercept a plot while patrolling Blyth. Once again action had eluded the squadron.

The weather in March was still bad, and by the 10th the airfield was in a terrible state, making it dangerous to operate Spitfires. The squadron was issued with a number of Gladiators, a type it had given up some years before, in order to continue operations from the muddy airfield. While Finland and Russia agreed an uneasy peace and the *Luftwaffe* bombed Scapa Flow anchorage in the Orkneys, uneventful patrolling continued, and on the 13th the squadron received orders that all aircraft were to be flown to Thornaby each night for dispersal and return to Acklington in the morning. This, of course, put an additional strain on the overworked ground crews trying to keep the aircraft serviceable.

The dispersal to Thornaby ceased on the 19th, and spirits were further buoyed by the news of a raid on the German seaplane base at Hornum on the island of Sylt in reprisal for the attack on Scapa Flow.

Sgt Winter was granted a commission in the rank of pilot officer on 1 April, but he was probably wondering how long he would have to enjoy it, as the 'Phoney War' became a little less phoney on 2 April, with Hitler giving the

Flt Lt 'Hiram' Smith, OC 'A' Flt at Acklington in 1940. (72 Sqn)

Sqn Ldr Lees, far right, visiting the sergeants' mess at Acklington. (72 Sqn)

Spitfire RN-B on its nose at Acklington in 1940. (72 Sqn)

order for the invasion of Norway and Denmark. The invasion of both countries commenced on the 9th, and over the next week the Royal Navy was engaged in fierce battles with the *Kriegsmarine*. The whole of April was taken up with interceptions of unidentified aircraft, all of which turned out to be friendly, and a series of uneventful convoy patrols. Flg Off Desmond Sheen, who had been with the squadron since 1937, was posted out on 20 April to 212 Sqn at Heston. He would be involved in some very dicey reconnaissance operations in France with this unit.

May 1940 saw a rapid withdrawal of British forces from Norway. Almost immediately 4,000 Norwegian troops had surrendered at Lillehammer, followed a few days later by the decision to withdraw British troops, leaving only a small force at Narvik, in the hope of preventing Norway's iron ore supplies falling into German hands. By the 5th the Norwegian government had gone into exile in London and the campaign was all but over. As the pilots and ground crew of 72 Sqn absorbed this information over the next few days and pondered their futures, the Germans commenced the *Blitzkrieg* in the West, quickly overrunning Holland, Belgium and Luxembourg. By the middle of the month the impregnable fortress at Eben Emael had been captured and Rotterdam had been subjected to 'terror' bombing, bringing about the collapse of Holland. German troops crossed the Meuse on the 13th and were on the Channel coast by the 20th, precipitating the evacuation of the British Expeditionary Force from Dunkirk, which began on the 26th.

Tom Thackray remembered the days preceding, during and after Dunkirk:

We fitters would maintain the pilots' cars for them and they would loan them to you if they were on standby, provided you put some petrol in. Naturally they were filled up with 100-octane aviation fuel. Not too good for the engines, but better than nothing. One day a fitter was filling up a car from a 400-gallon bowser, when suddenly the lot caught fire. Car and bowser were burnt out. Luckily the adjutant was a good chap and managed to smooth it all out with no charges being brought.

The ground staff had to do duty as aerodrome defence, and we had designated positions around the 'drome. Every time the sirens went it was 'action stations'. As

Ground crew at Acklington in 1940. (72 Sqn)

there were not enough rifles to go around we were issued with aircraft screw pickets (used to anchor aircraft down in windy weather). Not long after Dunkirk an Army officer used to have us on parade for training in aerodrome defence, complete with rusty old screw pickets at the slope. You can imagine the remarks when he told us they must be cleaned before the next parade.

For 72 Sqn May started as April had ended, with boring convoy patrols and fruitless interceptions of friendly aircraft. While the fighter squadrons of the BEF Air Component and the Advanced Air Striking Force (AASF) combined with those of No. 11 Group to provide cover for the withdrawal from Dunkirk, 72 Sqn continued to patrol the north-east from Acklington. The only light in an otherwise dismal month was the award of the DFC to the recently posted Desmond Sheen. Spitfire K9925 was stalled, the undercarriage collapsed and the Spitfire cart-wheeled on approach to Woolsington on 26 May 1940. Deacon Elliot witnessed some excitement during a supposedly routine journey to Cosford to collect some new Spitfires:

We were to get some new Spitfires from the MU at Cosford. Two Magisters set out, Flg Off Bob Walker and Sgt Pocock in one, Plt Off Robson and myself in the other. We landed at Cottesmore for fuel, but on landing Bob's aircraft decided to make a vicious swing slap into the nose of a new Hereford bomber. I must say it was a sorry sight, but with its humorous side. The Maggy's prop reduced to the boss and two jagged wooden stubs, the bomb aimers compartment of the Hereford dangling glass and aluminium and Bob Walker just sitting there with an expression on his face of complete bewilderment – 'Who? Me?' The Spitfire I collected was the first I had flown with the automatic undercarriage control replacing the awful pump handle on the earlier models.

With the collapse of France, Britain now stood alone, and things were about to become decidedly hot around the south of England. The country braced itself for the invasion and 72 Sqn was ordered south to Gravesend in Kent to bolster the defences against the imminent German onslaught.

Sqn Ldr Lees led the squadron south, and they landed at Gravesend in the afternoon of 1 June. Lees immediately took command of the station from the CO of 610 Sqn, which immediately left for Acklington. AVM Sir Keith Park, AOC No. 11 Group, was there to meet them, having just landed from a solo flight in his personal Hurricane. Immediately on arrival the squadron came to readiness.

The squadron made its first offensive patrol from Gravesend at 1940 that evening, twelve aircraft taking off, in company with four from 66 Sqn, led by Sqn Ldr Lees. As they patrolled the Kent coast they could see the fires of Dunkirk still burning across the Channel. The following day Plt Off Elliot and Sgt Else, who had remained behind at Acklington, flew down to rejoin the squadron. Plt

LONDON GAZETTE – 7TH MAY 1940

"The King has been graciously pleased to approve the following award. Awarded the Distinguished Flying Cross.

Flying Officer Desmond Frederick Burt Sheen (39470).

This award was made for attacks on Enemy aircraft on October 21st, 1939, and December 7th 1939, details of which are in the operations book for those periods, and during which time F/O D.F.B. Sheen was a member of No. 72 Squadron. This is the second award to No. 72 Squadron, the first being when F/O T.A.F. Elsdon was Mentioned in Dispatches for the same attacks."

Off Elliot sprang a fuel leak on the way and both diverted to Halton, where Sgt Else crashed Spitfire L1077 on landing.

That evening, at 1840 hrs, the squadron scrambled twelve Spitfires in company with four from 609 Sqn to provide cover over the Dunkirk beaches, and in particular to protect a hospital ship off Dunkirk. One of the 609 Sqn aircraft was forced to land at Manston while on the way, and the remainder of the formation continued towards the patrol area. The troops on the beaches complained bitterly about the lack of support from the RAF, but unseen by them 72 Sqn and others were there stemming the bombers' assaults. Red Section took up patrol at 10,000–12,000 ft, with Yellow Section at the same height, but to seaward. Blue Section provided cover a further 1,000 ft above, with 609 Sqn even higher providing top cover at around 14,000–17,000 ft. For the next hour nothing was seen, and then a formation of six Junkers Ju

Desmond Sheen receiving his DFC from the King. (D. Foster-Williams)

75

An ancient Vickers Valentia was used to transport the squadron to Gravesend to support the Dunkirk evacuation. (72 Sqn)

87 Stukas were spotted approaching Dunkirk. Red Section attacked one section of three Stukas, which had begun their dive onto targets below, while Yellow Section was ordered to seek out the second section of Stukas. Unfortunately this order went unheard and it remained above. Meanwhile Red 1, Sqn Ldr Lees (P9548), fired two bursts at one of the Stukas, which was seen to go into a steep right-bank spiral. Lees closed on the Stuka and fired another, longer burst from 75 yards range. The Stuka immediately caught fire and was observed to crash by Red 2 and 3. Turning his attention to his next potential target, Lees spotted an enemy aircraft attacking Red 2, and fired his remaining ammunition at it. Red 2, Flg Off Pigg (K9924), was busy attacking another enemy aircraft, opening fire at 300 yards and closing in, firing all the way; he had the pleasure of watching his victim crash in flames. Breaking away from this fight, Red 2 was hit by MG fire from another Stuka which hit his starboard wing, damaged his port aileron control and the air pressure system. On his return to Gravesend he landed wheels up, as he had no brakes, flap or aileron control. As a consequence of the fight and the crash-landing, the Spitfire (K9924) was severely damaged.

Red 3, Flt Lt Smith (K9942), attacked a Ju 87 but was moving too fast and overshot his target. Luck was with him, though, and he quickly latched onto another Stuka. Opening fire at 200 yards he quickly silenced the Stuka rear gunner, and white smoke began to appear from its engine. Red 4, Flg Off Villa (N3221), observed the stricken Stuka turn over on its back and dive vertically, but he lost sight of it at 200 ft. The aircraft that Red 3 had overshot was trying to make good its escape, but was quickly latched onto by Villa, who fired his first burst at 400 yards. A tail chase then commenced, and Villa struggled to close on the aircraft over the next twenty miles, during which he fired all his ammunition. The enemy aircraft was last seen disappearing with white smoke issuing from its engine.

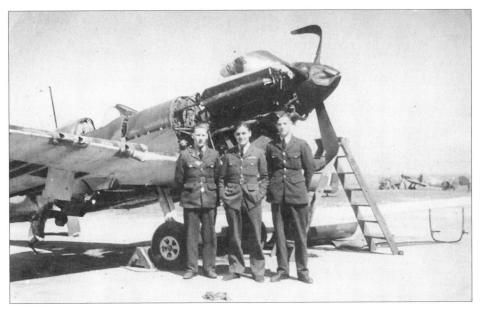

Flg Off Pigg and his ground crew with severely damaged Spitfire K9924 at Gravesend following the combat on 1 June 1940. (72 Sqn)

Another view of the badly damaged Spitfire K9924. (72 Sqn)

While Red Section was twisting and turning its way through the enemy formations, Yellow Section joined the fight. Yellow Section's Flg Off Elsdon (P9439) observed an enemy aircraft in a dive and followed it down, firing at 250 yards. The enemy aircraft lurched suddenly and went into a steep left-hand spiral. Elsdon followed it down almost to ground level until he was satisfied it

Sgt Else with Spitfire Mk I RN-P. Note parachute on tail awaiting a scramble. (R.D. Elliot)

could not possibly pull out of the dive. Flg Off Elsdon was Yellow 4 and reported on his return to base:

When the sections detailed to attack the Ju 87s dived down I saw a single Ju 87 diving down at about 30 degrees and 200–230mph. I attacked from the port quarter, opening fire at about 250 yards and 30 degrees to the direction of the enemy aircraft. I used full deflection on the sight, which is approximately ½ normal full deflection at 200 mph. After firing a burst of three or four seconds the enemy aircraft suddenly lurched to the left and went into a spiral. I followed it down and it was still spiralling down when I had to pull up sharply to avoid hitting the ground. It would be practically impossible for it to pull out from the spiral dive after I lost sight of it, and I could not see it in the air after I pulled out of my dive. Tracer fire from the ground nearby was getting very accurate on my machine and I decided I could serve no further purpose by staying to make absolutely certain that it did crash.

Blue 2, Plt Off Holland (K9959), observed two bombs dropped by a Stuka exploding close to a ship just off Dunkirk harbour, and dived to attack. He gave the Stuka a long nine-second burst from 200 yards and it immediately burst into flames. One of the crew escaped by parachute before the aircraft crashed. Holland then turned his attention to another Stuka. He opened fire but was overtaking at such a rate that he had to pull out to avoid a collision. None the less he had scored some hits, and the Stuka was observed with white smoke pouring from its engine, disappearing into the smoke from the fires of Dunkirk.

Plt Off Holland, Doc and Flt Lt Martineu (Adjutant). (72 Sqn)

With the fight over, the squadron returned to Gravesend. Flg Off Walker (L1056) diverted to Manston with engine trouble, but after repair was soon airborne and back at base. The squadron's claims tally was five destroyed and two disabled, one of which was presumed destroyed. It was not until some time after landing that Flg Off Pigg observed that he had been slightly wounded in the leg! The station medical officer dressed the wound and Pigg was declared fit for duty. Following the hectic battle the squadron was given the following day off.

The squadron came to readiness at dawn on Tuesday 4 June and prepared for another sortie over Dunkirk. The evacuation from the small French port would end this day with 338,226 troops rescued from its beaches. This time they would act as top cover and rearguard, in company with 64 Sqn, for 43 and 243 Sqns. The squadrons would rendezvous at Lympne before setting out for Dunkirk. To extend their time over the battle area they would return to Manston to refuel.

Almost immediately things began to go wrong. After twice reporting the poor visibility to Biggin Hill, the squadrons were ordered off, and 72 Sqn took off, led by Sqn Ldr Lees (P9548), into visibility of only 400 yards. Flg Off Walker (L1056) lost sight of the formation in the fog, but the rest of the squadron managed to re-form after climbing clear of it. Only 43 Sqn managed to join up with them, and the two squadrons proceeded towards Dunkirk. The patrol was uneventful and the squadron turned for Manston to refuel. As they approached the coast they could see that the fog stretched to about ten miles from the coast, and they almost ran into the cliffs trying to make an approach into Manston. Climbing away they began to look for an alternative, and attempted approaches at Littlestone, Lympne and Hawkinge, but all were fogbound. Lees turned the formation around once more and, with the assistance of homing from Manston, flew down the coast at sea level, parallel with the cliffs, in an attempt to get into the airfield.

Suddenly the cliffs and some shipping loomed up ahead, and the squadron was forced into a sharp turn, during which Yellow Section and one Spitfire of Blue Section lost contact with the rest of the formation. The remaining six Spitfires barely missed colliding with the towers at Ramsgate, and eventually, after a further three attempts, managed to land in the fog.

Flt Lt Smith (K9922) and two others managed to land at Shoreham. Smith had only 2½ gallons of fuel left when he landed. Twenty minutes later Plt Off Robson (K9929) also landed at Shoreham, almost out of fuel. Sgt Staples (L1078) could not find an airfield and successfully landed in a 600 yd long field near Lewes. Flg Off Walker, who had been the first to lose the formation, joined up with another squadron and ran out of fuel looking for an airfield, successfully force-landing his Spitfire in a field only 520 yards long near Lydd. He rejoined the squadron at Manston later that afternoon after obtaining fuel.

The six aircraft which had successfully landed at Manston held readiness there for the remainder of the day, flying two further patrols before they were rejoined by the stragglers late in the afternoon. Eventually all returned to Gravesend safely.

That evening the squadron was released, and they were entertained by the Chief Constable of Gravesend in the Police Club before returning to the station in a fire tender provided by the Gravesend Fire Master! Deacon Elliot was one of the happy passengers:

The whole squadron was entertained by the Chief Constable of Gravesend in the Police Club. Transportation was a problem quickly resolved by the Gravesend Fire Chief who provided us with one of his fire engines. We swarmed onto this huge red brute – with Oswald Pigg as officer i/c Fire Bell – which he rang continuously all the way home, and in doing so brought the whole camp to a state of readiness – the rest is a blank.

On Wednesday 5 June the squadron was airborne at 2053 hrs to intercept a raid over Dungeness at 20,000 ft. Arriving over Dungeness there was nothing to be seen, and they returned to Gravesend, where Sgt Hamlyn (K9942) landed with his wheels up. Sgt Else (L1056) and Plt Off Thomson (P9460) were involved in a taxiing collision after landing. The score for the day? Three damaged – all by 72 Sqn! Deacon Elliot was among those witnessing the arrival of the Spitfires back at Gravesend:

At 2245 (getting dark) the whole squadron was scrambled to patrol Dungeness at 20,000 ft – no interceptions – couldn't do much if we had – still in squadron formation and getting darker every minute. We were ordered back, then the fun began. I slid my hood back, to enable me to see better, and in doing so scraped the goggles from my helmet and they became wedged between the two layers of Perspex, holding my head firmly back in the process – most embarrassing. The fun was not over – on return to Gravesend it was quite *dark now – Sgt Hamlyn did not allow his wheels to become fully locked down so they went back up again – and Sgt Pocock when landing ran into Flg Off 'Happy' Thompson's machine and smartly cut off his tailplane. Fortunately no one was hurt. The party for that night was cancelled.*

The following day 72 Sqn's front-line adventure came to an end with the arrival of 610 Sqn, and Sqn Ldr Lees handed over the station to Sqn Ldr Smith before leading 72 back to Acklington. On arrival the squadron was brought to readiness and 'A' Flt was dispatched to Woolsington, returning the following morning. A raid was reported approaching in the afternoon, but the weather was too bad to allow the squadron to take off. A few days after returning to Acklington the squadron was visited by Air Marshal Lord

Sgt Sam Staples. (72 Sqn)

Plt Off Deacon Elliot flying Spitfire Mk IIa P7895:RN-N (R.D. Elliot)

Trenchard, accompanied by the AOC 13 Group. Trenchard spoke to the officers and congratulated them on the magnificent work they had accomplished. The visit was followed by night-flying practice. The squadron was about to embark on a new role in addition to its day-fighter role, that of night-fighting in defence of the cities and towns of the North-East.

Over the following days the squadron was busy with day and night readiness, night-flying training and the regular daily detachments to Woolsington. Acklington became somewhat quieter with the departure of 152 Sqn to Prestwick on the 15th, and 72 Sqn took up the slack by altering the normal readiness states to two sections at dawn readiness with another available, and at dusk three sections at readiness. By night one aircraft was at readiness, two were available and three sections were released. Only one section was released by day. All this meant a very busy time for the squadron, and although little action was seen the constant rounds of readiness with little time off to relax was very wearing on the air and ground crews. In Norway the situation was bleak as British and French troops began the evacuation from Narvik. The following day the aircraft carrier HMS *Glorious* was sunk, and heaping misery upon misery France was virtually defeated at this point, giving Mussolini the opportunity to share in the spoils by declaring war on Britain and France on the 10th. The last British fighting troops in France, fighting a brave rearguard action at St Valery, surrendered on the 12th. Two days later the Germans were in Paris.

The regular stints of readiness at Woolsington brought the squadron to the attention of the AOC 13 Group, Air Marshal Saul, who had his HQ nearby. He wished to see a typical turn-round drill. The squadron duly obliged, but not with the expected results, as Deacon Elliot recalls:

> *The carefully chosen ground crews were lined up in their clean overalls – all appropriate tools in the right place for a speedy turn-round. The AOC arrived, the Spitfire with Flg Off Pigg at the controls was in the circuit, made a perfect approach but unfortunately in direct line for the 'saucer', held off, held off a bit more – still no ground, stalled and on impact the aircraft broke in half just behind the cockpit – where do you go from here? I'm sure Oswald prayed for a large hole; there wasn't one of course, he did not even get a 'rocket', the AOC was speechless.*

The unusual readiness requirements returned to normal as 152 Sqn came back from Prestwick on the 16th. While the night-flying practices continued, Sqn Ldr Lees and Sqn Ldr Devitt departed for Farnborough to take part in tests of the new Spitfire Mk V against a captured Me 109.

On 19 June several new pilots arrived on the squadron, including Plt Off Males, Sgts Glew, Gilders and White, and Sgt W.T. 'Bill' Rolls. Rolls recalled their reception on arrival:

Plt Off Males, Sgts Glew, Gilders and White and myself filled in and signed the usual forms, and the adjutant took us to the squadron leader's office so that he could meet us. As he knocked on the door we saw the name Sqn Ldr R.B. Lees. The adjutant handed the CO our files, the CO then shook hands with us all and welcomed us to his squadron. He told us a bit about the squadron's history and hoped we would become valued members. 'For the purpose of getting familiar with the Spitfire you will come under Flg Off Elsdon who will ensure that you will learn the operational facts of the machine, I will test each one of you in a Harvard when he is satisfied that you are capable of flying a Spitfire.' With that he rang a bell and a sergeant came in and was told to take us down to flights to meet Flg Off Elsdon. After we had put our luggage into our billets we were soon on our way, passing several Spitfires in their pens, marvellous, in a few days we would be flying one of those machines.

The new arrivals were quickly introduced to their squadron compatriots and began their operational training on the squadron almost immediately, as Bill Rolls recalls:

Flg Off 'Jimmy' Elsdon soon put us at ease and introduced us to the flight commander of 'B' Flt, Flt Lt E. 'Ted' Graham; we were then introduced to 'A' Flt and met the members of it; one was nicknamed 'The Deacon' and another 'Pancho'. The next step was to meet some of the ground crew.

Flg Off Elsdon had impressed on us that next to the pilots, the ground crews were the most important people on the station. He told us, 'Every time you take up an aircraft you accept that it will be working properly and as efficiently as possible, and you have accepted this as part of the service and have not appreciated what the ground crew of a Spitfire have to do in order that your aircraft is serviceable. I suggest that during the coming weeks, while you are not operational, you make time to come down and watch these chaps at work and see how important their job is.' He introduced us to the flight sergeant in charge of the ground staff; he told Flg Off Elsdon he would arrange for a Spitfire to be near 'B' Flt so that we could get to know the cockpit layout.

Sgt White joined the squadron on 19 June 1940. (72 Sqn)

Flg Off Elsdon then gave the new arrivals their first Spitfire lesson, as Bill Rolls recalls:

Flg Off Elsdon asked Plt Off Males to climb into the cockpit and we could go through the cockpit drill. 'Jimmy' went through every item in the cockpit explaining their function and at the same time went and did a dummy take-off, telling Males exactly what he had to do to get airborne, one after another e all got the same treatment.

Our first lesson o over, we went back to our billets to unpack, where we met Sgts Plant and Gray who had been off duty for the day. We learned later that they were known as 'Laura' and 'Mabel' to the other pilots. We all got called the usual names, Johnny White became 'Chalky', Glew became 'Sticky', in time we all got called lots of other names.

Sgt Bill Rolls. (72 Sqn)

We made out way to the sergeants' mess; some of them were in the bar and as we were early we went in as well. We didn't get a chance to order a drink as one was pushed into our hands within seconds and a flight sergeant said, Cheers, welcome to Acklington, one of the outposts of the Empire.

After dinner we learned that we would do a couple of trips in a Miles Magister first, to get to know the area we would be flying over. It would also give us an idea of what a monoplane was like to fly, for after flying a Hart during our time at South Cerney it would be difficult to go on to a Spitfire without a single trip in a monoplane. Sgt Plant suggested that he could give us some instruction on the Harvard cockpit the next time he was off readiness; this we accepted. He also told us that the CO would give us a flight on the Harvard and he would expect us to take over directly we were in the cockpit. Over the next couple of days we did our trips in the Magister.

Less than a week after arriving, the new pilots flew their Harvard test flight with the CO. Bill Rolls remembers his test:

On the morning of 25 June 1940, Sqn Ldr Lees took me up for a test in the Harvard, and thanks to the cockpit drill I had received from Sgt Plant and Flg Off Elsdon, I had no trouble flying the Harvard, it felt nice and powerful. I felt at the time, if this is only a trainer what is the real thing, a Spitfire, going to feel like with all of that power? I did two take-offs and landings and climbed to 3,000 ft and did some minor and steep turns. After thirty minutes and having requested permission to land, we landed and taxied over to 'B' Flt. I climbed out of the cockpit after the CO and waited for him to tell me the result of the test, but all he said was, 'Put your parachute on the wings of that aircraft and come into the flight office.'

I finally reached the office and saw the CO talking to Flg Off Elsdon. He turned to me and said, 'Are you ready for your Spitfire solo?' I replied, 'Yes, sir.' He smiled: 'Thought you would be.' Flg Off Elsdon went to a locker and took out a Mae West and handed it to me. We walked out to the Spitfire and I put my parachute on over the Mae West and climbed into the cockpit. 'The aircraft has already been run up so you don't have to test the magnetos, the petrol is already turned on, push your R/T connection in tight and call control, for this flight your coding will be Green 3, the station code is Bluebell', said Flg Off Elsdon. I then had another run through the cockpit drill with Flg Off Elsdon, and when he was satisfied he told me to prepare to take off and said to me, 'This time I want you to do the exercise only.'

My exercise was to fly out to the coast and have a good look around, do some different-rate turns to get the feel of the aircraft, come back for a landing and then take off again for a complete circuit of the airfield. Time allowed was thirty minutes; I was to keep in R/T contact at all times.

I put my brakes on with the lever on the handle of the control column, primed the engine and called out to the trolley man, 'Switches on, contact.' He pressed the button on the trolley and with a bang the engine started. The man then pulled the cable out of the engine cowl. I knew I had to move as quickly as possible because the engine had a habit of heating up quickly as one of the wheels obstructed the vent radiator. I had to continually use my rudder on the rough grass to keep straight, and owing to the undercarriage the aircraft dipped its wing from side to side, and what with swinging the nose from side to side to see where I was going, it made the Spitfire quite a handful. During taxiing out I called control for permission to take off.

I did a quick check of the instruments, looked around to see that I was clear and then turned into the wind on the runway, set the radiator flap and the elevator trim, locked the gyro compass, put the airscrew into fine pitch and closed the hood. I opened the throttle fully, pushed the control column forward to get the tail up so that I could look ahead over the nose, a little rudder correction and I felt the aircraft leave the ground. I then pumped the undercart lever three times, selected wheels up, and continued pumping for about fifteen times and saw that the undercarriage lights came on and that the indicators on the wings were out of sight.

While I had been pumping with my right hand and holding the control column with my left, I had been performing a switchback motion, but putting my left elbow onto my thigh stopped the up and down motion. I then adjusted the radiator, put the airscrew into coarse pitch for cruising and unlocked the gyro compass. By the time I had done all this I found that I was at 2,000 ft near the coast cruising at 185 mph. I now had time to look around while I continued to fly straight and level, having trimmed the aircraft once more. I tried out the controls and was amazed at how light they seemed and how responsive almost immediately they were to the slightest touch of either elevator or rudder. Compared to the Hart, which I thought was the perfect machine; the Spitfire was like a greyhound, so sleek and fast. I climbed to 5,000 ft in no time at all and did various turns. I played with the controls to get the feel of them and waggled the wings from side to side. It was magic, I felt that I was an integral part of the Spitfire and that the wings were fixed to my arms and I could fly just like a bird. The cockpit was so small that there was no room to move and this made it feel as though you had it strapped on to you.

I decided to try some mild turns, and the smoothness of them and the grace of the aircraft in performing the moves was unbelievable. I had heard that in a steep turn it was possible to black out and so I decided to try one and see how far I could go before I felt myself blacking out. The sooner I learned what to expect the better.

I thought I would go into a shallow dive and go into my turn on the pull-out. As I went into the turn I pulled the control column over to the left and back at the same time, and then it happened. I felt a terrific pressure on my body and the nose was dropping. I had to give more rudder and a tighter hold on the control column. I didn't black out but I didn't like the feeling I had experienced. I was not prepared for such a quick reaction of the controls. I decided to come out of the turn in a half roll and so I throttled back, pulled hard over on the control column, and hey presto, I was coming out of the turn in a well-controlled bottom half of a loop.

Returning to base I called up on the R/T, 'Hello Bluebell, Green 3 requesting permission to land.' 'Hello Green 3, permission granted, over and out.' What a polite lot of chaps they are in control, I thought. I selected wheels down and pumped the lever until I saw the green light go on and the wing indicators were up and then I put the flaps down. This caused the Spitfire to drop its nose sharply and I had to correct it quickly. I adjusted the radiator and finally put the airscrew into fine pitch and turned into the wind over the runway approach. I motored in at 95 mph and gradually lost height. When just a few feet from the ground I cut the throttle and pulled back on the control column, I felt a slight bump and I was on the ground, using the handbrake on the control column to pull up and keeping straight with the aid of the rudder. I had done my first trip on a Spitfire.

I then taxied to the take-off point for my second trip, which was a repeat of the first. When I landed and was taxiing to dispersal I said my usual little prayer, 'Dear God, thank you.' Some pilots carry lucky charms, but the word had kept me safe all the other times I had flown and I didn't intend to change now.

As I approached the dispersal two airmen came running over and took hold of each wingtip to guide me in over the grass. They both put their thumbs up to me; I had been accepted by the boys who look after your aircraft. This was very important, as your life depended on these chaps every time you were airborne. I was to find out in the future just how brave and how important the ground crews of the RAF were. Up until now I had not taken much notice of them, I had been too worried about learning to fly to consider what other people had been doing to keep you in the air.

I switched off the engine and climbed out of the cockpit. Johnny White was waiting to take over for his solo flight. I wished him good luck and told him it was a piece of cake flying it. I went up to Flg Off Elsdon. 'Well, what do you think of the Spit?' he asked. 'Marvellous, I can't describe the feeling but I feel I've been flying it for ages, it's so easy to fly and what a graceful lady she is to look at.'

Over the days that followed, Bill Rolls and the other new pilots were given further training in height climbs and formation flying, and were becoming fully fledged members of the squadron, as Rolls recalls:

During these days every time Johnny and I went into flights some of the officers would say, 'Here come the sprogs.' It was meant in good fun. One night in the bar the four of us decided that we would paint on the back of our Mae Wests in bright lettering 'Sprog 1', which we decided should be for Plt Off Males, Johnny White was 'Sprog 2', I was 'Sprog 3', Johnny Gilders 'Sprog 4' and 'Stickey' Glew was 'Sprog 5'. We would show those officers that we were proud of being 'sprogs'. When we arrived at flights wearing our Mae Wests the officers had a good laugh and thought it a good idea. When the ground crew saw what we had done they thought it funny and very sporting of us. We had now been on the squadron ten days, and we were told to make up our logbooks for Sqn Ldr Lees to sign. My total flying time in those ten days was 11 hrs 10 min.

Rear L to R Sgt Gilders, PO Males, Sgt Rolls. Front L to R Sgt White, Sgt Glew (RD Elliot)

Just before midnight on 26 June three Spitfires were ordered off as a number of radar plots appeared on the ops table. Recently promoted Flg Off Thomson was first off at 2355 hrs in L1078, followed twenty-five minutes later by Flt Lt Graham in P9457. The third Spitfire, K9940, was flown off the darkened Acklington runway at 0040 hrs by Flg Off Jimmy Elsdon. The night sky was brilliantly illuminated by the anti-aircraft searchlights, which picked up a Junkers Ju 88 and managed to hold it in the beams.

Flg Off Thomson spotted the bomber in the lights, and closed on it. Thomson made his approach from astern and below. As he closed he observed that if he was at the same level as the apex of the searchlight beams he lost sight of the bomber, but if he descended about 1,000 ft below this level he could clearly see the Ju 88. Worried that any transmission he made might be picked up by the bomber, he maintained radio silence as he closed to fifty yards astern and twenty feet below the bomber before he opened fire with two bursts. After the first burst, smoke was observed coming from both engines. Maintaining a position behind and below, he was able to avoid overshooting, and after firing the second three-second burst a blinding white flash occurred as the Ju 88 exploded, throwing large pieces in all directions. Some of the fragments struck Thomson's Spitfire, a few lodging in the cowling and radiator. With the explosion Thomson broke away downwards and left and lost sight of the bomber. The whole fight had been clearly observed from Acklington as the Ju 88 was held in the searchlights throughout. On return to base it was found that Thomson had fired 1,029 rounds and that one of his guns had a stoppage with the first round fired. Deacon Elliot was among those observing the battle from the ground:

Happy Thompson's great success. Shortly after getting airborne to take up a position on his prescribed patrol line, the air raid warning sounded and seconds later searchlights illuminated and held onto the 'X' raid. Happy made the interception, and having identified the enemy, backed off a little and blew it to pieces. All this was witnessed by us standing at dispersal. On landing, which in itself must have been difficult, as the whole of his aircraft was covered in oil from the exploding enemy and pieces of the Ju 88 were lodged in his Spit's air intake duct, Happy, who at the best of times was frightfully modest, simply said, 'I think I got him.' Actually, at one stage we thought the searchlights, when pointing out to sea at a very low angle, would lose the enemy before Happy could intercept, and Flg Off Jimmy Elsdon made a hairy take-off in the hope of a kill – but no sooner was he off the ground than the most spectacular explosions occurred. That evening a lone raider dropped bombs in the area – some falling on the airfield and others near Warkworth station – other than a few sheep being killed there was no damage.

This success was due in part to the excellent work of the searchlight batteries in holding the bomber in the cone of lights, but mainly due to Thomson's exceptional flying. Not only had he had the blinding glare of the searchlights to contend with but the additional night-vision-destroying flames emanating from the Spitfire's engine exhausts. The Spitfire was not an easy aircraft to fly at night, and landing was all the more difficult when the exhaust glare and the narrow, stalky undercarriage are taken into account.

Bill Rolls had completed his training on the Spitfire by now and had been placed on the readiness roster and waited impatiently for his first scramble, which came on 29 June:

I was at readiness as Green 3. I looked out the window and wondered how long it would be before I actually had a chance to see the enemy. I had been waiting for that vital telephone call telling us to scramble, but although it rang several times, causing an awful feeling in the pit of my stomach, it was never for us to scramble. I looked at the Spitfires, which were at readiness with the ground crew sitting near their respective aircraft. The aircraft could be airborne within a couple of minutes if an alert was called. Suddenly, the telephone rang, with the call 'Green Section scramble!' This was it, the three of us in Green Section raced to our aircraft. By the time we reached them the ground crews had started the engines and the straps of our parachutes were open, ready for us to jump into the cockpit. The airman put the straps round you and hooked the leads up and the harness was put over you and the pin inserted in a matter of seconds.

The leader had started to taxi out, and number two and myself were soon in position ready for a formation take-off. The weather was very cloudy and at about 2,000 ft we were going through cloud in tight formation. A bandit had been reported off the coast at 6,000 ft. We received various directions as to which course to steer, when it suddenly appeared ahead of us. We could see, even from this distance, that it was an Avro Anson twin-engine trainer, but as yet we didn't know who was flying it. It could have been a captured one from the fall of France.

Green Leader tried to contact its pilot, but like control there was no reply from it. They didn't even fire a pistol giving the colour of the day. Green Leader ordered us to echelon port and number two came up under me on my left side. The leader then flew close to the Anson and you could see the pilot, but he couldn't understand what he was supposed to do. At the time I thought how dim the pilot must be, but it was not for me to reason why.

Green 1 flew ahead of the Anson and number two went underneath me and formatted on the port side and I closed in on the starboard. It was now hemmed in and short of committing suicide the pilot had to follow. Base was informed that the Anson was being escorted back to base. Green 1 changed course and we went down through the thin cloud and flew on to the aerodrome.

Green 1 put his wheels and flaps down on the approach and the Anson did the same. Green 1 then went in to land and Green 2 and myself motored in still in formation, until the Anson touched down. We then climbed away and landed in the normal manner. By now an RAF police van was waiting at the Anson door. We taxied back to dispersal and the Spitfires were soon refuelled and we were back at readiness. It was my first scramble and it was successful in the interception of another aircraft. I had learned a lot and it gave me a lot of confidence in the way control had handled the situation. If it had been a German aircraft it would have had three Spitfires shooting it down.

Further success was to come the squadron's way on 29 June, this time by day. Things were warming up in the North-East as the *Luftwaffe* began probing reconnaissance of the region looking for suitable targets. Just after 8 a.m. Yellow Section, Flt Lt 'Hiram' Smith (P9438) leading Sgt Gray (P9460) and Plt Off Winter (L1092), were ordered off to patrol base at 18,000 ft. About fifteen minutes later they were vectored to a bogey flying east at 20,000 ft about ten miles north-east of Holy Island. They soon sighted an aircraft at 20,000 ft and commenced a tail chase. Twenty minutes and 3,000 ft higher, Smith challenged the bomber, which failed to give a satisfactory response. The aircraft had, by now, been identified as a Dornier Do 17, though it was actually a Do 215 of *Aufkl Gr ObdL*, which immediately took evasive action with violent stall turns and dives. Smith positioned his section dead astern, and in turn he, Gray and Winter launched their attacks. After Smith and Gray had attacked, white smoke was observed pouring from both engines. Winter closed in and fired three short bursts as the Dornier stalled abruptly in front of him. His gunfire poured into the cockpit and he broke away at 100 yards range. The Dornier pulled out of the stall and Sgt Gray made a second attack, firing a full deflection burst as he descended through 10,000 ft chasing the bomber. He observed that the front of the bomber cockpit was breaking up. By now the bomber was at 6,000 ft and Flt Lt Smith closed in for his second attack. At close range, he opened fire, and the Do 215 went into a steep right-hand spiral and then dived vertically into the sea from 2,000 ft, where it burst into flames and broke up. The only return fire from the evading Dornier was during the first attack by Smith and Gray, during which one bullet hit Smith's engine. By the time Winter attacked, the Dornier's guns were silent. On their return to base they were able to relate their fight to the Secretary of State for Air, Sir Archibald Sinclair, who had arrived to visit the squadron. Sinclair added his congratulations to the squadron for its magnificent achievements. The following day invasion seemed even more imminent as the Germans occupied the Channel Islands.

As the first day of July 1940 dawned, Blue Section, led by Flt Lt Graham in Spitfire P9457, scrambled to intercept an unidentified aircraft just east of Sunderland. Flying in formation with Graham were Flg Off Wilcox (K9959) and Flt Sgt Steere (K9935). As they sped towards the coast the reported height of the intruder was given variously as 6,000 ft, 3,000 ft and then height unknown. At 0612 hrs Graham sighted the unidentified aircraft. It was a white-painted twin-engined Heinkel He 59 floatplane. This type was used by the *Luftwaffe* as an Air Sea Rescue aircraft officially, but more often than not they were used on reconnaissance duties, thus making them a legitimate target. Blue Section circled the floatplane three times, while it flew on three miles east of Sunderland at 500 ft. The Heinkel wore large red crosses on the wing upper surfaces and a black swastika on a red band on the tailplane.

Flt Lt Graham led the section into the attack, and opening fire at 200 yards he closed to thirty yards, rapidly overtaking the slow-moving floatplane, before breaking away to starboard. As he turned away he observed faint greyish smoke and vapour emitting from the aircraft fuselage. The Heinkel turned slowly to starboard as Wilcox and Steere attacked in turn. The Heinkel began to descend, shedding small pieces as it went, as Wilcox lined up for a second attack, but he only managed to get a short one-second burst in before the floatplane landed on the water about four miles east of Hartlepool.

Plt Off D.C. Winter.

While Wilcox and Steere were busy trying to down the Heinkel, Graham flew towards a cruiser he had spotted escorting a nearby convoy, and directed it towards the enemy aircraft. The Heinkel was now slowly sinking, tail first, and the crew had taken to their dinghy. The cruiser lowered a boat to pick up the crew as the nose of the Heinkel lifted clear of the water and it then sank. A jubilant Blue Section returned to base and landed just under an hour after taking off. The He 59 was from *Seenotflugkdo 3*, and its pilot, *Leutnant* Hans-Joachim Fehske, protested bitterly after his rescue at the destruction of an aircraft on a rescue mission.

With German plans for the invasion of Britain well advanced, there were a considerable number of probing and reconnaissance flights made over the following days, and with activity detected to the north of the Usworth sector four sections were scrambled on the 2nd to investigate. No. 152 Sqn provided cover to the airfield while 72 patrolled the area around the Farne Islands. Despite the activity observed by radar, only one Ju 88 was sighted momentarily, and the day's patrols ended inconclusively.

Over the following days numerous patrols were flown without result; however, the squadron almost lost Plt Off Elliot on a mid-afternoon patrol on 6 July. Elliot was flying Spitfire P9444 as Red 3 at 20,000 ft over the Cheviot Hills when he lost consciousness due to an oxygen problem. The Spitfire spun out of control for 17,000 ft and Elliot came to, to find himself only 1,000 ft above the hills. He managed to pull out in time and returned safely to base; a close call. The aircraft had been so badly overstressed during the descent and pull-out that it was a complete write-off. Deacon Elliot wrote of his experience:

Plt Off Robson was No. 2 and I was No. 3, and thus responsible for operating 'Pip-Squeak' [a transmitter usually operated by the No. 3 of the section to enable Ops to track and vector the leader for an interception], in the CO's Red Section when we were scrambled – my NEW machine would not start, so I quickly jumped into P9444 belonging to Flg Off Oswald Pigg. I must digress here to explain that the rubber oxygen tubes – usually on one's personal clothing card – were in extreme short supply. By pooling them there were enough for one per aircraft but not one per pilot. The CO therefore directed that the tube should become part of the aircraft equipment, and as a temporary measure a column was added to the Form 700 [aircraft logbook] for this purpose.

Graeme Gillard and Sandy Clay at Acklington in July 1940. (G. Gillard)

The cloud base was low and the tops unknown. On the way up, flying through thick and very dark cloud and thus in tight formation to keep contact with the CO, he checked with us at about 10,000 ft for 'oxygen on' – this is when I discovered there was no tube in Oswald's aircraft. I felt all right so I went on, hoping we would soon be on top – this eventually was the case but not until we were at 20,000 ft. I was still with my section but well astern, 'Pip-Squeak' pushing out our position, but now my vision was deteriorating. The two aircraft in front became four – then two – then four. That was it; the stick thrashing round in all directions and the effect of excessive G crumpled me down in the cockpit – but I was still able to transmit that I was spinning down completely out of control in thick cloud. I resigned myself to death, and I so vividly recall that I was quite happy, content, and at peace with the world, with no vestige of fear. At this stage the Lord must have taken over, for after an undetermined lapse of time I found myself below cloud in pouring rain – very close to the ground and – fortunately – climbing rapidly. I thought I was over the Lammermuir Hills so I headed east, turned south down the coast to Coquet Island and cut inland back to Acklington. I noticed the flying characteristics of the plane were most peculiar – perfectly all right flying straight and level but skidded badly in turns.

On landing, a technical inspection revealed the aircraft to be buckled, twisted and corrugated to such a degree it was a complete write-off. Supermarine technicians when stripping the Spit found the wing root bolts, which normally are straight, to be like little boomerangs. (They were of the opinion the aircraft had performed a series of manoeuvres involving excessive G forces – almost to the limit of destruction. Oswald was furious at losing his beloved Spitfire – the CO was furious with Oswald for not complying with the instruction to leave his oxygen tube in the aircraft instead of

The ground crew readiness hut at Acklington in 1940. (G. Gillard)

having it sewn around his helmet. My feelings were a combination of fear, elation, delight and intense surprise to find myself still alive.

At 1648 hrs that afternoon the whole squadron was brought to readiness to move to Drem when a strong enemy force was reported approaching the Firth of Forth. No. 152 Sqn took over the readiness at Acklington to allow this, and quickly scrambled a section for aerodrome defence. However, the probing force approaching the Forth dispersed and the squadron was stood down.

Probing by the Germans and counter-patrols continued over the next few days, and on the evening of the 8th Red Section, led by Sqn Ldr Lees (P9458), was ordered

Cpl Graeme Gillard at Acklington in July 1940. (G. Gillard)

off to intercept a raid approaching the airfield from the direction of Berwick. Working their way through a very cloudy sky they fleetingly saw a Heinkel He 111, but it was lost again in the cloud and no interception was made. The enemy activity continued on the 9th, but the Spitfires made no contacts. The pilots waited impatiently for action. It was obvious to all that the large amount of probing would soon come to an end, followed by all-out attack.

CHAPTER THREE

The Battle of Britain

Wednesday 10 July 1940 is now recognized as the official start date of the Battle of Britain, but while convoys were attacked by day off Dover and North Foreland and further attacks were made during the night on target on the east coast, the home counties and western Scotland, it might as well have been any quiet day for 72 Sqn. Bad weather prevented any flying. Over the following days, despite day and night patrols and attempted interceptions, little occurred in 72's sector. On the night of 15/16 July several patrols were made in an attempt to intercept enemy raiders, and though searchlights illuminated several none were intercepted. The poor weather continued to play a hand in frustrating interception efforts for the rest of the month.

On the 24th a farewell party was held for Sqn Ldr Lees, who was posted to No. 13 Group. His replacement as commanding officer was Sqn Ldr A.R. Collins, who took over the squadron the following day. Another pilot rejoined the squadron when Flg Off D.F.B. Sheen returned on the 29th. Throughout July the *Luftwaffe* had concentrated on shipping attacks in an attempt to draw Fighter Command into battle, but it was largely unsuccessful, except for a fight on 19 July when Dover was raided and No. 141, a Defiant squadron, was largely destroyed. For 72 Sqn it had been a month frustrated by poor weather, inconclusive patrols and failed interceptions.

August began as July had ended, with little activity other than routine patrolling. The tedium was broken on the 6th when Green Section returned from a patrol over Acklington and one Spitfire (L1078) of Green Section was crashed on landing by Sgt R.J.C. Staples. The following day saw widespread raids around the coastline from Liverpool in the west to Aberdeen in the north-east; however, 72 Sqn was unable to report any action during its only sorties of the day.

On the 9th the *Luftwaffe* concentrated their efforts on Channel convoys, and over the following days they continued to carry out convoy attacks, reconnaissance and minelaying sorties. No. 72 Sqn continued to patrol the north-east but encountered no enemy activity. The same can be said for the next four days, when the squadrons of 10, 11 and 12 Groups were being heavily engaged during raids on Portland, Dover, Portsmouth and Channel convoys, while 72 Sqn kicked its heels in the north.

Goering had planned his main assault on the RAF, *Adlertag*, to commence on the 13th. However, despite large forces raiding Portland and Southampton and attacks on airfield in Hampshire in Kent, the results were poor. Inadequate intelligence had targeted Eastchurch, Odiham, Farnborough, Andover and Middle Wallop. Most of these airfields were not fighter stations, and the *Luftwaffe* had squandered its chance to destroy the RAF fighter force on the ground by attacking the wrong bases. The *Luftwaffe* suffered heavy losses, particularly those units equipped with the vaunted Junkers Ju 87 *Stuka*. No. 72 Sqn could only watch with envy as its southern counterparts began to rack up scores.

Little occurred in the north-east on the 14th, but the 15th was to be a decisive day during the Battle of Britain. It was also to be a successful day for 72 Sqn. Goering threw all three of his *Luftflotten* into the battle, their targets the RAF's airfields. In the process he would lose seventy-five fighters and bombers. No. 72 Sqn made a major contribution to the *Luftwaffe* losses. The radar stations in 13 Group began to see plots building off the Firth of Forth about ninety miles out. Estimated at twenty aircraft, the number quickly rose to thirty, in three sections, as they turned towards Tynemouth. The sector controller called 72 Sqn and advised them that 'a very large group of Huns' was approaching and there was every indication that they were 'coming to town'. As the squadron came to readiness, off-duty pilots began to stream in, and as Desmond Sheen recalls, 'They begged for aircraft to fly.' No. 13 Group scrambled 72, 79, 605 and 607 Squadrons to intercept. No. 72 Sqn was directed to patrol the Farne Islands, while 605 covered Tynemouth. The Spitfires of 72 Sqn, led by Flt Lt Graham, lifted off from Acklington at 1215 hrs and sped towards the enemy. It came as something of a shock when the formation was spotted. The approaching German force was much larger than Ted Graham's formation, and on sighting it he hesitated for a moment, uncertain of the best tactics to deal with it. Unable to bear the suspense, one pilot called on the R/T and asked Graham whether or not he had seen the enemy force. Ted Graham had a slight stutter and replied, 'Of course I've seen the b-b-b-bastards, I'm trying to w-w-w-work out what to do.' Ted Graham later wrote:

The following moments are difficult to describe because they were so completely full. I remember seeing clearly that the long line of Huns ended abruptly some miles north of us. They were obviously the right flank of the pack and were well below us at 18,000 ft. Turning left I led the squadron across the face of the rapidly approaching armada. We reached the right flank at about the right time – some moments before the Huns passed to the west of us. I had seen another line of aircraft above and behind – well behind, thank goodness – the first mighty wave and had given the order: 'Prepare to attack. Rearguards look out for escort fighters.' I had determined to make our attack into the flanking aircraft of the armada. This would leave us less exposed to crossfire.

Instead of the thirty aircraft reported, there were in fact sixty-five Heinkel He 111s of *III/KG26* escorted by thirty-four Messerschmitt Bf 110s of *I/ZG76*. Undaunted, Graham led his squadron into the attack from the flank, directing one section to fend off the fighters, while the remained went for the bombers. The Me 110s, which had been vaunted by the *Luftwaffe* as mighty destroyers, had already been found wanting in combat against Spitfires and Hurricanes, and their pilots knew they were at a disadvantage in air combat. To counter the disadvantage they used the tactic of forming a defensive circle to give mutual fire support to each other. *I/ZG76* quickly formed a circle on sighting the approaching Spitfires, leaving the bombers to their fate. The Heinkels quickly split their formation, some jettisoning their bombs into the sea, while others turned tail and fled for Norway. No. 72 Sqn had a field day, returning to base only forty-five minutes after take-off with claims of eleven destroyed, three probably destroyed and one damaged. Those bombers which had managed to evade 72 Sqn and press on were met by 79 and 605 Squadrons, which inflicted more damage before the survivors turned tail and fled, leaving most of their bombs in the sea. Desmond Sheen, who had returned to the squadron after a stint with the Photographic Development Unit (PDU) and Photographic Reconnaissance Unit (PRU), was involved in the battle flying Spitfire X4109. He recorded in his logbook:

Intercept 100 Bomb's 50 Fit's – Squadron bag 11 – Mine 1 Ju 88, 2 Me 110. [The Ju 88 was scored through in the logbook.]

He reported:

I was detailed as Green 1 with two sections of two aircraft each, patrolling both flanks as rearguard. When Blue and Red Sections attacked, Green Section remained behind until the enemy formations had split up. I ordered individual attacks. Formations of Ju 88s and Me 110s were forming defensive circles while other aircraft jettisoned their bombs and escaped into cloud. I attacked a straggler in a circle of seven Ju 88s. This aircraft carried one very large bomb underneath the fuselage. Fire was opened at about 200 yards range, dead astern and slightly below. The second burst of about three seconds hit the bomb. The enemy aircraft disappeared in minute fragments. Six enemy aircraft believed Me 110s were then observed in a similar formation and an attempt was made to pick one out. Another showed signs of attacking me and a deflection shot approaching head on was tried. This was not successful, but another enemy aircraft appeared in my sights head on and another deflection shot was made. Immediately flames and smoke appeared near the inside of the port engine. The enemy aircraft, either with the pilot shot, or in a deliberate attempt to ram me, approached head on and left wing low. Violent evasive action was taken and the enemy aircraft disappeared over my head with the flame and smoke greatly increasing in volume. No evasive action was taken by the Ju 88 and no return fire of any description was encountered from either enemy aircraft. The remaining enemy aircraft were then lost in cloud and attempts to locate the main body failed. I therefore returned to base and refuelled. A further short patrol of 20 minutes was made but no contact was made.

One of the Messerschmitts, coded M8+AB, claimed by Desmond Sheen, was that flown by the *Gruppe Kommandeur* of ZG76, *Hauptmann* Werner Restemeyer. The fighter crashed into the sea off Newcastle. The exploding large bomb was actually a very large long-range fuel tank known to the Germans as a *Dachshund*. Restemeyer and *Unteroffizier* Werner Eichert were both killed. Deacon Elliot gave an equally detailed account of the action:

The whole squadron was at readiness and Flt Lt Ted Graham was acting CO when we were ordered to scramble and proceed out to sea at 25,000 ft off the Farne Islands. We intercepted a raid of I should think at least 200 enemy aircraft at about 40 miles out to sea, made up of every type we knew of. Led by the He 111 and Ju 88 bombers, with a long-range escort of Me 110s well to the rear.

None of us had ever seen so many aircraft in the sky at one time. Just what attack to make was difficult for Ted Graham to decide. In any case he stuttered badly, and by the time he got it out the attack was on. There was a gap between the lines of bombers and the Me 110s coming up in the rear, so in there we went. I do not think they saw us to begin with. When they did, the number of bombs rapidly jettisoned was fantastic. You could see them falling away from the aircraft and dropping into the sea, literally by the hundreds. The formation became a shambles – big as it was. No. 72 Squadron was, I am certain, the first to intercept this raid, but it was later joined by 79 Sqn, 41, 607 and 605 Sqns flying from Drem and Catterick.

It really was a terrific scrap – I saw two separate Huns literally disintegrate, and later I was able to confirm as having fallen to Flt Lt Hiram Smith and Flg Off Desmond Sheen DFC. Some of the enemy, but only a very few, crossed our coast and forced on almost to the Clyde, while others attacked Newcastle and turned sharply out to sea again. We had hoped to get the stragglers on the way back, but no luck.

Ted Graham, leading the attack, engaged a Heinkel at 250 yards range and received accurate return fire from the bomber's rear gunner:

I continued to pour bullets into the Heinkel until its tail looked enormous through my windscreen. I didn't see her go down as avoiding action had to be taken to save a collision, but she seemed to me to be done for, as she was lurching about and losing height.

Graham then had to take further avoiding action on sighting an enemy aircraft behind him:

So fast was my speed that I entered the cloud layer before I was able to pull out of the dive. Emerging a few seconds later from the cloud, I was in time to see an aircraft very like an Me 110 spinning down to enter the cloud from which I had just emerged. Was that the one which had been on my tail?

Following the combat, Ted Graham filled in and submitted his combat report:

Encountered over 110 enemy aircraft of He 111, Ju 88 and Me 110 type, 30 miles east of Farne Isles. The squadron was flying at 22,000 ft on course 020 degrees with the enemy well below flying west in many vic formations, line abreast and line astern – decided to attack the enemy on his right flank which was approx 3 miles northward. Circling the flank I warned the rearguard of escort fighters and then ordered the squadron to attack, leading my Blue Section in a No. 3 Stern Chase on to three He 111s which were flying behind and slightly above the enemy preceding vics. I opened fire at 250 yd closing to about 30 yd, and saw smoke burst from the fuselage and port engine. Intense return fire was encountered but this was inaccurate. On diving away from the Heinkel I spotted an Me 110 circling above me, so dived straight for the clouds 9,000 ft below.

Before entering the cloud I could still see this Me 110 spiralling down, but this time I got the impression that it might have been out of control – though no smoke was issuing from it. Coming out of cloud I found I was about 20 miles out to sea. I made for home and landed. On refuelling and rearming I took off again on orders to patrol base at 10,000 ft but was ordered to pancake after 15 mins.

Plt Off D.C. Winter was acting as rearguard for the squadron as it approached the enemy formation, and wrote later in his combat report:

…Green 1 and 2 were then on the port side of the enemy aircraft. They then attacked and I was left on my own – Green 3 having attacked himself by then. Still acting as rearguard I flew back and forth over the combats which were then taking place, looking for more fighters, which did not appear.

Then I decided to attack myself, at the same time seeing a He 111 with its wheels down gliding seawards. I followed it for a while until I saw it hit the sea and disappear. Climbing up again I saw about 2,000 ft below me at 16,000 ft a circle of six Me 110s with a Spitfire in the circle. I waited until one Me 110 was detached a little from the circle on the Spitfire's tail and dived to attack. I waited until I was about 100 ft from it and opened fire. I saw the bullets entering the pilot's cockpit. The enemy aircraft turned on its back and dived seawards, eventually crashing in the sea. I observed no return fire.

Climbing up again I found another ring of six Me 110s with three Spitfires in the circle. One of the Me 110s flew to one side and I again dived to attack. In the first combat I fired at about 150 ft and the port engine started to smoke. I fired two more bursts which entered the pilot's cockpit. The enemy aircraft dived vertically for the sea. I followed it through the cloud and saw it crash in the sea. No return fire was observed and no markings on the second enemy aircraft. On the other undersurfaces – pale blue.

Flg Off T.A.F. Elsdon of 'B' Flt was flying as Green 2, and found that the enemy kept trying to include him in their circling defensive formations, as he wrote in his combat report:

This they succeeded in doing, but I managed to get away before they fired a shot at me. After extricating myself I found the circle had broken up completely and I was in a position to attack individuals. I attacked one with 30 degrees deflection from the starboard quarter and above with two short bursts. Smoke came from the starboard engine and the machine spiralled into the clouds. I could not confirm his destruction as I did not see him crash into the sea. Then I saw another Me 110 diving for the cloud in an easterly direction. He disappeared before I could get within range. He did not appear again above or below the cloud although I waited for a short time in the hope of finding another target.

Not once during the engagement did I observe an Me 110 put itself in a position for its rear gunner to fire nor was any return fire experienced from them. I consider, therefore, that the rear gunners had been sacrificed for an overload of petrol (carried in the bulbous tanks under the fuselage) to obtain the necessary range.

Flg Off E.J. 'Willie' Wilcox latched onto an He 111 and shot it down, describing the action in his combat report:

On receipt of the order to attack I sighted an He 111 bomber and observed the rear gunner firing at me. As I was at a range of about 600 yd I put my lead a little above the rear gunner of the Heinkel. After a short burst I observed no more enemy fire from this machine. I closed to point-blank range and fired at the port engine until black smoke poured from it and the undercarriage dropped. I then transferred my attention to the starboard engine and fired until black smoke appeared. The enemy aircraft glided down towards the water. My windscreen was splashed with oil from the engines of the Heinkel. As I had expended all my ammunition I returned to base.

Following the excitement of the 15th, the focus of *Luftwaffe* activity returned to the south and south-east, while the Norwegian formations wiped their bloody noses. For 72 Sqn the boredom of patrolling, with nothing to show for it, returned. The squadron continued to carry out night-flying, and on the 27th a Spitfire (K9922) was crashed on landing. Bill Rolls was night-flying that night, and recalls the incidents which resulted in damage to a number of Spitfires:

Night flying in a Spitfire was about the most dangerous thing you could do in an aircraft. Owing to the long nose and the proximity of the two exhausts it was almost blind flying until you were airborne and if you had no horizon to look at it was head down in the cockpit most of the time. On my second night's flying I was over Newcastle having been vectored by control that enemy aircraft were in the region. I was at 23,000 ft and it was bloody dark and I was on instruments quite a lot of the time. If there were any enemy aircraft about I had no chance of seeing them unless I was behind them and could see their exhaust. I was ordered to descend to Angels 12 and given a course to vector, which I was sure would take me right over Newcastle. I saw a dark shape ahead which according to control was an He 111. I dived down and the shape suddenly grew much larger and then I realised it wasn't an aircraft but a balloon I could see. At the same time I saw ack-ack flashes way ahead of me. I thought for a moment that the ack-ack was firing at me, but I realised it was too far away. I was now getting low on fuel as I had been airborne for almost an hour.

On the R/T I heard that one of the other Spits had crashed on landing and didn't make me feel very good. I didn't know if it was Johnny White or one of the officers or how bad the crash was. After about ten minutes I got the order to return to base and as I was turned towards home I heard the all-clear for landing given to one of the other aircraft. It was not long before I had another instruction to orbit base as the runway was obstructed by another crash. I was now getting very worried. If I didn't land soon I would be out of petrol and I would be number three on the runway. I had now been airborne for 1hr 15 mins out of 1½ hours' duration. Taking into consideration that I had done a speed climb to 23,000 ft, I doubted I could last 1½ hours.

I could see that the crashed aircraft was now clear of the runway and so I called up control and told them I was getting low on fuel, and the only reply I got was that they had everything under control. Which was more than I had as I watched the seconds ticking away on the clock. 'Hello Green Two are you receiving me?' What a bloody silly question. Quick as a flash I replied, 'May I now pancake?' 'Hello Green Two, permission to land, watch out for obstacles at the south side of the runway.'

By the time he had finished talking I had my wheels and flaps down and short-circuited the approach leg and straight onto the runway. I taxied to the far end and saw two damaged aircraft at the side of the runway. At least I had made it, I had landed safely. Because of my shortage of fuel I opened my throttle and raced back to dispersal, whistling because I was so happy, when there was a sudden jolt and a noise of twisted metal and I came to a full stop. The engine cut out and there was this terrible silence for a moment or two. I jumped out of the cockpit and saw to my utter confusion that I had gone head on into another Spitfire which was taxiing for take off. I had damaged two Spitfires through sheer bloody negligence.

The other pilot, an officer, was out of his aircraft and said quietly, 'Wait for it, here it comes.' The flight commander had reached the scene and I knew what he implied, and was waiting for a rocket from the flight commander. To my surprise he looked very concerned and asked us if we had been hurt at all. He took us back to dispersal in his car and immediately I was given a cup of coffee by one of the officers. I was trembling, not from fear but because I was wondering what was going to happen to me after such a silly accident. The telephone rang and the flight commander answered it and spoke to the CO of the squadron.

After he put down the phone he came into the room and sat down near me: 'You have had a nasty experience tonight what with the searchlights and waiting to land with very little petrol. I think we can safely say that your accident on the ground was caused by circumstances beyond one's normal control. I suggest that you stand down for the rest of the night.' I was only able to mutter, 'Thank you, sir', my mouth had dried up.

When he returned to his office I asked one of the other officers what would happen to me because of my carelessness. 'Nothing', he said. 'You see it was as much the fault of the officer in the other aircraft, he is a far more experienced pilot than you and should have seen you coming.' He looked at the office door and quietly said, 'The CO has settled it with the flight commander so you will not hear any more about this matter.' It took me some time before I realized that even after I had done all that damage I was still going to be allowed to fly.

The following day, having had little time to recover from his frightening night-flying experience, Bill Rolls was airborne in another frightening episode:

The next day I was back on duty and we had a scramble. There were only two of us, Green 1 and myself, Green 2. We were ordered to 25,000 ft, as bandits were coming in from the east at that height. It was bad weather with ten-tenths cloud when we took off. I had to keep my eyes on Green 1's wingtip every second as the slightest shift in my position and I wouldn't be able to see the other aircraft. I was not unduly worried because I thought that after about ten minutes we would break cloud and see a nice blue sky. Ten minutes passed and we were still climbing in cloud. I had never been so long in cloud and I was getting worried. There was no R/T talk so I just had to follow the leader, whatever he did. At last we broke cloud and continued to climb to 25,000 ft. This didn't take long and we vectored out to sea for some fifteen minute and were then told by control that the bandits had gone back, so we could return to base.

That sounded a simple order but we had about 18,000 ft of cloud to go through with a cloud base of about 4,000 ft. All kinds of thoughts were going through my head. I was thinking, suppose you lose Green 1 in the let-down and suppose you dive much too fast and can't control your descent, will you have enough room to pull out of a dive at 340 mph?

Green 1 brought me back to my present situation by asking me if I felt confident enough for a formation let-down. 'Yes', I replied. 'OK, then; if you lose me turn to starboard and continue in a straight line.'

I tucked myself in as close as I dared and we went into the cloud at a shallow angle, the airspeed reading 200 mph. This continued for a while and then I noticed that the airspeed was increasing; when I looked at the artificial horizon I knew why, we were now in a steep dive. I watched the other aircraft more than ever now; at one *point we reached 340 mph and then gradually dropped to about 250 mph. This was more like it, a few more minutes and we should break cloud, which we did. What a glorious feeling that was.*

We landed and taxied back to dispersal. We had been airborne one hour exactly. I could have sworn it was at least two hours. As we went into dispersal the officer said in front of the other pilots, 'Bloody good show, Rolls.' If he had given me a medal I could not have been more pleased, especially as it was said in front of the other sprogs. I told them about the clouds and that I had kept formation all the time and that it was fear more than skill that made me do it.

Bill Rolls's luck was running out, though, and on the 30th inexperience and the bad weather finally caught up with him:

Two nights later I was again on readiness and was told to patrol Blue Line, which was an imaginary line, about 100 miles off the Northumberland coast. The weather was not very good. As I started to climb through the cloud towards the coast it seemed to get darker and darker and I didn't like it at all. I had been flying for about twenty minutes when I had a call on the R/T to return to base as quickly as possible as the weather was getting worse. I turned back on a reciprocal course as the aircraft started to buffet and became hard to control. I opened the throttle to offset the bumps and called up control for a QDF – this gives you barometric pressure for the height of the aerodrome. Normally you get it when you take off, but because of the bad weather coming up I knew it must have changed since take-off. I set the millibars of my altimeter and I was at about 2,000 ft. I thought the glim lamps were bright for that height – normally you could hardly see them. I decided to come in on a long approach on engine because of the bumpiness. I was about to lower my flaps when it happened.

I felt a terrific bang on my head and back and heard a rending sound of metal, the aircraft pitched up into the air and I saw a blinding light go past me. I saw the front of the aircraft fall away and felt the bang as my right wing hit the ground and tore itself away from the fuselage. I was bouncing up the runway and then my left wing was torn off. I vaguely remember a howling wind as the fuselage went up the runway, and a lot of noise, but by then I was too dazed to care.

The first I remember when I came to was a voice saying, 'Don't touch him, don't move anything, wait.' I then saw the fire engines and ambulance and a lot of running airmen. Then an officer, I think it was the medical officer, was undoing my harness very slowly, asking if I had any bad pains. I told him I only had a bad knee, as it was bleeding, and a headache, but I could get out of the cockpit with a bit of help. With this help I got out of the cockpit and into the ambulance and off we went to the hospital wing.

After a full examination the only damage I had sustained was a piece of skin taken off my right kneecap, and this was soon plastered. Both our CO and my flight commander came to see how I was and I convinced them that there was nothing wrong with me. The CO told me not to worry about it as long as I was all right; they could replace the Spitfire, but not me.

At the back of my mind was thinking of the artificial horizon; there was something I had to do about it, but I couldn't think what it was. I remember thinking at the time I crashed that someone had made a cock-up and it wasn't me. When I went back to the billets the sergeants were all awake and discussing the crash, and I quickly learned that the Spitfire was a complete write-off. 'That's right, you bastards, rub it in', I was thinking. My biggest worry was that Spitfire K9959 was the one I had done my solo in, and now I had killed it stone dead.

The next morning at about 5 o'clock Johnny White and myself walked over to the other side of the aerodrome. I could hardly believe my eyes, to think that I had escaped from that crash with only a minor cut. We walked along the runway and I saw the wings away on the grass approach to the runway. The biggest shock was to come because the engine was on the grass approach to the runway. I must have hit well before the floodlight that must have been the blinding light I saw as I bounced past. Johnny took some pictures of the wreck, but I didn't accept any prints, as I didn't want a reminder of how I lost my first Spitfire.

During the morning I went to see the CO and my flight commander and filed in the report, stating the change of barometric pressure I had been given and also the one I had been given prior to take-off. I also told the CO that I didn't have my landing light on as my altimeter was reading 1,100 ft and I did not use a landing light above 500 ft. I asked the CO if I could go on readiness at the afternoon session, as I was quite able to fly and would like to do so. One reason I asked for this was because I was anxious to see whether I was grounded pending an investigation into the cause of the accident. He agreed and said to the flight commander, 'You have a visit to Woolsington this afternoon, he can go with you.' I felt relieved as I knew that if he had thought the crash was due to my own carelessness, he would not have let me fly until after an inquiry.

Not all of the excitement was in the air, and the pilots still found time to seek out entertainment of one sort or another, as Ted Graham recalled:

Deacon Elliot was the man who invited the visiting Warkworth copper to a pint of ale (in fact a pint of champagne) at the farewell party for Ronnie Lees, our CO, and a drunken Aussie. He quite forgot that the bobby had an incredibly steep bicycle run down the main village street back to the police station. There was one hectic flip, but no prang, thank heaven.

Acklington was somewhat inaccessible, so the pilots would often travel far and wide to seek out entertainment, as Des Sheen remembered:

Like many other RAF stations, Acklington was known for its inaccessibility. Indeed, as the Edinburgh to London express stopped at a nearby railway station it was sometimes easier to go to London for recreation than to places only a few miles away. On the station itself, our entertainment was limited to the occasional but very welcome ENSA show, invariably followed by a party in the mess.

Everything was about to change for the squadron, though, as 13 Group ordered it south to Biggin Hill, to reinforce 11 Group, on the last day of the month. The order came through at 0715 hrs, and by 1230 hrs the squadron was airborne and on its way. Biggin Hill had been attacked earlier in the day, and the squadron landed to a rather chaotic scene at 1520 hrs, having refuelled at Bicester on the way, as Deacon Elliot recorded:

On the way to Biggin Hill the squadron stopped at Bicester to refuel. The station commander and his reception party were simply terrific. The luxury of a separate starter battery and crew for every aircraft was unbelievable. Then there were the soft drinks, fruit and food served by the wives, and all this in the brilliant sunshine of that Saturday afternoon.

Bill Rolls was among the pilots who flew down to Biggin Hill, and he recalls the scene when they arrived:

On the morning of 31 August 1940 we were on our way to Biggin Hill. We were flying all the aircraft we could muster and would refuel on the way. We arrived at Biggin Hill after lunch. I was shocked to see the number of bomb craters which had been hastily filled in and which littered the grass field. I could see clearly the hangars, which had been blown up the day before, and several buildings were just a pile of rubble. My immediate thoughts went out to those poor buggers who had been in the thick of it for the past month while my pals and I had been enjoying ourselves at Acklington. The landing took a bit longer than usual, having to pick a path through the bomb craters. We were all conducted to the far corner of the airfield to our dispersal area. Here our aircraft were taken over by our ground crews, who had travelled down the day before. When we went into the dispersal office we saw the squadron had been put on thirty minutes readiness. We were now in the thick of the Battle of Britain.

Deacon Elliot also recorded his impressions on arriving at Biggin Hill:

We landed at Biggin Hill at 1530. As we flew in, No. 610 – or what was left of them – flew out; they seemed in a hell of a hurry and we were soon to find out why. We were ordered to readiness as soon as refuelling was complete. Then within minutes we were to take off on our first mission in what we all know as the 'Battle of Britain'.

The pilots had no chance to settle in, as they were scrambled to patrol Biggin Hill at 1745 hrs. The *Luftwaffe* was out in force once again, and its main target was the airfields, Biggin Hill included. Patrolling at 10,000 ft the squadron sighted a huge formation of approximately 160 aircraft, including Dornier Do 17s, Dornier Do 215s and Messerschmitt Bf 109s. Flt Lt Graham led the Spitfires into the attack near Dungeness. Concentrating on the bombers, the squadron was able to claim four damaged; two by Flt Lt Graham (X4034), one by Flt Sgt Steere and one by Sgt Pocock (L1056). On the debit side the squadron suffered its first loss when Plt Off Wilcox (P9457) was killed when he was shot down near Dungeness, and Flt Lt Smith was wounded when his Spitfire (P9438) was damaged by Bf 109s off Dungeness and crash-landed at Biggin Hill. A further aircraft loss was Spitfire

Sgt Maurice Pocock. (M.A. Pocock via L.J. Barton)

R6928, which was destroyed in an air raid at Biggin Hill. The fighting in the south was going to be very different for 72 Sqn. From the point of view of the ground crew the arrival at Biggin Hill was also an eye opener, and almost as dangerous, as Graeme Gillard recalls:

September '40 we got the order to move quickly to Biggin Hill, action was expected. An Imperial Airways Hannibal arrived, a few ground crew complete with tool boxes and home-made wheel-spanners were loaded. The Spitfires were dispatched and Biggin Bump here we come. It was straight into work: we fuel, arm and snags cleared. It seemed that almost immediately RDF did its work and we were warned of a German raid. Squadron was dispatched (all except one) and then we saw the Luftwaffe. They certainly hit Biggin. From our bomb shelter we saw our lone unserviceable Spitfire just curling up under the bombardment. One of our electricians, a very brave but silly man, ran out to pick up an unexploded bomb. It exploded half way to the perimeter woods. Many casualties, mostly WAAF, occurred. The runway was out of action.

Deacon Elliot set down his memories of that first sortie from Biggin Hill. It was a very different battle from those fought in the north of England, and 72 Sqn discovered that the *Luftwaffe* fighter pilots were as determined to shoot them down as they were to get at the bombers. Likewise, the bombers made determined efforts to destroy the squadron on the ground:

Shortly after take-off the squadron ran into a large number of enemy, and during a hectic fight that followed claimed three enemy destroyed and two badly damaged.

Unfortunately we suffered our first fatality – Flg Off Willie Wilcox killed, riddled with bullets. Other casualties included the new CO, Sqn Ldr Collins, on his very first operational mission, who was shot down and crash-landed near Hawkhurst between two trees and a haystack. Although very shaken, he came back for more. Flt Lt Hiram Smith shot down – with a terrible wound – a cannon shell entered the back of his neck, just missing the spine, and came out by his left ear. Flg Off Desmond Sheen was posted missing but turned up later, having been forced down elsewhere.

No sooner had the squadron landed and refuelled than the Germans bombed the airfield – this the second time in two days running, and the place was in a terrible shambles. Twenty-nine killed yesterday – most of them WAAFs in an air raid shelter – another seven today. The armoury, water supply, lighting, communications, many domestic buildings had all been knocked out. The ops block received a direct hit, injuring the station commander, Gp Capt Grice. I saw at least two dispersed aircraft burning from direct hits with incendiary bombs. Bomb craters everywhere.

The most amazing thing about it all was the human factor – no panic – everyone doing their utmost to keep the aircraft in the air. Bomb craters on the airfield being quickly filled in, food being delivered to dispersals to avoid waste of time returning to messes. Land lines installed to run out from ops to squadron dispersals to replace those destroyed. But Biggin had been hit very hard and conditions were at a low.

The squadron had barely had time to settle into Biggin Hill when it was dispatched to Croydon on 1 September. Graeme Gillard recalls the ferocity of the air fighting at this time, and the effect it had on the pilots and their tactics:

Ted Graham I knew very well (as officer to airman) in those days. His marriage in Sheffield was quite a big affair and he threw a beer party for the lads in a hangar at Church Fenton. After the bombing of Biggin Hill we bussed out to Croydon. I marshalled Ted Graham in. He looked shattered and said to us that he must go into town and make his will. We were instructed to go into Woolworths to buy some

72 Sqn pilots playing football in full flying gear while at readiness during the Battle of Britain. (72 Sqn)

A 72 Sqn Spitfire, showing the black underside to the port wing and large yellow ring around the roundel during the Battle of Britain. (72 Sqn)

more small mirrors to fit to the windscreens as rear-view mirrors. Later marks had them fitted.

Deacon Elliot wrote of the conditions at Croydon:

Here the facilities were very limited, but Croydon had not received the punishment of Biggin Hill. Field kitchens were soon established, and much grass and dust found its way into the soup each time we scrambled. The ground crews, led in the main by Sgt Barnard, remained extremely cheerful, and they continued throughout to be a great source of encouragement.

The officers' mess was established in the Airport Hotel, and it was here we were able to get a shave and a bath, the first for most of us for three days. The weather continued to be brilliant sunshine every day – oh, for a cloud or two.

The airfields of Biggin Hill, Detling and Eastchurch, as well as Tilbury Docks in London, were the targets for the *Luftwaffe*'s first assault of the day. Radar began to detect activity from *Luftflotte 2* at around 1015 hrs, when three raids totalling sixty plus aircraft were plotted in three groups. The numbers grew until 120 aircraft overflew Dover before splitting up to make their attacks. No. 72 Sqn, led by Flt Lt Graham (X4034), was scrambled at 1054 hrs, and fifteen Spitfires took off to search for the bandits over Tunbridge Wells. The enemy was sighted over Tunbridge at 30,000 ft, and a stern chase developed between Maidstone and Beachy Head. Here one fighter, claimed as a Heinkel He 113 (no He 113 aircraft took part in operations over Britain) was destroyed by Plt Off Winter (K9958), while Sgt Douthwaite (L1092) shot down a Bf 109 and another was probably destroyed by Flg Off 'Pancho' Villa (P9338). Plt Off Thomson (P9448) was wounded during the fight and Flg Off Pigg (P9458) was missing. Plt Off Winter submitted a report which gives an interesting comparison between the capabilities and tactics of the Spitfire and Messerschmitt Bf 109 and an aircraft

72 Sqn pilots at Croydon during the Blitz. L to R: Flg Off Villa, Flt Sgt Steere, Flg Off Robson, Sgt Staples, Sgt Plant, Plt Off Norfolk, Plt Off Elliot, Sgt Glew, and Plt Off Holland. (72 Sqn)

reported as a Heinkel He 113, but most likely another Messerschmitt, as the Heinkel type never saw operational service:

Then six more Me 109s came down on me and as I turned port an He 113 pulled up in front of me and I had a good bead for about 2 seconds during which time I was firing. The He 113 turned over and dived seawards. By then I was being attacked by six more Me 109s, and by doing steep spiral turns I managed to avoid their fire. After a while I saw the He 113 I had shot at, plane down into the water and sink about 2–3 miles off Beachy Head. This was confirmed by Red 3. Meanwhile I was still spiralling steeply, and the Me 109s followed me down to about 1,000 ft, and then I got down to about 50 ft and they left me. It was impossible to get a bead on them owing to their numbers.

Deacon Elliot wrote of these first combats from Croydon:

Soon in the thick of it again. Enemy aircraft everywhere, it seemed. A terrific scrap with Me 109s and once more we suffered a setback. Flg Off Oswald Pigg missing and many days later confirmed killed. He was found buried under his Spitfire in some remote wood in Kent. A most cheerful fellow and an aggressive fighter in the air. Flg Off Happy Thompson missing but later we traced him to Sidcup hospital. He had been shot down and severely wounded in the knee and body. Flg Off Desmond

Sheen had his machine so badly shot up he was forced to bale out, and he returned to Croydon for more. Sgt Pocock, too, was badly wounded in the leg by a cannon shell and a bullet in his wrist.

During this combat Desmond Sheen, who was shot down, recalled:

Flg Off O. St J. Pigg.

I was lining up a bomber when I glanced behind and found six Me 109s bearing down on me. Despite my frantic twisting and turning my engine was hit by a cannon shell and burst into flames. I was left no option and quickly baled out. Floating down I could see bombs bursting over Dover on my right with Ack-Ack fire from the answering defence. On my left I could see bombs falling on London docks. Not far away I saw an Me 109 burst into flames. The pilot baled out and his parachute opened. Suddenly he fell away; I guess his harness may have been burnt. I quickly looked down to see how far I had to go. On looking up I was horrified to see another Me 109 turn towards me. We had all heard tales of pilots being attacked after baling out. Suddenly a Spitfire appeared on his tail and the two quickly disappeared from view. Before I had time to look around again I found myself landing lightly in the middle of a field.

Desmond's Spitfire, X4109, crashed at Court Lodge Farm, Ham Street, and was excavated in 1981 by an aviation archaeology group.

Landing at Croydon at 1150 hrs, the Spitfires were quickly rearmed and refuelled and were scrambled once again an hour later to patrol Hawkinge at 15,000 ft. This time the Spitfires waded into a large formation of bombers escorted by Messerschmitt Bf 110s and Bf 109s. In the ensuing fight Flg Off Jimmy Elsdon (K9940) shot down two Bf 110s. Plt Off Elliot (P9460) damaged a Bf 109, and once again Flg Off Villa (P9338) was able to make a claim; this time for a Bf 109 damaged. Sgt Pocock was wounded in the arm and leg during the engagement and force-landed his Spitfire (L1056) at West Malling. Deacon Elliot recorded the speed

Flg Off Oswald St J. Pigg, killed in action on 1 September 1940. (G. Gillard)

of turn-round between combats and the ferocity of the fighting during this stage of the battle:

Sgt Duffy Douthwaite. (72 Sqn)

Within five minutes of refuelling from our first mission for that day we were off again heading south-east. We soon intercepted a huge raid, estimated at 150 enemy aircraft. We were split up by enemy fighters as we closed with a bomber formation, and now it was every man for himself. In the process my aircraft was badly mauled by an enemy fighter, tearing a gap the size of a dinner plate in the port wing, damaging the tailplane and punching numerous holes in the other wing. I recognized it, in my mirror, as an He 113 by the cannon which, installed close to the wing root, were 'winking' flame from their barrels. I was able to nurse the Spit back to Croydon to find with relief we had suffered no other losses on that mission. The plane was a write-off.

We also heard some splendid news today – our old CO, Wg Cdr Lees, had taken a week's holiday so he could come and fly with us.

Flg Off T.A.F. Elsdon was also in the thick of it, and filed his combat report later that day:

When I first saw the formation of about 20 Messerschmitts, Jaguars and 110s they were flying in two vics. North-east at the same time I saw two Me 109s in my rear-view mirror. While watching them I became separated from my Section and the Me 109s dived away. As I approached the Me Jaguars they formed a circle in tight line astern. I attacked from slightly above and towards the centre of the circle, gradually decreasing the deflection to about 30 degrees. Range about 400–200 yds. This produced no result –except that the aircraft closed up in line astern.

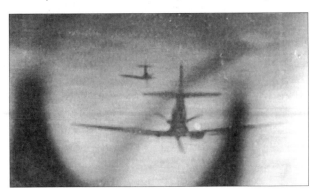

72 Sqn Spitfires seen through the gunsight of the third aircraft of a formation during the Battle of Britain. (72 Sqn)

A 72 Sqn Spitfire streaks along the shoreline at low level during the Battle of Britain. (72 Sqn)

A Spitfire being refuelled and rearmed during the Battle of Britain. (72 Sqn)

In my second attack I decided to keep a steady burst into the circle and let them fly through. I finished my rounds in this manner, and during one burst two of them just dropped out of formation and went down. An eye-witness, Sgt Rolls, on the ground saw the machines falling and crash into the ground, and confirmed that they were from a circle of aircraft very high up and to the south-east of Croydon. Apart from the two 109s in the first instance no other fighters were encountered. No other pilot reported seeing bombers forming a circle as an evasion tactic.

Sunday 2 September dawned fine and warm, and early morning mist and fog patches cleared quickly. Nine Spitfires took off from Croydon at 0745 hrs and climbed to 15,000 ft. They quickly latched onto a formation of Dornier Do 17s escorted by Bf 110s and Bf 109s at 13,000 ft over Maidstone. The Dorniers broke formation as the Spitfires approached, and turned for home. Losing the opportunity to immediately attack the bombers, 72 Sqn's Spitfires waded into the Messerschmitt escort. By the end of the engagement three Do 17s and one Bf 110 were destroyed, and one Do 17 and one Bf 110 were damaged.

The second patrol of the day, consisting of nine Spitfires, took off at 1206 hrs to patrol Dover at 15,000 ft. Over Herne Bay, led by Flt Lt Graham in a borrowed 610 Sqn Spitfire (DW-S), they spotted a tight formation of enemy aircraft, consisting of Do 17s, Bf 109s and Bf 110s. Once again 72 ploughed into the enemy, and this time succeeded in claiming three Bf 110s destroyed, one Do 17 and one Bf 110 probably destroyed and one Bf 110 damaged. Five of the squadron's Spitfires landed at Hawkinge.

Further 72 Sqn Spitfires arrived at Hawkinge, and at 1552 hrs eight of them took off to patrol Dungeness at 10,000 ft. They soon sighted Do 17s escorted by Bf 110s five miles east of Dungeness, and attacked them from astern. Wheeling round they made another attack from the beam and in total managed to damage four Bf 110s. Sqn Ldr Lees was wounded during the engagement.

The last sortie of the day was also flown from Hawkinge, by six Spitfires, ordered to patrol over the base at 15,000 ft. Seeing bursts of anti-aircraft fire over Chatham, they turned to investigate and soon sighted a formation of Do 17s escorted once again by Bf 109s and Bf 110s. Attacking the formation, 72's pilots managed to shoot down one Bf 109 and damage two others. On the debit side Sqn Ldr Collins was wounded in the fight. Among those involved in the day's fighting was Sgt Basil Douthwaite, who reported:

I then turned to port and attacked a Me 109 who was turning steeply to port. I could easily out-turn him, and fired until he broke away in a steep left-hand dive. As I had expended my ammunition I did not follow him but returned to Hawkinge.

Deacon Elliot recorded the events of 2 September in his diary:

A quiet night with lots of sleep for a change found everyone refreshed and ready to go. Flt Sgt Steere led the first scramble with most of the 'sprogs' in his formation, all of whom, during the ensuing battle, did remarkably well.

The squadron then moved to a forward base at Hawkinge, on the south-east coast, for the remainder of the day's operations. A day of successes thwarted by more tragic incidents. Wg Cdr Lees was there – for a short while anyway. Several of us were released for the day, but I recall how hectic it had been for those operating from Hawkinge. The CO, Sqn Ldr Collins, was shot down for the second time, and unfortunately this time badly wounded in his knee and hand – he never returned to the squadron, and Flt Lt Ted Graham assumed command. Wg Cdr Lees was shot down early in the day's fighting, crash-landed on Hawkinge, and it was only with great difficulty he was released from the cockpit. It appeared a cannon shell struck his canopy frame, 'welding' it to the frame of the windscreen. Later, when attacking a gaggle of Me 110s he was shot down again. This time being well and truly hit, both his aircraft and himself in the thigh, which led to a spell in hospital. This was bad luck – all of us were very disappointed as we had hoped he would be with us for a whole week. Flt Sgt Norfolk was shot down, and as he crash-landed his aircraft burst into flames, but he escaped unhurt. Flt Lt Ted Graham was also shot down; his aircraft riddled with lead, he crash-landed at Lympne. The weather continued to be brilliant sunshine – still no clouds – as the squadron returned to Croydon in the evening.

Most of the squadron was stood down on the 3rd, while heavy attacks took place on many airfields during another fine and sunny summer day. However, T.A.F. Elsdon, flying Spitfire X4262, was forced to take to his parachute when he was shot down. On the 4th the squadron was back at Croydon and back in action. After an early raid by *Luftflotte 2*, which saw the *Luftwaffe* introduce a new tactic of splitting its forces between the airfields of Fighter Command and the factories constructing the much-needed fighters, 72 Sqn was scrambled at 1255 hrs on a patrol. Twenty-five minutes later the nine Spitfires sighted an enemy formation over Tenterden and Tunbridge Wells. The formation was reported as Junkers Ju 86s (most likely Ju 88s) escorted by Bf 110s at 15,000 ft. The Spitfires swept into a quarter attack, during which claims for six Bf 110s and three Ju 86s (Ju 88s) destroyed, two Bf 110s probably destroyed and one Bf 110 damaged were made. Elated with 72 Sqn's results, AVM Park, AOC 11 Group, wired his congratulations. Deacon Elliot wrote of the day:

Not so busy today – flew only two missions. Flg Off Desmond Sheen joined up with some 'Hurricanes' only to find they were Me 109s, and immediately spun his way out of trouble. Flg Off Jimmy Elsdon was hit by our own flak, baled out, landing near Stapleford – he was not hurt and returned the same evening to Croydon.

The pace of operations was beginning to take its toll of the pilots, and they were becoming increasingly tired, as Deacon Elliot recorded on the 4th:

The weather was still hot and cloudless. Our second mission proved more successful. Ran into about 30 Me 110s; nine of which were shot down and confirmed by the Army in the area. Plt Off Males, one of our new pilots, was badly hit and baled out. Plt Off Dutch Holland, after attacking an Me 110 head on, limped home with a machine that looked more like a pepper pot than a Spitfire – there were even several holes in the blades of his prop. That evening several of us went up to London but just could not get going, so we bathed, fed and tumbled into bed early, feeling rather exhausted.

The squadron commander's report, recorded by Flg Off Elsdon, stated:

72 Squadron was ordered on patrol and took off with 9 aircraft, 6 in main formation and 3 rearguard. We were vectored onto enemy and we intercepted between Tenterden and Tunbridge Wells when we were at 18,000 ft and they were proceeding north-west. I ordered Red and Yellow Sections into individual line astern for the attack. As we did this the enemy broke up their vic and echelon formation and went into line astern also, and prepared to form a circle. I led the six aircraft of my main formation into the first six of the enemy before they could join up in a circle.

In this attack I shot down the leader, confirmed by Sgt Rolls, and two others were shot down in this first attack. Subsequently a dogfight ensued and the Ju 86s joined in, although the pilots who engaged them did not consider they helped the Me 110s.

During this dogfight no further enemy appeared, and the rearguard came in to assist my main formation. Three Ju 86s were shot down confirmed, and a further four Me 110s confirmed shot down from the fight. One Me 110 was probably destroyed but has not yet been confirmed.

We then saw Me 110s breaking away from the fight and flying 'flat out' for France. Two of us followed, and one, Flg Off Villa, caused his to smoke, but it continued to fly on and was afterwards engaged by Hurricanes.

Flt Lt Smith and Plt Off Holland. (72 Sqn)

I followed one which went very low over Bexhill. I attacked from dead astern and it started smoking from the starboard engine but continued to fly about 100 feet over the sea. I followed, giving short bursts from 400–150 yards, and as I expended my ammunition it lost height and dropped into the sea about 20 miles SSE of Bexhill. This makes a total of 9 enemy aircraft shot down confirmed and 2 probables from this engagement. One pilot, Plt Off Males, was shot down but baled out and has returned uninjured. One other aircraft was damaged by cannon fire but is repairable at unit. The squadron returned individually to base and landed around 1350 hrs.

Following the attacks on the aircraft factories on the 4th, No. 11 Group ordered special cover for them on the 5th. However, the *Luftwaffe* concentrated on attacking airfields once again, the main targets being Biggin Hill, Croydon, Eastchurch, Lympne and North Weald. To counter these attacks 72 Sqn was moved forward to Hawkinge in the afternoon, and after refuelling there the squadron's seven Spitfires were airborne and patrolling the airfield at 25,000 ft. At 1425 hrs they engaged two formations of Bf 109s and came off worst. Although one Bf 109 was destroyed and another damaged, Plt Off Winter (X4013), shot down by Bf 109s at Elham, Kent, and Sgt Gray (L1093) were killed, and Flg Off Sheen (X4034) was wounded and shot down again:

I heard a shout in my earphone, but before I could react I was bounced. Cannon shells poured into my aircraft and I was hit by flying metal in my leg, hand and face. My next recollection is coming to and finding my Spitfire going down at great speed. Panels and bits were missing from the port wing and I had no flying controls whatsoever. I had no idea of height but released my harness ready to bale out when I was immediately sucked out of the cockpit. Unfortunately my boots caught on top of the windscreen with me lying on top of the fuselage. After what seemed an age my feet came free and I at once pulled the ripcord and my parachute opened with a terrific jerk. I just had time to see treetops underneath and then I was in them. These broke my fall and I landed on my feet as light as a feather. But for the trees I am sure it would have been a different ending. A policeman cycled up and produced a welcome flask. 'Why didn't you bale out earlier, lad?' he asked me.

Desmond Sheen's Spitfire, X4034, crashed at Wildage Farm, Bladbean, and he was taken to hospital in Sidcup for treatment, remaining there for six weeks. The speed at which aircraft losses were mounting made it difficult for the squadron to field anything like full strength, and they had scraped together every aircraft fit to fly that day, as Deacon Eliot remembers:

Down to nine Spitfires, all of which flew down to Hawkinge for the day. First patrol ran into lots of Me 109s at 27,000 ft, and into lots of trouble. Our losses once again were tragic. Plt Off 'Snowy' Winter was shot down, tried to bale out but left it too late and was killed. Sgt 'Mabel' Gray was seen to catch a terrific 'packet' from an Me 110, apparently being killed instantly, his aircraft dived vertically into the deck. Sgt Gilder's aircraft was a write-off from enemy fire but he managed to get away with it. Flg Off Desmond Sheen was wounded once again and taken off to hospital in Sidcup.

The 6th dawned fine but a little hazy to the east of London, but 72 Sqn was inactive until the afternoon, when four Spitfires took off at 1255 hrs. They encountered the Germans over Maidstone, and in the subsequent mêlée destroyed one Bf 109 in exchange for two damaged Spitfires. The squadron's ability to put aircraft into the air had become even poorer, and still there was no sign of any replacement aircraft. Deacon Elliot, who was shot down, recorded the fighting on the 6th in his diary:

Only five Spitfires available first thing today – the lowest number the squadron had operated since the war began. We were up on an early patrol, saw a lot of enemy aircraft but did not engage – they were out of reach and well on their way home, acting as rearguard protection for some straggling bombers.

Only four aircraft for the next mission, so we joined up with 66 Sqn and the Kenley Wing. It was over Ashford that we ran into some bombers, escorted as usual by many Me 109s. We were terribly outnumbered. In making two consecutive head-on attacks on an Me 109 he went down smoking and crashed near Marden, killing the pilot. In the process my aircraft too was badly damaged, the bullet-proof windscreen splintered, the leading edges of the wings were holed and torn, and very shortly afterwards, when down to 1,000 ft, something exploded, blowing off the engine cowling. My Spitfire caught fire. I baled out from about 800 ft, landing in a hop field, only to find I was being covered by a shotgun in the hands of a member of the Local Defence Volunteers (LDV). The hop pickers gave me their one remaining bottle of beer – how refreshing. They seemed very perturbed at the number of RAF planes being shot down around their area – they had hoped for more Germans. The Army kindly collected me and had me driven back to Croydon.

Having failed to subdue Fighter Command with its heavy attacks on airfields and aircraft factories, the *Luftwaffe* now sought to bring the fighters to battle by attacking London in strength. The attacks commenced on 7 September, and Goering personally directed the attacks from Cap Gris Nez, throwing every available fighter and bomber into the battle. Following large raids in the morning, another large raid was seen developing over the Calais at 1600 hrs. Over 300 bombers escorted by more than 600 fighters were sweeping towards the English coast as 72 Sqn were scrambled from Croydon at 1700 hrs and headed for the Thames estuary. Targets along the estuary and in the East End of London were heavily bombed by the German formations, while 72 Sqn, with only seven Spitfires available, attempted, in company with other squadrons, to turn the enemy back. During the fight one Bf 110 was destroyed and one Heinkel He 111 probably destroyed, but at the cost of Flg Off Elsdon's Spitfire (X4254), which he was forced to bale out of, severely injured. A further Spitfire (X4022), flown by Sgt White, crashed on landing. The first group of Spitfires was reinforced by a second wave from 72 Sqn getting airborne from Croydon at 1755 hrs. They engaged the Germans over the Dartford–Maidstone area at 15,000 ft. The small group of fighters were up against forty Dornier Do 17s and sixty Bf 109s and Bf 110s, and gave a good account of themselves, claiming one Do 17 destroyed and five more damaged for no losses. Deacon Elliot recalled the wounding of Jimmy Elsdon and a visit from an old CO:

Another loss today for one Me 109 destroyed and another damaged. Flg Off Jimmy Elsdon was again shot down – he baled out but this time received a terrible wound, an incendiary bullet lodged in his knee. I often visited him in Farnborough Hospital, and it was here, for fun, Jim started to grow his famous moustache, which I believe he has to this day.

Wg Cdr Lees called in to see us all at Croydon on his way to Halton Hospital – he looked dreadfully pale and ill, and we learnt he was also in great pain. I so well recall that in the ante-room there was a juke box and for a coin you could play the tune of your choosing – frightfully advanced in those days. 'Begin the Beguine' and 'Fools Rush In Where Angels Fear To Tread' were the most popular. New pilots arrived to replace our losses – all of them very young and inexperienced. The first few replacements had only an average of nine hours' flying on Spitfires before being subject to daily combats with the enemy. Some lasted longer than others – some even survived.

Elsdon dictated his combat report from his hospital bed to Plt Off Whitaker:

No. 72 Squadron was ordered by Sector Control to join with a Hurricane squadron from Kenley at 5,000 ft over Kenley. This interception could not be effected and No. 72 Squadron proceeded on patrol alone, with seven aircraft. At about 20,000 ft a formation of enemy bombers escorted by Me 109s was seen proceeding toward London.

I saw no other fighter squadrons in the vicinity so I decided to lead the squadron into the leading sections of the bombers, which were flying in section line astern, stepped up, in an attempt to break up the formation.

I put the squadron into echelon starboard and led the attack onto the port quarter of the bombers, each machine in my squadron taking the port bomber in the first five sections, and two remaining rearguard.

I shot down an Me 109 or Jaguar which formed the leading section (confirmed by Sgt Rolls) but was hit in the knee and shoulder and forced to retire before I could see any further result of the attack.

I attempted to get back to Croydon, but over Biggin Hill I began to feel faint from loss of blood and decided to land there. The undercarriage, I found, had been jammed up, so I was forced to land the machine on its belly.

The following day the squadron was scrambled once but did not make contact with the enemy. On the 9th the Germans threw their weight against London again, and in the evening the squadron was scrambled to patrol Biggin Hill. Twelve Spitfires were airborne from Croydon at 1735 hrs, climbing to 15,000 ft. Near Biggin Hill they spotted a formation of Do 17s with Bf 109 and Bf 110 escorts. Due to a faulty radio, Flt Lt Graham's order to form line astern for an attack was not heard, and the opportunity for a co-ordinated attack was lost, with only the 'tail-end Charlie' of the Spitfire formation able to engage an Me 110. This was Flg Off Elliot flying Spitfire P9460, who submitted the following combat report:

I was Yellow 1 in my section and was acting as rearguard to the squadron. We were climbing up to 15,000 ft to engage enemy aircraft, when at 8,000 ft I saw an Me 110 2,000 ft below and flying on a south-east course. I was astern of the enemy aircraft, and with max boost gradually closed with it. After giving two 6-second bursts the port engine caught fire and the enemy aircraft started to lose height. I followed up to fire all remaining rounds into the enemy aircraft fuselage. The enemy aircraft continued its downward course and crashed near Lewes about twelve miles from the south coast. The whole enemy aircraft was in flames and completely destroyed.

The upper fuselage was of a greenish grey camouflage with white crosses with a white circle around. I did not notice crew jump, and think this rather improbable. Return fire was experienced at first but not after second 6-secs burst.

A successful interception was made on the 10th, when five Spitfires took off at 1705 hrs to patrol over Redhill. The controller notified them of bandits approaching at 10,000 ft, and they were vectored to intercept them just east of Biggin Hill. The enemy aircraft were two unescorted Do 215s which were quickly dispatched, one crashing at Weybridge and the other at East Grinstead.

Wednesday 11 September saw the *Luftwaffe* make three large raids, including attacks on the important naval targets of Portsmouth and Southampton. It was also the day that Hitler first postponed Operation *Seeloewe*, delaying the planned invasion until the 14th. Mid-way through the afternoon 72 Sqn was ordered to patrol over Croydon at 15,000 ft, and shortly afterwards it was vectored towards the Maidstone–Gravesend area, where the eleven Spitfires encountered a large formation of about sixty Do 17s and He 111s escorted by ninety Bf 109s and Bf 110s. Wading into the formation, the squadron made claims for three Do 17s, one He 111 and one Bf 109 destroyed, two Do 17s probably destroyed and one Bf 109 damaged. The squadron escaped lightly, with only Sgt Douthwaite (R6710) slightly wounded. With the recent losses to the squadron through death and wounding, the squadron needed reinforcements, and they arrived on the 11th in the form of Plt Offs Lindsay, Ritchie and Walker and Sgt Bell-Walker. The following day saw only one inconclusive scramble, after which the Spitfires landed at Biggin Hill, where they would now be based, and on the 13th the squadron was mostly stood down, which allowed it a little time to settle in to the new base and gain some respite from the hectic fighting that had gone before. Only a few sorties were flown, but the pilots were now dreadfully tired, as Deacon Elliot recorded in his diary:

Friday 13th September – what a day to fly. Did two trips with Robby – apart from running into some Me 109s – both were uneventful. Feeling very tired these days cannot think why.'

The first sorties of the 14th were by five Spitfires ordered to patrol over base at 15,000 ft, taking off at 1055 hrs. A lone He 111 was sighted over Hailsham and the Spitfires gave chase, catching it over Eastbourne, where it was shot down into the sea in flames. The day wore on with showers of rain accompanied by thunder as the pilots waited for the next patrol or scramble. Then, at 1800 hrs, they were ordered off to patrol over the Ashford area. Nine aircraft lifted off from Biggin Hill and found seventy Bf 109s. They scoured the sky for the bombers, but none were to be seen. The Messerschmitts were looking for a fight, and turned into the 72 Sqn Spitfires, breaking formation as they did so and setting up a series of individual dogfights. The Messerschmitt pilots probably thought they had the advantage of numbers over the Spitfires, but 72 Sqn escaped to make claims for two Bf 109s and one Bf 110 destroyed for no losses.

Sunday 15th September, now celebrated as Battle of Britain Day, saw the *Luftwaffe* carry out its heaviest attacks on London and also suffer its highest losses since 18 August. By the end of the day Fighter Command had lost twenty-six aircraft and London had been heavily bombed, but in return the *Luftwaffe* had also suffered heavy losses. No. 72 Sqn was ordered into the air to patrol Canterbury at 20,000 ft, and the first three Spitfires were airborne at 1035 hrs, soon followed by seven more in company with 92 Sqn. A German formation consisting of Do 215s and Bf 109s was seen over Canterbury at 22,000 ft. Giving them cover was another group of Bf 109s 3,000 ft below. The Spitfires stormed into the attack between Canterbury and Dungeness, and when the fight was over the pilots landing back at Biggin Hill made claims for two Bf 109s destroyed, two damaged and a Do 215 also destroyed. One of the successful pilots was Flt Lt J.W. Villa, who wrote in his combat report:

The Me 109 which I attacked half rolled as I opened fire, and before he could dive away he caught fire and exploded. I was then attacked by five other Me 109s. I did a step turn to starboard and continued to turn until I out-turned one Me 109 which was on my tail. I gave him two short bursts and he burst into flames.

Deacon Elliot flew again on the 15th, and wrote of the effect that the constant scrambles and dogfighting was having on him and his compatriots:

Three missions today. The whole German Air Force seemed to be airborne. Action everywhere and on every mission. By the end of the day I was tired, annoyed at being shot at so frequently and feeling rather sick. I was not alone in these feelings. Also, my aircraft P9460 for some unaccountable reason was most difficult to fly.

Every day there was activity and more activity, and it seemed much better to stay with it rather than take allotted days off. I found it was far less disturbing to fly on most days and on as many missions as possible than to take a break and be faced with the unsettling problem of getting re-acclimatized – mentally a painful process for some.

The second patrol of the day consisted of eight Spitfires, ordered to patrol over base at 15,000 ft in company with 66 Sqn. It was not long before they encountered a large formation of He 111s escorted by Bf 109s. As the enemy bombers passed over the Dartford–Maidstone area it appeared that the Bf 109s were in a poor position to provide any cover, and 72 and 66 Squadrons waded into the bombers. All eight of 72's Spitfires returned to Biggin Hill, and the successful pilots made claims for three He 111s destroyed, one probably destroyed and one damaged.

After the mauling of the *Luftwaffe* on the 15th, the Germans only came in penny packets by day, concentrating on heavy night raids on London, Merseyside,

Glasgow and the Midlands on the 16th and 17th. The Spitfire was not well suited to night-fighting, and as a consequence the squadron was able to gain a breathing space, with only two uneventful patrols over both days. On the 18th the squadron was back in the thick of it and took more casualties. Eleven Spitfires took off from Biggin Hill, led by more from 92 Sqn, and set up a patrol over Gravesend. It was not long before they got into a fight during which Plt Off Lloyd and Sgt Bell-Walker (R6704) were both seriously wounded. Only nine of the Spitfires returned to Biggin Hill.

The 19th was another quiet day, but the following day saw more action and another loss for the squadron. In company with 66 Sqn, eight Spitfires took off at 1020 hrs to patrol over Maidstone. They were joined there by two more squadrons from Hornchurch. A group of Bf 109s and Bf 110s were sighted over the Canterbury–Ashford area, and a fight commenced. The squadron scored one Bf 109 destroyed and one probably destroyed, but Plt Off Holland was killed in the battle. The squadron lost one aircraft on 20 September, R6881:RN-M being shot down by a Bf 109 near Canterbury, but Plt Off Lindsay was safe. Deacon Elliot was flying one of the squadron's more unusual missions of the battle, and did not hear of the death of his friend, Dutch Holland, until he returned:

Three pilots were required to escort an Anson from Hawkinge over the Channel to a point where the Army officers in it could spot the impact positions of heavy shells being fired from Dover to Calais. All pilots' names were put in the hat, and the 'lucky' ones were Robson, Staples and myself. The first mission, flying at no more than 1,000 ft, took us half way across the Channel, and it was quite eventful. Ops were keeping us and the Anson informed of local enemy activity, and it was on the second mission, when about ten miles out, we lost contact with the Anson, but soon spotted it heading almost vertically for the sea and home.

On landing at Hawkinge, it appears the Anson pilot heard what he thought was a warning of enemy aircraft in the vicinity and took the appropriate protective steps. The effects of his action left large sections of the Anson's fuselage completely void of canvas – one could see through the aircraft from stem to stern. To the best of my knowledge this operation was a first and last.

That evening on return to Biggin Hill I learned the very sad news of the death of my closest friend, Dutch Holland – we had joined the squadron together at Drem in December 1939. It is thought he had a direct hit from our own flak when over the Thames Estuary. He baled out, was conscious on landing, but his legs had been shot away and he died in Chatham hospital.

No. 72 Sqn next saw action on the 23rd, when eleven Spitfires took off from Biggin Hill, led by Flt Lt Graham (X4481) to rendezvous with 66 and 92 Sqns over Gravesend. No. 72 Sqn did not manage to join up with the other two squadrons, but it did manage to get into a fight during which Plt Off Brown was forced to crash-land his Spitfire (X4063) after being shot down by Bf 109s near Gravesend,

Kent. On the credit side the squadron scored one Bf 109 destroyed and one probably destroyed. Ivor Cosby and 'Sticky' Glew shared the Messerschmitt, as Cosby reported:

I was No. 3 of the Section which was ordered to patrol Gravesend at 25,000 ft. The enemy fighters were above and dived to attack. I then took evasive action and found myself alone. On looking round I noticed a Spitfire engaging an Me 109. There was another Me 109 on the Spitfire's tail, so I got on his tail and gave him a 3-second burst. The Spitfire then became aware of the enemy aircraft and turned to engage him. I followed the original Me 109 and gave him a 4-sec burst. Petrol immediately gushed out of the port side of the fuselage and he began to lose height rapidly. Making sure that it was all clear behind, I followed him down over Folkestone, gave him a final short burst and he went into the sea about 400 yards from the pier.

Cosby's victim was Messerschmitt Bf 109 W.Nr.1969 coded 2+ of 4/JG2 flown by *Unteroffizier* Dilthey. Dilthey was wounded in the shoulder and leg and just managed to escape from the fighter before it sank. He was rescued from the sea by 2/Lt M.E. Jacobs and another soldier who swam out and helped him into a fishing-boat. Deacon Elliot was on the receiving end in this dogfight:

A huge mixed raid just south of the Estuary, heading due west for London. Me 109s everywhere. I was just closing in on an Me 109 when unbeknown an Me 109 was doing precisely the same thing to me – he fired first. His cannons ripped off a piece of my port wing, leaving the aileron twisted and jammed. The rudder and elevators were reduced to a crumpled frame and my engine, streaming glycol,

Plt Off Lindsay in cockpit of Spitfire in classic fighter pilot pose. (Lindsay)

was failing rapidly. Fortunately, Sgt Norfolk saw it happen and acted as protective escort during a glide descent to the time I crash-landed, just prior to which all my controls seized. Yet another lucky break.

A further attempt was made to join up with 66 and 92 Squadrons at 1525 hrs that afternoon at Swanley Junction, but by the time 72 Sqn arrived there the other two squadrons had been ordered to land. Left on their own, the ten Spitfires patrolled over Maidstone and the south coast at 3,000 ft. No enemy aircraft were encountered and all of the Spitfires returned to base. The last sortie of the day followed a similar pattern, and the only highlight was the announcement of the award of the DFC to Flt Lt J.W. Villa.

With early morning fog beginning to clear over Northern France on the morning of Tuesday 24 September, the German bombers and fighters began to rise from their airfields until some 200 of them were plotted on radar at 0830 hrs. No. 72 Sqn were already airborne, having lifted from Biggin Hill at 0820 hrs to join 92 and 66 Squadrons at Swanley. The three squadrons intercepted more than a hundred Do 17s, Ju 88s and Bf 109s over Rochester at 19,000 ft. No. 72 Sqn attacked in line astern and shot down one Ju 88. Two Bf 109s were probably destroyed, and two Do 17s and a Bf 109 were damaged in exchange for one Spitfire damaged.

The next two days were relatively quiet for the squadron, but they were to see much action on the 27th, when the *Luftwaffe* made heavy attacks on London and Bristol. Having taken off at 0853 hrs, the twelve Spitfires were patrolling between Maidstone and Sevenoaks in company with 92 Sqn, which was leading, when a large formation of Do 215s, Do 217s and Ju 88s with Bf 109 escorts was sighted between 18,000 and 25,000 ft. The two squadrons quickly engaged the 100+ enemy bombers and fighters, and in the mêlée Flg Off Davis-Cook

(N3068) and Plt Off Males (X4340) were killed. Males was shot down by Bf 109s, crashing into Shadwell Dock, Stepney, London. Two further Spitfires were damaged in return for one Ju 88, one Bf 109, one Do 17 and 3½ Do 215s destroyed, one Ju 88 and two Do 215s probably destroyed and one Do 215 damaged. Plt Off J.J. O'Meara (RN-J) claimed a Do 17 damaged. After a brief respite ten Spitfires were airborne again at 1145 hrs to rendezvous with 92 Sqn over

Flt Lt Bernard Walter Brown.

Biggin Hill before heading for Maidstone to intercept an inbound raid. Between Dungeness and South Foreland they encountered a formation of more than forty Bf 109s at 25,000 ft. In the fighter *v.* fighter combat the squadron emerged victorious, damaging three Bf 109s for no loss. The final fight of the day for the already exhausted pilots came in mid-afternoon. Eight Spitfires lifted from Biggin Hill at 1514 hrs and climbed to patrol over the base at 25,000 ft. The Germans soon put in an appearance in the form of twelve to fifteen He 111s escorted by forty Bf 109s over the base at 14,000 ft. With the advantage of height the squadron swooped down on the enemy, catching them between Biggin Hill and the Channel, where they destroyed two He 111s and one Bf 109.

In addition to the day's victories, and taking some of the sting out of the day's losses, it was announced that Flg Off Jimmy Elsdon had been awarded the DFC.

The 28th found the *Luftwaffe* targeting London again, and also the Solent area. To counter this, 72 Squadron's ten Spitfires took off at 1319 hrs to patrol the Sevenoaks area with 66 Sqn. They sighted over thirty Bf 109s slightly above them over Canterbury, and climbed to engage. A series of dogfights developed, but aside from one Bf 109 shot down, most were inconclusive. No. 72 Sqn landed back at Biggin without loss. On the 29th Plt Off J.J. O'Meara (RN-K) was again in the thick of it, and claimed one Ju 88 destroyed, one probably destroyed and one Bf 109E damaged. The squadron returned to the fray on the 30th, when eleven Spitfires climbed away from base at 1626 hrs to patrol at 25,00 ft. They found several groups of Bf 109s flying north-north-west, slightly below, and ran in line astern to attack. The Messerschmitts climbed and made a half-hearted attempt to attack, firing at extreme range before climbing away. Only one Bf 109 probably destroyed resulted from the encounter. By the end of the month the squadron had had several aircraft lost and damaged and lost pilots shot down or wounded. The aircraft were replaced, as were the pilots, with the arrival during the month of Plt Offs Case, Secretan, Davy and Sutton.

October opened with 72 Sqn still based at Biggin Hill and the Battle of Britain moving into a new phase. After the heavy losses for little gain in September, Goering had decided that the day arena would be given over to high-flying fighter-bombers carrying out 'tip and run' raids, while the bombers concentrated on night raids. Consequently the month was relatively quiet for Fighter Command's day-fighters, with few interceptions or victories. The first four days of the month were taken up with uneventful patrols for 72 Sqn, but it did allow some of the new pilots to gain experience and for replacements to be posted in. Two pilots, Plt Off J.J. O'Meara DFC and Sgt M.A. Lee, were posted out to 421 Flt at Gravesend on the 3rd. This flight was equipped with a high-altitude variant of the Spitfire designed to counter the *Luftwaffe* high-level raids. Posted in were Plt Off P.D. Poole and Sgt P.H.R.R.A. Terry, followed the next day by Sgt Morrison.

The first sorties on the 5th began tragically. Twelve Spitfires got airborne at 0935 hrs, but immediately on take-off Plt Off Sutton (K9989) collided with Sgt Staples

(X4544). Sutton crashed and was killed, while Staples managed to maintain control of his damaged Spitfire and land back at Biggin Hill. The remainder of the Spitfires continued to climb towards Maidstone and were then ordered to continue their climb to 30,000 ft. They intercepted a formation of thirty Bf 109s at 24,000 ft, but were then attacked by another formation of twenty Messerchmitts lurking above. Flt Sgt Steere (X4337), acting as the 'tail-end Charlie' rearguard weaving behind, took the brunt of the attack but managed to escape with only slight damage. The ten Spitfires made it back to Biggin, having had a lucky escape. Deacon Elliot recalled the tragic incident:

> A new pilot, Plt Off Sutton, arrived on 30 September, but the poor chap only lasted four days – lack of experience cost him his life. He was late in getting airborne during a scramble, and on catching up with the squadron at about 1,500 ft he was attempting to manoeuvre into his allotted position when he flew through Sgt Staples's propeller. His tail was chopped off. Sam Staples managed to land his badly damaged aircraft back at Biggin Hill, but he was a terribly shaken man. I borrowed a Master from 92 Sqn and flew Sam up north to my home for the weekend. Sam had a very kind nature and he was always a gentleman.

On the 8th ten Spitfires took off to patrol over Maidstone, but Sgt Glew (K9847) had engine trouble and made a forced landing at Holstead. Communications between the formation and the controller at Biggin Hill were lost, and Plt Off

J.J. O'Meara as a squadron leader.

Plt Off Holland's grave.

Elliot (X4483) was dispatched back to base to re-establish communications. This was achieved by telephoning orders from the control room to the squadron dispersal, from where they were relayed by radio. Reaching 20,000 ft, the squadron was suddenly bounced, out of the sun, by Bf 109s, which damaged two of the Spitfires before making their escape.

DFC Citation

LONDON GAZETTE, 8TH OCTOBER 1940

Acting Flight Lieutenant John Wolferstan Villa

Since 31st August, 1940, this officer has destroyed at least six enemy aircraft. One day in September, 1940, he was successful in destroying three enemy aircraft unaided and assisted in the destruction of a fourth. Flight Lieutenant Villa has consistently led his flight, and frequently the Squadron, with great dash and eagerness, and has proved a keen fighter and a good leader.

DFC Citation

LONDON GAZETTE, 8TH OCTOBER 1940

Flying Officer Thomas Arthur Francis Elsdon

Since 31st August, 1940, this officer has destroyed six enemy aircraft, bringing his total to eight. On 4th September, 1940, when leading his Squadron, his method of attack was successful in destroying nine enemy aircraft and probably three more. A few days later, he brought down the leading aircraft of a bomber formation. His record is outstanding and he has led his section and flight with distinction, showing complete disregard of danger and personal injury.

On the 10th the squadron received another pilot replacement in the shape of Sgt R.E. Plant, posted in from 611 Sqn. On the following day it almost lost another pilot. Eleven Spitfires took off at 0735 hrs for a convoy patrol off Deal, where about thirty Bf 109s attacked them. Plt Off Pool (K9870), who had been on the squadron just over a week, had his Spitfire shot down in flames, though he managed to bale out successfully. Having taken to his parachute, Peter Pool felt the need to write to the Irvin parachute company to thank them:

22.10.40

Dear Sir

I am extremely indebted to your company for saving my life on Friday 11 October at 8 a.m. As I was shot down by a Me 109 without seeing him (the dirty dog!)

I was flying on Patrol at 22,000 ft with my squadron – No. 72 from Biggin Hill. When I was shot without any warning. I was flying at the back of the squadron.

My Spitfire caught fire and the fumes in the cockpit got rather thick. I decided to leave and found this easier than anticipated as my hood had been shot away. The plane was inverted and I fell out easily. I should have made a delayed drop but being my first I pulled the ripcord after the required three seconds.

The jerk – though surprising – wasn't so intense as I anticipated but my foot caught up in the parachute for one long agonising second – then I found myself the right way up – floating down slowly – very slowly.

I saw a plane approaching and feared it was an Me, but luck was with me and two of my friends circled me the whole way down.

It was a very very warm uncomfortable descent due I suppose to my own fault of having my parachute too tight. It was painfully tight and bruised me below the belt considerably. I was drifting in the opposite direction to the ground wind towards some water so I pulled at the cord above my head. I succeeded in getting a terrific pendulum motion on the 'chute which was most unpleasant – about 45 deg each way and hurt considerably.

So I stopped this and resigned myself to the slow but sure descent. At about 6,000 ft I thought I would land on a large factory – but the wind thought otherwise and in the end I landed safely in a field – having turned the release box before landing – the parachute was quickly detached.

I bent my legs on landing but fell rather sideways and nearly broke my right leg but I was lucky and just hurt it a little.

I have been in hospital since with a few leg and arm wounds and some superficial burns but I am nearly mended.

Thank you very much for the safe descent, I believe I qualify for your Caterpillar Club by this. I shall be pleased to consider any other questions you would like to know. This is rather long winded but I thought you might like a full account of my exploit.

I should estimate that I pulled the cord at 20,000 ft (approx) and that it took me well over 20 minutes to come down. I came down about a mile away from Sittingbourne in Kent and after going to an Army Medical Station I was taken to Chatham County Hospital.

I am just off to Torquay to recuperate now.

Yours sincerely,

Peter D Pool
Pilot Officer

At 0900 hrs Flt Lt 'Pancho' Villa (X4419) took off alone to intercept an enemy bomber over the Thames estuary. Climbing to 30,000 ft, he found a Do 17 heading for home. He claimed it shot down, having watched it dive into low haze over the sea east of North Foreland. The 11th also saw the return of Flt Lt R.A. Thomson to the squadron, having recovered from his wounds.

There was another tragic loss on the 12th. Seven Spitfires in company with five of 92 Sqn took off on patrol, during which they observed a squadron of Hurricanes in a fight with Messerschmitts. They had joined up with a squadron of Hurricanes, but in deteriorating weather the formation split up and Plt Off Case (P9338), who had joined the squadron in September, became separated. He did not return to Biggin Hill and was later reported to have crashed near Folkestone and been killed.

Peter and Diana Pool. (D.E. Pool)

After four more inconclusive patrols on the 13th, the squadron ended its sojourn at Biggin Hill and departed for Leconfield for a period of rest and re-equipment. Flt Lt Villa remained at Biggin, having been posted to 92 Sqn, while Flt Lt D.F.B. Sheen DFC returned to the squadron as a flight commander. During the first few days at Leconfield Plt Off A.L. 'Archie' Winskill was posted out to 603 Sqn at Hornchurch. Deacon Elliot remembers Leconfield as a different world from the terror and excitement of Biggin Hill:

> *What a different world it seemed up in the Yorkshire area, quiet and peaceful. One could fly around without looking over your shoulder every second for Me 109s – the gun button could now be left on 'safe' – R/T procedure was more relaxed, in fact it was a joy to be alive. The Beverley Arms in Beverley provided most of our eats and drinks during 'released' periods.*

Hardly had the squadron had time to settle in at Leconfield than they were moved again on the 20th, to Coltishall. On the 22nd it was announced in the *London Gazette* that the former squadron commander. Wg Cdr R.B. Lees, had been awarded a bar to his DFC. At this point they were classed as a 'C'-Class squadron, non-operational and tasked with training and bringing the squadron's replacement pilots up to operational standard prior to being thrown back into battle. This did not mean that they were to have an easy life of it. The Germans were still active and occasionally wandered into No. 12 Group's area looking for a fight. No. 72 Sqn was happy to oblige on the 25th. Blue Section took off from

Coltishall at 1400 hrs to patrol, and over Aylsham it was vectored to intercept an intruder at 27,000 ft over Cromer. It closed with the intruder, which was identified as a Bf 110, and as Blue Section climbed to intercept, a square, flat object was jettisoned from the Messerschmitt. This object left a trail of smoke as it fell. The Bf 110 waggled its wings, then fell into a stall turn, diving towards a cloud bank in an attempt to escape, heading out to sea. Blue 1, Plt Off Norfolk (X4601), was in the best attack position, and opened fire, observing a flash, then a puff of smoke from the Bf 110, which dived through the cloud and was last seen at about 1,500 ft north-east of Great Yarmouth. On subsequent examination of the evidence, Fighter Command allowed the Messerschmitt as destroyed. The Messerschmitt Bf 110C-5 coded F6+MK of *2(F)/122* crashed fifteen miles north-east of Great Yarmouth. The pilot, *Leutnant* K. Wacker, was picked up by HMS *Widgeon*, but his gunner, *Gefr* G. Gneist, was killed.

Fitter IIE, Jack Lancaster, joined the squadron at Coltishall:

I joined 72 Sqn at Coltishall as a Fitter IIE in October 1940 and was placed in Maintenance Flt. Having previously worked on Fairey Battles, the work was not so different, but to me, more exciting. The squadron were in a bit of disarray because they had a very, very rough time at Biggin Hill in September and October and we had lost a great number of pilots during that Battle of Britain period. In a matter of a few weeks the squadron moved to Leuchars, Maintenance Flt went to Turnhouse, but within a month, the whole squadron moved to Acklington.

Deacon Elliot also wrote of the brief time spent at Coltishall:

We moved to Coltishall and continued routine operations. Patrols investigating the occasional 'X' raid and lots of training flights. Norwich was the main centre for our entertainment. The Angel and the Bell both provided – or rather sold – excellent food.

Two days later it was Yellow Section's turn to get into a scrap. Patrolling over Great Yarmouth, it was vectored to a position twenty miles west, where it sighted a Bf 110 at 26,000 ft. Flg Off Robson (X4486), Plt Off Secretan (X4413) and Sgt Staples (X4595) all made attacks on the high flyer and observed whitish smoke coming from the Messerschmitt's starboard engine before it disappeared into cloud and escaped. They claimed it damaged. The remainder of October passed uneventfully, with only a large influx of newly posted pilots to make things interesting. Those posted in were Plt Offs R.S. Smith and L.B. Fordham and Sgts J. Hurst, S.A. Hibbert, W.H. Lamberton, A.J. Casey, D.S. Corser, W. Gregson and S. Hamer. All were posted straight from training at No. 7 OTU, Hawarden. On the last day of the month the squadron moved out to Coltishall's satellite airfield at Matlaske. Deacon Elliot recalls the brief idyllic – and alcoholic – sojourn at Matlaske:

On 30 October we moved a few miles across the way to Matlaske, a satellite of Coltishall. The officers' mess was in a magnificent old country house called Itteringham Mill. It was built over a trout stream and you could hear the water flowing under the house and toppling down the other side into a deep pool, from which our breakfast was caught on numerous occasions. Flg Off Slim Farmer, the intelligence officer, was messing officer, but we had joint accounts with the main officers' mess at Coltishall.

We lived so well at Matlaske and became so frightfully in debt that on 3 November we were all ordered back to Coltishall. Actually, there was another reason for this move – after two Spitfires were tipped on their noses the airfield was declared unserviceable.

Portrait of Sgt Allan James Casey. (via E.J. Mannings/72 Sqn)

Plt Off Gregson. (R. Gledhill via 72 Sqn)

CHAPTER 4

Leaning into Europe

Operations commenced from Matlaske on Friday 1 November with a series of convoy patrols, but the airfield soon had to be abandoned due to waterlogging, and the squadron moved back to Coltishall on the 2nd. During the 1st the *Luftwaffe* made five attacks on the London and Kent areas. In the third raid of the day thirty-six Bf 109s made landfall at Folkestone, and the Bromley and Biggin Hill areas were attacked. In defence 46 and 17 Squadrons were ordered off from North Weald to Maidstone, followed about forty-five minutes later by 222 and 603 Squadrons from Kenley. Ten minutes later 229 and 302 Squadrons were ordered to patrol Croydon. The last pair of squadrons airborne were 72 and 92 Squadrons to patrol Biggin Hill and take over the readiness patrol after another interception. They then went on to intercept a raid on a convoy in the Thames estuary.

Flg Off Cosby was posted out on the 4th to 222 Sqn at Hornchurch, but in his place came an influx of new pilots from 57 OTU: Plt Off J.F. Reeves and Sgts W.J. Rosser and B.C. Webber. Desmond Sheen was airborne in Spitfire X4596 on 5 November and encountered an enemy bomber, recording:

Attacked Do 215 30 [miles] NE Yarmouth. No result.

DFM Citation

LONDON GAZETTE, 8TH NOVEMBER 1940

Rolls, William Thomas Edward, 745542, Sergeant, RAFVR

This airman, after a very short experience of operational flying, has taken his place with the best war pilots in the squadron. In each of his first two engagements, he shot down two enemy aircraft, and has, in all, destroyed at least six.

The 8th saw another flurry of postings, with Sgts G.E. Camplin and E.W. Perkins arriving from 611 Sqn. Sgt A.C. Leigh was sent in the opposite direction, and Sgts N. Glew and J.S. Gilders were sent to 616 Sqn at Kirton in Lindsey.

The first action for the squadron in November occurred on the 9th, when Green Section, consisting of Plt Off Douthwaite (X4643), Plt Off Smith (N3228) and Flt Sgt Steere I (X4483), took off to patrol base at 5,000 ft. They were vectored toward Great Yarmouth where an He 111 was sighted heading towards the coast. Douthwaite led the section into the attack, and though the He 111 returned fire this quickly ceased under the hail of bullets from the Spitfires. The Heinkel was last seen heading seawards with both engines smoking. The rest of Green Section returned to Coltishall to claim it destroyed. More movements occurred on the 9th, with Flg Off Robson posted to CFS at Upavon and Sgts T.E.J. Ream and S. Wilson arriving from 616 Sqn. Further postings occurred with Sgt Squiers posted in from 64 Sqn on the 21st, and on the 28th Flt Lt F.M. 'Hiram' Smith arrived from Biggin Hill. Deacon Elliot remembers this period as one of rest, re-equipment and reinforcement:

Lots of pilots began to arrive now – three officers and eleven sergeants in the course of a few days – while some of the regular squadron pilots who had survived were posted out to training posts. This included Plt Off Robson, who was promoted to acting flight lieutenant. Most of our flying now was devoted to training the new arrivals – this was invigorating and most rewarding as they were all so incredibly keen.

We still spent endless hours at readiness in addition to operating an intensive training programme; this meant heavy work and rather tiring for the few of us considered 'experienced'.

The days of November were filled with boring patrols and convoy escorts until, on the 29th, the squadron was moved to Leuchars in Fife. Deacon Elliot wrote of the first few days at Leuchars:

We were all confined to camp for a day or two, not for bad behaviour, but because our cars being driven up by airmen had not arrived. It was very cold at Leuchars, but nothing like as bad as when some of us were at Drem this time last year.

On 4 December Plt Off Slim Farmer, Desmond Sheen and myself were invited to a pheasant shoot by Air Commodore Cochrane on his magnificent estate, the family seat of which was Crawford Priory. There were a number of expert 'guns' there. We took up our allotted positions and shot when the opportunity arose, and finally returned with our respective 'bags'. I shot a pigeon and a rabbit, Slim Farmer a very small duck, but he was thrilled and claimed its relative value equal to at least six brace of pheasant. Then I spotted Desmond literally staggering under a load – I thought he was carrying everyone else's for them – but not a bit of it – he had shot them all himself.

The mess arranged a huge dance on the evening of 6 December, in the midst of which who should breeze in but Hiram Smith – out of hospital and on sick leave. This just made matters worse – the party was extended.

The stay at Leuchars was intended to be brief, as another move to Turnhouse was planned when the runways there were ready for operations. In expectation of this the adjutant and orderly room staff and the ground crew moved to Turnhouse by road, while seven of the squadron Spitfires made the first flights to Leuchars. They began patrols from the Fife base the next day. The planned move to Turnhouse was cancelled and the squadron would stay at Leuchars through December.

There was little excitement at Leuchars until the 8th, when Green Section, led by Plt Off Norfolk (X4601), was vectored south from Leuchars while on patrol. Norfolk sighted a Heinkel He 111 as they approached Holy Island. The bomber was flying north, but turned east at high speed on spotting the Spitfires. Norfolk opened fire at extreme range and continued to close on the Heinkel. He was only 150 yards away when it disappeared into cloud. The Heinkel had not returned fire, and Norfolk saw many hits on the bomber, but no visible damage. This one got away.

On the 14th the squadron received orders to move once again, this time to Acklington. Once again the adjutant and his orderly room staff and the ground crew set off on a long road journey. The aircraft were to have followed immediately. However, bad weather delayed the move until the 19th, when they finally flew down to their new base, the spare pilots being ferried in two Handley Page Harrow bomber-transports. Over the next two days several pilots were posted away; Sgts Hurst, Raw, Squier, Webber and Wilson all went to 603 Sqn at Drem, Sgt Ream to 92 Sqn at Biggin Hill and Sgt Hamer to 610 Sqn at Tangmere. With little operational flying, the squadron was able to celebrate Christmas and the New Year at Acklington, but more than a few would wonder what the next year would bring.

DFM Citation

LONDON GAZETTE, 24TH DECEMBER 1940

White, John, 741363, Sergeant, RAFVR

Within a period of eight days in September 1940, this airman destroyed two enemy aircraft and assisted in the destruction of three more. His courage and efficiency over a long period have set a splendid example to his fellow pilots. He has personally destroyed four enemy aircraft and possibly four more.

Poor weather and heavy snow curtailed flying in the early part of January, with the first large patrol, over the Farne Islands, not occurring until the 9th. Two pilots, Plt Offs N.A. Doobyn and G.N. Marshal, were posted in from 57 OTU on the 8th, but just as quickly posted out again to 253 Sqn on the 9th. More new faces arrived from 258 Sqn in the form of Sgts E.A. Southey, J.R.T. Dykes, W.A. Lack and T.R. Mallett. While these pilots were moving to and fro, Flt Lt Sheen and Flt Lt Smith were detached to operate from Prestwick in a scheme designed to provide cover for airfields where the resident squadron had to be moved urgently elsewhere; they returned on the 13th. Another of the recently arrived pilots, Sgt Allan Casey, had a lucky escape in a forced landing with Spitfire X4602 at Brancepeth Castle on the 11th. The CO annotated his logbook: 'INEXPERIENCE – forced to land by bad weather. Crashed on landing.' Flt Lt R.A. Thomson, who had only recently returned to the squadron after recovering from wounds, was posted out again to No. 2 CFS at Cranwell for flying instructor training.

Fitter Tom Thackray recalls the winter of 1940/41:

In 1940/41 a lot of airmen, not squadron personnel, were billeted in the Co-operative Hall in Broomhill, and they had special passes to get into and out of camp. As there were armed guards at the barriers at all of the entry roads, passwords were also in use. When we booked out at the guardroom for an evening out we were given the password. People would forget the password after a few drinks, so you can visualise the chaos when they tried to get back into camp.

If you went to a dance in Ashington you would have to leave the dance early to enable you to catch the last bus to Broomhill. We would try and get hold of the SOPs (sleeping-out passes) which the airmen who were billeted in the Co-op Hall were issued with, we could then get the first bus back in the morning and use the SOP.

In the winter of '41 four of us were stranded in Ashington, snowbound. It was three days before we decided we had better walk back, as there were still no buses running. We walked back from Ashington in about nine inches of snow, and when we arrived the Flight Sergeant gave us all a dressing-down, starting with the words,

---

DFC Citation

LONDON GAZETTE, 7TH JANUARY 1941

Pilot Officer Norman Robert Norfolk

Throughout a long period of operations, Pilot Officer Norfolk has shown himself to be a most determined fighter pilot, pressing home his attacks on every occasion. He has displayed great courage and has destroyed at least four enemy aircraft.

'I know why you buggers have come back – it's pay day.'

The squadron would lay on liberty wagons sometimes to take personnel to Ashington and pick us up at about 11.15 p.m. at a pre-arranged point. One night this 3-ton Bedford was so crowded it was unstable and didn't recover on one of the many bends, and tipped over into the ditch; luckily no one was hurt. On one of these liberty wagons was a flight sergeant of the RAF Service Police, who was not a very nice man to know and disliked the squadron personnel, as we were a bit scruffy and didn't like discipline. He was well inebriated one night and he came to get a lift back to camp. 'Jump on', said the lads, seeing a chance to get their own back for the way he had treated them in the past.

Sgt Allan James Casey. (72 Sqn)

Everyone was swaying about under the canvas cover, with the flight sergeant in their midst. First his gas mask went overboard, followed by his hat, and someone had slit his boots all around the tops. When we arrived back at the guardroom he was rolled over the backboard onto the ground, protesting in a slurred voice, 'I'll get you for this, you're that 72 Squadron lot.' Nothing more was ever heard about this incident. Sometimes we would go to dances in Broomhill at the Primrose Hall, more commonly known as 'The Sweatbox'.

January continued with a distinct lack of enemy activity in the north of the country by day, and 72 Sqn resigned itself to training flights and the occasional fruitless patrol. The pilots continued to come and go, with Sgts C.E. Camplin, W.T. Rolls and T.R. Ritchie posted out to 145 Sqn, 56 and 58 OTUs respectively. Flg Off T.D.H. Davy was posted to No. 315 (Polish) Squadron as a flight commander. On the 16th a Spitfire crashed with Cat. 3 damage at Acklington when returning from an early-morning defensive patrol.

From the operational point of view, February was even quieter than the preceding month. Desmond Sheen flew a night operation on the 15th in Spitfire X4855, and noted:

Night Operational Patrol. 70 Jerries. No interception.

Snow hampered operations on several days, and on the 20th the heaviest snowfall recorded since 1886 left eighteen inches of snow on Acklington's runways. The squadron had its fair share of movements again during the month, with the posting-in of a medical officer, Flg Off H.B. Jones, on the 1st, and two new pilots from 57 OTU – Plt Off R.B. Newton and Sgt D.J. Prytherch. Plt Off R.S. Smith was posted away on the 25th.

Since the end of the Battle of Britain in October 1940, there had been little to cheer about, as the Allies suffered reverse after reverse. Throughout November the *Luftwaffe* had continued to bomb British cities, striking Coventry, Birmingham and Southampton in heavy night raids, against which the day-fighter Spitfires could do nothing. Only the Fleet Air Arm attack on the Italian fleet in Taranto gave a fillip to home morale. December found the Italians invading Greece and very quickly looking for German assistance when things began to go wrong for them, and they suffered similar humiliation in North Africa, with British forces gaining much ground. At home the *Luftwaffe* bombed Bristol and London. British successes continued in North Africa throughout January, and by February they were in Benghazi, although the situation was about to change with the imminent arrival of Rommel's *Afrika Korps*.

March 1941 saw 72 Sqn still at Acklington and still making uneventful patrols. However, one patrol on the 3rd almost ended in disaster. Flt Lt Sheen (X4104), Sgt Staples (X4167) and Sgt Pocock (X4643) were sent off on night patrols, but soon after they had taken off the weather closed in, reducing visibility to 1,000 yards. The Spitfire was a difficult aircraft to fly at night, with the glare of the exhaust blinding the pilot, and the weather only made it worse. The controller diverted the three pilots to Catterick, but then changed his mind and told them to return to Acklington. The squadron operational record noted that it was more by luck than judgement that they managed to return safely, as the controller seemed to have little idea of their position, and it was only the pilots' intimate knowledge

72 Sqn in formation from Acklington in 1941. (72 Sqn)

The squadron over the Northumberland coast in 1941. (72 Sqn)

Spitfire Mk IIs in formation low over the Northumberland coast in 1941. (72 Sqn)

Graeme Gillard astride the nose of a Spitfire at Acklington in 1941. (G. Gillard)

of their sector that got them down at base. Desmond Sheen commented in his logbook:

Night Operational Patrol!!! Bad.

He recalled this sortie some years later:

I remember one night in March 1941 heading for a bomber in the Newcastle searchlights, when suddenly all was blotted out in a snowstorm. I was told to divert to Catterick, but the radio went out in static. I flew north, coming out near the Farne Islands. I then crawled down the coast at sea level until the River Coquet appeared. I did a sharp right turn straight into the flare path almost out of fuel".

Three new sergeant pilots arrived from 57 OTU on the 11th, Sgts Gledhill, Harrison and Collyer boosting the squadron strength. Finally, on the night of 13 March, the squadron had its first contact with the enemy since December. Flt Lt Sheen (X4596) was airborne at 2126 hrs, patrolling at 6,000 ft, when he was directed to climb to 12,000 ft. As he passed through 10,000 ft he spotted an aircraft silhouetted against the high, thin cloud and lit up by the moonlight. A chase began, and as Sheen closed he identified the aircraft as a Ju 88. Sheen managed to carry out two attacks on the bomber in the darkness, and left it with its starboard engine blazing. The Ju 88 was later confirmed as destroyed. Desmond Sheen's victim was Ju 88 W.Nr.2234 coded M2+JL of *3/HG106*, piloted by *Leutnant zur See* R. Dietze, with his crew, *Obergefreiter* W. Wesseres, *Obergefreiter* H. Vandanne and *Oberleutnant* Hildebrandt Voightlander-Tetzner. All were killed, with the latter's body being recovered from the sea. Desmond Sheen was once more heard on the radio relating this combat:

Plt Off Newton. (R. Gledhill via 72 Sqn)

There was brilliant moonlight and I could see the coast for several miles in each direction. The conditions were ideal for night-fighting in a Spitfire. When I first saw the raider, he was at about 1,000 ft above me so I opened out and climbed after him. When I was about 100 yards behind and below, I saw he was a Junkers 88. As I opened fire I could see my tracer bullets bursting in the Junkers like fireworks. Soon the old familiar black smoke that you've heard so much about came pouring out of the raider. With it was a lot of oil, which covered my windscreen and forced me to

Spitfire RN-E and ground crew at Acklington in 1941. L to R, Jim Foot, Johnny Urquhart, Jock ?, others unknown. (G. Gillard)

Cpl Graeme Gillard in the flight van at Acklington. (G Gillard)

break away. When I turned in for my next attack I saw one of the Hun's engines was beginning to burn; but just to make quite sure of him I pumped in a lot more bullets, then I had to dive like mad to avoid ramming him. I had been so keen on giving him as many bullets as I could that I almost collided with him. In the dive I lost quite a lot of height, several thousand feet in fact, and when I pulled out I had lost sight of him, but before I went down one of the enemy's wings was burning like a bonfire so I felt certain that the Junkers would not get home. Actually, confirmation came fairly quickly. Members of the Observer Corps had watched the fight and had seen my tracer bullets hitting the raider. I think my first burst must have killed or disabled the gunners, for there was no return fire. Apparently the Hun went down like a flare; as he hit the sea there was an explosion.

To balance the influx of pilots earlier in the month, two were posted away, Sgts Mallett and Dykes both going to 74 Sqn at Manston. The next small excitement for the squadron occurred on the 22nd, when Flt Lt Sheen (X4596) was scrambled to go to the aid of an incoming Whitley returning from a raid. Sheen escorted the bomber back to Acklington, where it landed with less than ten gallons of fuel remaining.

April was another month of reverses for the Allies, with Rommel pushing the British forces all the way back to Egypt, and the British withdrawal from Greece. The Germans were also actively supporting a coup in Iraq, which was another strain on the already slender resources in the region. At Acklington the squadron could only watch these events with frustration. With little activity

A 72 Sqn Spitfire climbs away from Acklington in 1941 with RN-N in the foreground. (G. Gillard)

other than sector and convoy patrols, it seemed far out of the war. The month had opened to wild gales, and there was a wind of change on the squadron too. Flg Off R.D. Elliot was promoted to flight lieutenant, and took over 'B' Flt. Flg Off D. Secretan was likewise promoted, and took over command of 'A' Flt, and Sqn Ldr Graham relinquished command of the squadron, being posted to Catterick. He was replaced by Flt Lt Sheen DFC, promoted to squadron leader on the 17th. Other movements during the month included Sgt Mason and Plt Offs E.P.W. Bocock and F. Baldwin from 58 OTU, Plt Off J. Godlewski, a Pole, arrived from 57 OTU and Plt Off Pool was posted to ACME. More Poles arrived when Plt Off J. Stabrowski and Sgt Biel were attached from 317 Sqn. Sgt Rosser also returned to the squadron.

The German activity over the North-East had been almost dormant through

Plt Off Bocock arrived from No. 58 OTU in April 1941. (72 Sqn)

72 Sqn pilots clay pigeon shooting. L to R, Flg Off Bocock, Sgt Rosser, Sgt Pocock, Flg Off Fordham, unknown WAAF officer. (72 Sqn)

the winter months, but they became much more active in April. No. 72 Sqn was not long in getting in on the action. Late in the evening of the 10th, two Spitfires of Green Section, flown by Sgt Allan Casey (R7069) and Sgt Dalton Prytherch (R6752), took off at 1844 hrs to patrol over Acklington. During the patrol they intercepted a Ju 88, which they shot down. The bomber crashed about one mile below low-water mark off Boulmer. Their victim was a Ju 88A-05 coded F6+NL of *3(F)/122*, flown by *Leutnant* Rolf Braose, who was lost with his crew, *Unteroffizier* E. Helmart and *Feldwebel* D. Graobke. Shortly before, two Spitfires of Blue Section, flown by Sgt Gregson (X4918) and Sgt Lack (X4551), were patrolling just below the cloud base when they sighted another Ju 88. Giving chase, they intercepted it and opened fire. It was last seen, falling apart, with its port engine on fire, in a vertical dive towards the sea north-east of Long Houghton. They claimed it as probably destroyed. The squadron began to re-equip with Spitfires Mk II in mid-April, and flew the first sorties with them on the 14th, losing their first Mk II, P8231, on the 29th.

On the 28th Green Section got into another fight, this time with tragic results for the squadron. Plt Off Bocock (P8146) led Sgt Collyer (P8231) and Sgt Perkins (P7376) off from Acklington at 1510 hrs for practice flying. Shortly afterward the controller reported a 'bogey' (enemy aircraft) five miles east of Blyth. Bocock led the attack and got in a four-second burst. Sgt Perkins followed with a very short burst. Sgt Collyer was last seen following the Ju 86 into cloud, and was then heard to say that his engine had failed and that he would have to ditch. Bocock and Perkins searched for their compatriot but found no trace of him. His body was recovered later in the day.

The last day of April saw more combat for the squadron. Once again it was Green Section in action. Control vectored Sgt White and Sgt Harrison to intercept a Ju 88 south of the Farne Islands. They first saw two bomb bursts in the sea, and then saw the Ju 88 above. The bomber had probably jettisoned its bombs in an attempt to escape the Spitfires when the crew sighted them. As the Ju 88 fled eastwards, the Spitfires began to overhaul it. The Ju 88 was on the deck and Green Section made numerous attacks, leaving it with both engines smoking as it disappeared into

Sgt Allan Casey and two other SNCOs in full flying gear. (72 Sqn)

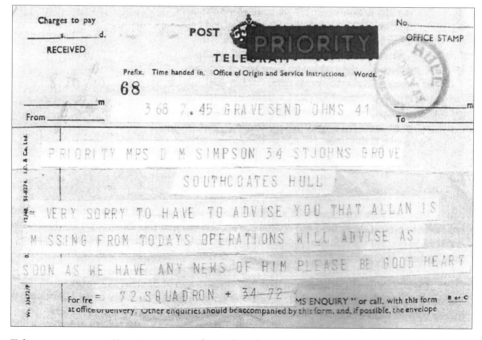

Telegram sent to Allan Casey's mother when he went missing. (Casey via 72 Sqn)

Presentation Spitfires paid for by contributions from Ulster. 72 Squadron's 'Enniskillen' is 4th from the right. (72 Sqn)

cloud at only 500 ft. They returned to base to claim the bomber as damaged. The Ju 88A actually crashed into the sea off the Farne Islands, killing the crew.

Another bomber, S4+JH, a Ju 88A-1 flown by *Leutnant* H. Jark, was shot down by 72 Sqn on 1 May. The bomber crashed into the sea, and Jark and his crew, *Fw* K. Pahnke, *Uffz* J. Schaare and *Obergefreiter* J. Schumacher, were all killed. Schumacher's body was recovered from the sea and buried at Brandesburton.

During May 1941 Plt Off Douthwaite and Sgts White, Lack and Gledhill were all posted to 213 Sqn at Turnhouse, while Plt Off Baldwin went to 260 Sqn at Drem. Sgt Bell-Walker returned to the squadron from Biggin Hill on the 7th.

The squadron kept up its routine of convoy and sector patrols, but saw some action on the 5th when Sgt Gregson (P8146) and Plt Off Godlewski (P7376) of Blue Section intercepted a Ju 88 and managed to damage it before it escaped. Plt Off Gregory and Sgt Gregson intercepted a Ju 88 near Seaham on the 6th, and each claimed a half-share in the victory. Yellow Section was next to have some luck when it intercepted a Do 17 while patrolling over a convoy east of Blyth on the 18th. Sgt Harrison (P8200) and Sgt Rosser (P8045) managed to damage

Poor photo of Spitfire Mk II RN-A. (J. Corbin)

this one too, but like the Junkers earlier in the month it escaped. The last few days of the month saw some exceptionally bad weather, which curtailed any flying. On the 15th Sgt Allan Casey continued his run of bad luck, colliding with another Spitfire. The CO noted in his logbook, 'Gross carelessness – collided on runway with another Spitfire which was landing.'

Plt Off Rosser. (R. Gledhill via 72 Sqn)

While 72 Sqn was busy defending the North-East from the *Luftwaffe*, events elsewhere were taking a more serious turn. On the 10th there was a huge raid on London by the *Luftwaffe*, and Rudolf Hess, Hitler's deputy, had arrived in Scotland by parachute, hoping to arrange for peace between Britain and Germany. No. 72 Sqn was involved in the Hess incident. Hess's aircraft was detected by radar over the North Sea, and two patrolling Spitfires were ordered to intercept the aircraft. However, an error in control resulted in them both being vectored onto each other. Sgt Maurice Pocock was scrambled from Acklington to intercept, but was scrambled too late to make a successful interception. Later, Defiant night-fighters from Ayr were scrambled to intercept, but Hess abandoned his aircraft and parachuted into captivity and notoriety. In the Middle East the Iraqis had been soundly defeated, but the defenders of Crete had received their last reinforcements and were awaiting the inevitable German attack. The invasion began on the 20th, and it was all over by June. May also saw the sinking of the *Hood* and the *Bismarck*.

June was a month taken up by convoy and sector patrols with no action, and the only things to hold the pilots' interest were a rash of postings. The last Mk I Spitfire had departed and the squadron was now fully equipped with Mk IIs. The Poles began to leave, and a group of Australian pilots arrived in their stead. Sgts Rutherford, 'Tiny' Falkiner and Merrett arrived from 57 OTU at Hawarden on the 9th. Plt Off Godlewski was promoted flying officer on the 16th and fellow Pole Sgt Biel left to join 308 (Polish) Sqn at Middle Wallop the same day. On the 22nd it was the turn of Plt Off Stabrowski to leave for a Polish squadron, No. 317, and the last day of the month saw Flg Off Farrar posted to 23 Sqn at Ford, while Plt Off Bishop arrived from 74 Sqn at Gravesend. On the international front the British were being hard pressed in North Africa by Rommel, and Hitler made the mistake that would be a turning-point in the war when he invaded Russia on the 22nd. On the 27th, Sgt Allan Casey in his third incident crashed Spitfire P8166 into the boundary hedge on landing.

July 1941 began much as June had ended, with convoy and sector patrols and yet another rash of postings. Plt Off N.E. Bishop and Sgt Mallett arrived from 74 Sqn, and Sgt Gledhill returned from 213 Sqn. Sgt Prytherch went to 603 Sqn at Southend, Sgt Southey went to Heston and Sgt Bell-Walker, who had only recently returned to the squadron, was posted to 602 Sqn at Ayr. Plt Off Bishop, who had only been with 72 for a week, returned to 74 Sqn on the 8th. The 8th was to be the squadron's last day at Acklington, as it moved south to Gravesend the following day – a little nearer the action. Jack Lancaster recalls the move to Gravesend:

Sgt Merrett joined the squadron from No. 57 OTU on 9 July 1941. (72 Sqn)

In July the whole squadron moved to Gravesend, but Maintenance Flt became Station Echelon and so I stayed behind. However, I was made up to corporal within a few weeks and I was posted back to the squadron. Gravesend in 1941 was a tiny airport, taken over by the RAF, and there were some interesting aircraft lying around, including an old de Havilland Comet and Flamingo.

The CO drew a big circle in the middle of Gravesend airfield, took his Spitfire up and fired his guns into the middle of the circle. He was mad.

While at Gravesend we were billeted in Nissen huts at Laughing Lester near Bobham Hall (officers' mess). A number of Australian ground crew arrived and I was given the 'honour' of being NCO i/c Hut. Our adjutant told me to arrange a kit inspection, to ensure that the Aussies were kitted out OK. He needn't have bothered, because they had more kit than I had ever seen, including a set of civvies.

The inspection next day was a scream, as not only the many items of uniform, but civvies and photos of their girlfriends, dogs, etc. were conspicuously displayed. The adjutant didn't linger long, and with a laugh and shrug of his shoulders wished me the best of luck. Those lads were great guys, but boy, did they drink!

The first patrol from Gravesend on the 9th was a search by eight Spitfires for an aircraft down in the sea. The aircraft was located, but there was no sign of the crew. All aircraft returned to Gravesend. The following day was 72 Sqn's first taste of life on the front line since the end of the Battle of Britain, and it ended badly for them. Eleven Spitfires took off from Biggin Hill as part of a wing sweep (*Circus* No. 42) which was to follow a route to Hardelot, on to Fruges and St Omer and return, providing high cover for three No. 3 Group Stirlings. Between Fruges and St Omer 72 Sqn was attacked by two groups of Bf 109s, six in each group. A second encounter with the enemy occurred after passing Gravelines

72 Sqn at Gravesend in July 1941. Spitfire 'Basuto' at left with RN-N next in line.
(R. Gledhill via 72 Sqn)

Another view of the pilots and their mounts. (R. Gledhill via 72 Sqn)

Head-on view of a Spitfire Mk V at readiness, with power cable from trolley accumulator attached for quick scramble. (R. Gledhill via 72 Sqn)

on the return leg, and the result of the two meetings with the *Luftwaffe* was the loss of Flg Off J.M. Godlewski (W3411), Sgt Allan Casey (P8600) and Sgt C.L. Harrison (P8604). The remaining aircraft landed at Coltishall, though Sgt Rosser (W3229) crash-landed, escaping uninjured. German claims for this raid were eleven shot down by pilots of *JG2* and *JG26*, which included the aces *Oberleutnant* Josef 'Pips' Priller and *Hauptmann* Hans 'Assi' Hahn.

On the 11th six Spitfires from the squadron took part in *Circus* No. 44, flying to East Dunkirk–Poperinhe–Cassel–Gravelines and return. (A 'Circus' operation involved a small number of Bomber Command aircraft, escorted by a large number of fighters, making short-range incursions into enemy territory with the intention of drawing the *Luftwaffe* fighters into battle. It was hoped large numbers would be shot down.) No flak was encountered on the sortie, and four Spitfires landed safely at Detling. Sqn Ldr Sheen (W3380) landed at Biggin Hill, and the only aircraft loss was the Spitfire flown by Sgt Lamberton (W3171), which he crash-landed at Lympne.

Circus No. 47 was mounted on 12 July, and the squadron provided eight Spitfires taking off from Biggin Hill at 1255 hrs. The route for the sortie was Gravelines–Hazebrouck–Ambeltuese in a diversion sweep to cover the flight of a single 60 Group Blenheim IV. The weather played a hand, and the cloud obscured the French coast. The only things of note on the sortie were the lack of flak and the sighting of six German R-boats in the Channel. The weather scattered the formation, and Sqn Ldr Sheen (W3380), Plt Off Fordham (P8069) and Sgt Rutherford (R7219) all landed at Biggin Hill, while Flt Lt Elliot (R8544), Plt Off Newton (R7228) and Sgts Merrett (W3256) and Perkins (W3170) landed at Manston. Sgt Gregson (P8750) landed at Hawkinge. The following day Flg Off Nicholson arrived from Turnhouse to take up the post of squadron intelligence officer.

The squadron provided eleven Spitfires as target support for *Circus* No. 48 on 14 July escorting the bombers to Hazebrouck marshalling yard. Just after crossing the coast large numbers of enemy fighters were encountered and many skirmishes took place. The scattered fighters landed back at Biggin Hill, Gravesend and West Malling; however, Sgt Lamberton (R7219) failed to return. He was later reported to have been captured, badly wounded, having been shot down by the *JG26* ace, 'Pips' Priller.

Sgt Merrett. (R. Gledhill via 72 Sqn)

While at Gravesend George Coggle, one of the ground crew involved in the 'flight on the tailplane incident' at Acklington, was involved in another potentially deadly accident, as Jack Lancaster recalled:

The aircraft had just returned from a sortie and the ground crew were doing their checks, when suddenly the silence was shattered by a burst of cannon fire, which disappeared across the Thames.

Aircraftman Coggle had jumped in the cockpit and pulled the stick back; unfortunately the pilot had not put the firing-button on safe.

There were a number of postings in mid-July, with Plt Offs Gosling and Clive, Sgts McCann, Lewis, Stone, Breckon, Ingham and Cox all posted in, while Flt Lt Elliot was posted out due to problems with his eyesight. Later, on the 14th, the squadron supplied twelve Spitfires as an escort to air-sea-rescue Lysanders searching for a pilot in the sea between Dungeness and Boulogne.

The squadron was able to find some relief from the daily strain of the *Circus* operations on the 16th, when Sqn Ldr Sheen married Section Leader M.M. Russell of the ATS at the registry office in South Acton. The respite was a short one, as the squadron was back on operation the next day with an offensive patrol routeing North Foreland–Gravelines–St Omer–Hardelot–Dungeness. The weather intervened, and a revised plan saw the twelve Spitfires fly to Le Touquet before returning to Biggin Hill. At 2000 hrs that evening the Spitfires were airborne again on a second sweep from Biggin Hill to cover Gravelines–St Omer–Le Touquet. A few enemy aircraft were sighted as they crossed the French coast, but too far away to engage. The flak, however, took its toll, and Plt Off Fordham (P8544) was shot down by it. As he descended he transmitted a distress signal, which was picked up by the air-sea-rescue organization, which went to his assistance. Unfortunately he was found dead of drowning in the Channel.

Plt Off D. Clive was posted in during July 1941. (72 Sqn)

Circus No. 51 on 19 July saw twelve Spitfires airborne from Biggin Hill at 1310 hrs to escort the bombers to Lille. Several Bf 109s of *JG2* and *JG26* were tangled with, and the Spitfires returned in small groups, landing at Gravesend, Manston and Martlesham Heath. Sgt Breckon (P8751) force-landed on Ramsgate beach,

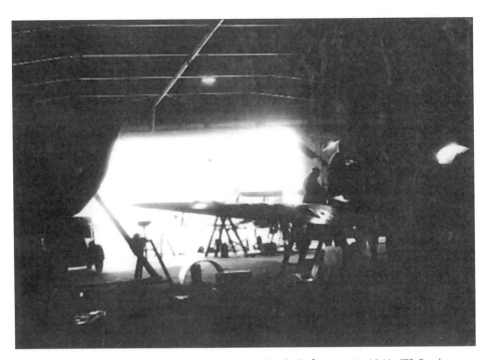

72 Sqn Spitfires undergoing maintenance in a dimly lit hangar in 1941. (72 Sqn)

which was mined, and having survived the landing made his way through the minefield to safety. Sgt Lewis (W3181) failed to return.

There were further new arrivals on the 19th and 20th, with the posting-in of Flt Lt D. Stewart-Clark and two Czech sergeants, Sika and Valenta. While the new personnel arrived the squadron was busy on a *Roadstead* operation to the area off Le Touquet. A *Roadstead* was an operation by fighters, or bombers escorted by fighters, to attack ships at sea or in harbour. The twelve Spitfires attacked a single ship, and all returned safely to Biggin Hill except one, which landed at Gravesend.

On the 21st the wing leader, Wg Cdr 'Sailor' Malan, led nine Spitfires from 72 Sqn on *Circus* No. 54 to Lille via Dunkirk. All ten Spitfires returned safely to Biggin Hill. In the evening twelve Spitfires left Biggin Hill for *Circus* No. 55, and headed for the target at Mazingarbe. One again they all returned, landing at Gravesend, with one diverting to Biggin Hill. The following day an offensive patrol was mounted from Gravesend over the area of the Forêt de Neippe, Aire and St Omer. Several Bf 109s were encountered, and Plt Off Gosling (W3229) probably damaged a Bf 109F, receiving a wounded leg in return. Accurate flak was encountered over Dunkirk on the return leg; however, all returned safely. Two more Poles arrived to swell the ranks during the month – Flt Lt Kosinski, from 145 Sqn, and Flg Off Skalski.

Wg Cdr Malan again led the squadron from Biggin Hill on the 23rd for *Circus* No. 59. After rendezvousing with the bombers and other escorts over Manston, they proceeded to the target in the Forêt D'Eperlecques. During the sortie Wg Cdr Malan, Sqn Ldr Sheen and Red Section dived down to attack two small vessels west of Dunkirk. The results of the attack were not observed. The second operation of the day was *Circus* No. 60, and once again Malan led the squadron's twelve Spitfires. The target was Mazingarbe, and the squadron was intercepted by many formations of Messerschmitts over St Omer, and a large mêlée ensued in the Le Touquet area. The honours were equal, with Czech Sgt Sika (W3418) destroying a Bf 109F north of Boulogne and the squadron losing Sgt Perkins (W3259). Perkins was later reported to be a POW and wounded.

The war of attrition with the *Luftwaffe* continued, and on the second operation of the 24th eight Spitfires acted as high cover to *Circus* No. 61. On the way to the target at Hazebrouck marshalling yard, heavy flak was encountered over Mardyck, and Sgt Breckon (W3316) failed to return. He was later reported a prisoner.

The squadron moved from Gravesend to Biggin Hill on the 26th, and there was another rash of postings with the arrival of Sgts P.T. Grisdale and D.A. White, a New Zealander. Operations for the month ended with a two-aircraft *Rhubarb* to Le Touquet and Boulougne on the 29th, but weather was poor and nothing was seen. A *Rhubarb* sortie was an offensive operation carried out by small groups, usually of two fighters aimed, at harassing the Germans in occupied Europe and making them retain large fighter forces in the West. Jack Lancaster moved to Biggin Hill with the squadron:

Soon we were off again to Biggin Hill and stayed until September. While we were there, Ben Lyon and Bebe Daniels visited the station and Plt Off Bocock was asked what he would like most. He told them he would like a fresh egg each morning. Soon after a young chicken was delivered to the flight. Unfortunately it turned out to be a cockerel and was christened Ben.

The first few days of August 1941 were quiet, and it was not until the 5th that the squadron recommenced operations. Twelve Spitfires took off from Biggin Hill with the rest of the wing for *Circus* No. 65. The target was St Omer and Longuenesse. However, extremely bad weather was encountered, and 72 Sqn failed to join up with the rest of the wing. After twenty minutes patrolling over the Channel the squadron returned to base. The following day two Spitfires from the squadron attempted a *Rhubarb* sortie, but once again the bad weather intervened and they were forced to return. Later that afternoon twelve Spitfires from the squadron attempted to link up with bombers for *Circus* No. 66, but the operation was again thwarted by bad weather. The bombers turned back before reaching the French coast. No. 72 Sqn continued over France but returned having sighted no enemy activity.

Polish Flt Lt Kosinski joined the squadron from 145 Sqn on 21 July 1941. (72 Sqn)

Spitfires RN:L and RN:M at Biggin Hill in 1941. (72 Sqn)

Des Sheen in the cockpit of his personally marked Spitfire. The boomerang shows his Australian roots. (72 Sqn)

The target for *Circus* No. 67 on 7 August was Longuenesse airfield, and eleven Spitfires took part in escorting the bombers via Gravelines and St Omer. Just after crossing the French coast the formations were targeted with fairly accurate flak; all the Spitfires returned safely, though, landing at Biggin and Manston. Later that day the squadron took part in *Circus* No. 62 to Lille, but once again the success of the operation was marred by poor weather. The bombers were not met, and they were not seen until they were on the way back over Mardyck; no engagements took place.

72 Sqn pilots in 1941. (72 Sqn)

Plt Off Rosser on left introducing Nigger, a dog owned by one of the sergeant pilots, to Ben, the cockerel, held by Plt Off Bocock, which was presented to the squadron by Ben Lyon and Bebe Daniels. (72 Sqn)

The squadron was kept busy with convoy patrols on the 8th and 9th, and later that evening took part in an offensive sweep along the route Ambeltuese–St Omer–Gravelines. All of the pilots experienced radio interference, and no enemy aircraft were seen. It was a different matter on the 10th, when another sweep was carried out over the same route. This time the *Luftwaffe* came up to meet the wing, and there were several engagements over Calais and St Omer. Plt Off Newton (W3321) damaged a Bf 109F over St Omer, while Plt Off Bocock (P8560) damaged another east of Calais. Not content with this, Bocock attacked a 500-ton ship off the coast on the way back, and in the process experienced considerable flak from the coastal batteries.

L to R: Flt Lt Ken Campbell, Plt Off De Naeyer and Sgt Watson in August 1941. (72 Sqn)

On 12 August two operations were flown, *Circus* No. 70 and a wing sweep. Although enemy aircraft were sighted on both, none were engaged. The 14th was similar, with *Circuses* No. 72 and 73 flown. Many enemy aircraft were sighted, but none were engaged. On the 16th the squadron carried out three operations. In the morning a wing sweep of St Omer–Gravelines was flown, but cloud and the position of the sun made the operation difficult. Enemy fighters were seen but declined to fight. Just after noon the second sortie was flown. This was a repeat of *Circus* No. 73 to the Shell factory at Marquise. In excellent weather this time many enemy formations were encountered; however, 72 Sqn was not engaged. The operation was not altogether successful, though, as Plt Off Skalski (W3170) crashed on landing. At 1740 that evening twelve Spitfires took off for *Circus* No. 75 to St Omer and Longuenesse airfield. As the formation crossed the French coast south of Hardelot, the *Luftwaffe* was sighted and a general mêlée ensued. Sgt Stone (W3431) was most successful, destroying a Bf 109F and damaging another between Boulogne and Calais. Plt Off Rosser (3441) descended to low level and shot-up a sound detector at Gris Nez, while Plt Off Bocock (W3429) did likewise, shooting up a gun post near Hardelot. All returned safely to Biggin Hill. Cedric Stone returned, but only by the skin of his teeth:

On 16 August 1941 flying Spitfire W3431 I avoided colliding with the neighbouring aircraft as the squadron turned sharply to attack the enemy and to meet his attack. I went down in a spin. The squadron was out of sight, but a black spot on the horizon soon appeared. This spot split as it came nearer to me. I prepared for battle, to find two pairs of Me 109s, yellow nosed, coming towards me. One pair one side and one on the other for a coordinated attack on me. It was kill or be killed. The first dived on me as I entered my aerobatics. A barrel roll, loop, turns and twists. As they came past my sights I fired. The first went down. I didn't see the second. Then the second pair attacked. Again I was conscious that only one was left. I had avoided their fire! One to go! I tried, but had no more ammunition. I immediately, in the heat of the battle, decided to ram him. However, by the time I was about to start my next thrust to ram him he had turned tail and fled. With heart beating like mad and leaping up and down from my seat I tried to control myself to review the situation. I had to calm my compass to find where England lay in relation to me. The compass was difficult to see through misted goggles and in the darkness deep down between my feet. All this at some twenty to thirty thousand feet. Alone in a vast clear sky. My eyes were glued to the sky from horizon to horizon looking for anything suspicious. I decided where north was when the compass swings were settling down. I throttled back to cruising as soon as I thought the dangers had subsided. Nose down slightly and with some one to two hundred miles to the Channel I set course. The control room said I crossed the Channel in one minute! I think that very unlikely, but I was certainly travelling between three and four hundred miles per hour. Was I pleased to see the white cliffs of Dover on the Kent coastline!

On 17 August the *Luftwaffe* was up providing cover to ships in the Channel between Cap Gris Nez and Calais. No. 72 Sqn was tasked to engage them, and twelve Spitfires took off from Biggin Hill at 1530 hrs. Numerous combats took place over the ships, with Sgt Stone (W3431) destroying a Bf 109F, while Sqn Ldr Sheen (W3380) damaged another, recording in his logbook, '*Circus*. 1 Me 109 Prob. Attacks on N. France. German Convoy Escort.' Once again all returned safely to Biggin Hill. The following day the operations were *Circus* No. 78 to the Fives–Lille engineering works, where accurate flak was encountered over the target and one Spitfire crash-landed on return to Biggin Hill, and *Circus* No. 80 to the Shell factory at Marquise where, once again, heavy flak was encountered. Desmond Sheen, flying Spitfire W3380, noted, '*Circus* 1 Me 109 damaged. Escort to Lille.'

The first operation of the 19th was a little more unusual. The target for *Circus* No. 81 was the Gosnay power station. Taking off at 1025 hrs, twelve Spitfires joined the wing and crossed the French coast over Dunkirk. During the operation many German fighters were seen but none engaged, and one of the bombers involved dropped an artificial leg for Wg Cdr Douglas Bader, who had lost one baling out of his stricken fighter on a previous sortie.

The second sortie of the day was *Circus* No. 82, during which the wing leader, Wg Cdr Robinson, flew with the squadron. The target for the bombers was Hazebrouck marshalling yard, and heavy flak was encountered in the target area. The *Luftwaffe* came up to challenge the incursion, and many dogfights took place. All twelve of the squadron's Spitfires returned safely.

In the days that followed, the squadron continued to fly *Circuses* in the well-established routine: enemy fighters seen, few engaged and heavy flak encountered. *Circuses* No. 83 and 87, two wing offensive sweeps and a *Roadstead* were flown between 21 and 26 August with no losses.

Circus No. 85 on the 27th was a different prospect. Ten Spitfires, led by Wg Cdr Robinson, lifted from Biggin Hill at 0618 hrs, heading for St Omer and Longuenesse airfield. The four 139 Sqn Blenheim bombers aborted their attack on Longuenesse, and meeting heavy flak throughout the route over French territory the Spitfires became embroiled with ten Bf 109s over Dunkirk. Sgt Rutherford (P8609) damaged a Bf 109 but sustained damage to his own Spitfire. He managed to nurse it with a rough-running engine to within three miles of the English coast near Ramsgate, when the engine stopped and he parachuted into the sea. Luckily he was picked up within a few minutes. Rutherford's damaged Messerschmitt was a Bf 109F-4 (7121) of *III/JG26* which crash-landed near the village of Desvres in the Pas de Calais. Flg Off Skalski (W3170) failed to return from this sortie, becoming a POW.

On the 29th it was back to Hazebrouck marshalling yard as escort to the bombers of *Circus* No. 88. Twelve Spitfires, led by Sqn Ldr Sheen, took part, and as they crossed the coast near Hardelot a large number of Bf 109s were sighted. Sqn Ldr Sheen decided that they were a distinct threat to the squadron, and led the Spitfires

L to R: Plt Off Rosser, Plt Off Ingham, Plt Off Daniel, Plt Off Kitchen following the sortie to drop Douglas Bader's new leg. (72 Sqn)

into a running battle, which stretched into the middle of the Channel. During the fight Sqn Ldr Sheen (W3380) damaged a Bf 109, Plt Off Rosser (W3441) destroyed one, Flt Lt Kosinski (W3511) destroyed one Bf 109 and probably destroyed another, while Plt Off Bocock (W3429) also destroyed one and probably destroyed another. On the debit side of the battle Sgt Grisdale (P8713) called up on the R/T to inform his squadron mates that he was force-landing in France. Grisdale was

This photo is believed to be Flt Lt Campbell. (R. Gledhill via 72 Sqn)

Flt Lt Kosinski and Flt Lt Campbell. (R. Gledhill via 72 Sqn)

killed. Sheen recorded, '*Circus!? 1 Me 109 damaged. Attack on N. France. Sqn versus 250+ 109s 30 miles inland.*'

The month ended with uneventful convoy patrols. Several postings occurred during the month: the Czech, Sgt Sika, went to 57 OTU at Hawarden, Plt Off Bishop returned from 74 Sqn and Sgt Rosser was promoted pilot officer. Flt Lt Secretan left the squadron for medical treatment of a poisoned foot and Sgt Gregson was commissioned. Flt Lt K.N.T. Lee arrived from No. 59 OTU, Crosby-on-Eden, and Sgts A.B. Binns and S. Croft arrived from 123 Sqn at Drem.

The first few days of September 1941 allowed the squadron a brief respite, with no operational flying. They rejoined the fray on the 4th in a wing-strength operation to escort bombers on *Circus* No. 93. The bombers' target was Mazingarbe, and the force came under fighter attack from the *Luftwaffe* from crossing the French coast at Gravelines, all the way to the target and back.

No. 72 Sqn's contribution to the battle was one Bf 109 probably destroyed by Plt Off Clive (P8757), and all returned safely, landing at a number of airfields.

Following this operation, the squadron had another break of almost a week before embarking on an uneventful *Rhubarb,* by two pilots, which was curtailed by poor weather. Uneventful patrolling continued until the 17th, when twelve Spitfires acted as escort cover wing for *Circus* No. 95 to Mazingarbe. Crossing the French coast east of Gravelines, the squadron split into fours as a series of attacks by the *Luftwaffe* developed, and running battles continued all the way

Squadron adjutant Flg Off Melhuish. (R. Gledhill via 72 Sqn)

Sgt J. Rutherford with Spitfire 'Matlama'. (72 Sqn)

Sgt S. Croft, seen here with Spitfire 'Thaba Bosiu', was posted in from 123 Sqn at Drem in August 1941. (72 Sqn)

Flt Lt W. Gregson with Spitfire 'Maseru'. (72 Sqn)

Spitfire RN-T running-up at Biggin Hill in September 1941. (72 Sqn)

Biggin Hill, September 1941. Rear, L to R: Plt Off Stone, Plt Off Bishop, Plt Off Bocock, Plt Off Clive, Flt Lt Campbell DFC. Middle, L to R: Plt Off Rosser, Sgt Falkiner, Sgt White, Sgt Jemmett. Front, at window, Sgt Ingham. Front, L to R: Plt Off Rutherford, Sgt Grisdale, Plt Off Newton, Sqn Ldr Sheen DFC*, Flt Lt Kosinski, Flg Off Melhuish (adjutant), Flg Off Nicholson (intelligence officer) Sgt Merrett, Sgt Gledhill. (72 Sqn)

Biggin Hill, September 1941. Flt Sgt Hilton, Flt Lt Kosinski, Sgt Barnardo, Plt Off Crook, Sgt Ingham, Plt Off Clive, Plt Off Gosling. (72 Sqn)

The Biggin Hill wing leader, Wg Cdr Jamie Rankin DSO DFC*, in 1942. (72 Sqn)

Plt Off Clive in a humorous moment. (R. Gledhill via 72 Sqn)

to the target and back to the coast. The operation resulted in no claims and no losses. Later in the day the Spitfires was airborne again for *Circus* No. 96 to Marquise. The *Luftwaffe* intercepted the force in the Bris-de-Guines area, and a number of engagements occurred; once again, however, no claims or losses were made.

On the 18th, Wg Cdr Jamie Rankin led the squadron and the wing to the power station at Rouen on *Circus* No. 99. The wing failed to rendezvous with the bombers, and after some discussion between the wing leader and the controller, Rankin led the Spitfires to the target area. The Spitfires crossed the coast at St Valery and flew towards Rouen. When they were twelve miles from the target there was still no sign of the bombers. There were, however, thirty Bf 109s near Dieppe, and Rankin led the wing towards them. The *Luftwaffe* was not keen to fight on this day, though, and fled towards Abbeville before contact could be made.

The following day was a lower-key effort, with two pairs carrying out *Rhubarb* ops. The first pair, Plt Off Bocock (W3771) and Sgt Falkiner (AB922), crossed the coast between Berck-sur-Mer and Le Touquet, and turned north towards St Etaples. Falkiner found a truck loaded with cables and shot it up, and on the way out Bocock had a go at an anti-aircraft emplacement, causing casualties among its crew. The second pair, Flt Lt D. Stewart-Clark (W3516) and Sgt Merrett (P8560), swept over the coast and flew from Gravelines down to Calais.

Sgt Merrett with ground crew flight sergeant. (R. Gledhill via 72 Sqn)

Sgt Merrett with squadron dog Nigger. (R. Gledhill via 72 Sqn)

Australian Sgt 'Tiny' Falkiner prepares for flight at Biggin Hill. (72 Sqn)

Sgt F. Jemmett. (72 Sqn)

'Tiny' Falkiner of 'B' Flt climbs into the cockpit of Spitfire RN-T at Biggin Hill, September 1941. (72 Sqn)

Servicing the cannon of Spitfire RN-T at Biggin Hill in September 1941. (72 Sqn)

On the return leg, midway between Calais and Dover, Sgt Merrett engaged a Bf 109E and shot it down. Unfortunately, Flt Lt Stewart-Clark failed to return from the sortie.

On the 20th and 21st respectively, the squadron took part in *Circus* Nos 100B and 102, with no loses and no claims, and followed this with a few days of uneventful convoy patrols before taking part in *Circus* No. 103B to Mazingarbe on the 27th. The squadron's twelve Spitfires crossed the coast at Mardyck, and about fifteen miles inland, to the south-east of St Omer, were attacked by a large enemy formation. The honours were equal at the end of the fight, with Flt Lt Hall (W3704) probably destroying a Bf 109F, while Sgt Falkiner (AB922) shot down a Bf 109E. The *Luftwaffe* downed Sgt Binns (AB843) and Sgt Merrett (P8560). Sqn Ldr Rankin claimed one Bf 109F destroyed, one probably destroyed

Sgt 'Tiny' Falkiner forecasting Allied victory at Biggin Hill. (R. Gledhill via 72 Sqn)

165

and one damaged. Once again the month ended with uneventful convoy patrols.

October began with an offensive sweep led by Sqn Ldr Sheen on the 1st. The squadron provided twelve Spitfires to sweep east of Dunkirk, on to St Omer and out via Gravelines. Cloud cover thwarted the plan, however, and the wing carried out the sweep down the Channel instead. Between Calais and Dover Flt Lt Kosinski (P8763) destroyed a Bf 109F and damaged another. All twelve pilots landed safely back at base, to find the squadron had a new intelligence officer in the form of Flg Off H.V.C. Gibbs, who had previously been with 457 Sqn at Jurby on the Isle of Man.

In the afternoon the squadron was engaged in a large ASR search involving three other squadrons, all searching for two pilots missing while escorting a rescue launch off Calais. Nothing was seen and all returned safely.

After a break of almost a week the squadron once again became involved in *Circus* operations. The Biggin Hill wing provided a diversion for *Circus* No. 104, as the rendezvous with the twelve Blenheim bombers of 2 Group was not made, by sweeping around Berck and Abbeville. Crossing the coast at Le Crotoy, led by Sqn Ldr Sheen, the wing flew towards Abbeville and pounced on a formation of fifteen Bf 109Es. Soon several dogfights ensued, and Sqn Ldr Sheen (W3380) probably destroyed a Bf 109F. No. 92 Sqn was badly mauled on the same operation, losing three Spitfires shot down with pilots killed, and one crash-landed near Ashford. The following day the target for the bombers on *Circus* No. 105 was Ostend power station. Wg Cdr Parkin led twelve Spitfires of 72 Sqn and the wing as escort, crossing the French coast at Neiuwport before turning

72 Sqn pilots with Spitfire and mascot. Sgt Maurice Pocock holds the mascot. (G. Gillard)

towards the target. The wing then encountered heavy flak, which continued to harry them until over the sea. The flak had some success, with pilots reporting seeing one Spitfire going down with its tail cut off.

Following these operations the squadron had a week without any, and during this time Sgt Stone was commissioned as a pilot officer, Sgt Pocock was promoted flight sergeant and Sqn Ldr Sheen was awarded a bar to his DFC. Cedric Stone recalled his promotion and a reprimand at the same time:

Sqn Ldr Masterman called me into his office on 4 October 1941 to congratulate me and award me the DFM (won as a SNCO). It was also at this time that I had a 'ticking-off', a reprimand. As a result of my being attacked in France by the four Me 109s, and surviving. I was in an exceptionally tense and excited state when I landed for refuelling and rearming. Once the aircraft was serviceable again it needed testing. Rather than have lunch I took the aircraft for test so that I would be ready for the next squadron scramble. Excitedly I took off across the all-grass field of Biggin Hill. Thinking I was airborne I raised the undercarriage. Alas, I raised it too soon. The aircraft slumped back towards the ground and the propeller ploughed into the grass, bending the propeller tips and reducing the rate of climb. This had the effect of my tailwheel catching the perimeter fence. Instead of climbing away above the trees I sank between them! My wings caught the trees and were left behind, while the fuselage continued. It came to a halt in a field, but the engine and propeller continued another twenty yards. I remained, dazed, sitting in the cockpit, still strapped in, with the wings and tailplane torn off. I surveyed the situation, and there at the field gate was the ambulance to pick me up. I undid the straps and walked to it. It took me to the station medical officer. He examined me and said, 'No bones broken, but you had better have a 48-hour pass to overcome your nerves.' I borrowed a cycle from the hangar and cycled to my parents' house in Handcross, some 20 miles away. My mother said I talked continuously for some fifteen or more hours then dozed off. I slept for 24 hours. I then returned to the squadron.

I received a letter of congratulations, stating not only that His Majesty the King awarded me the DFM but that I was granted a King's Commission.

Circus operations recommenced on the 12th, with No. 107 to Boulogne docks. This time Wg Cdr Rankin led 72 Sqn and the wing, covering the bombers all the way in to the target in what turned out to be an uneventful sortie, with no losses or claims. The following day the much-attacked Mazingarbe power station was the target once more for *Circus* No. 108B. The formation crossed the coast east of Gravelines and was met by small numbers of Bf 109Fs near Mazingarbe. Later, on the return leg, they were bounced by a group of Bf 109Es. Sqn Ldr Sheen (W3380) reacted quickly, turning on the Messerschmitts and firing a short burst at them as the rest of the squadron broke up into sections of fours. Having disengaged from the Messerschmitts, the wing continued homewards, sighting more Bf 109s out to sea. Due to fuel shortage these were allowed to escape

---

DFM Citation

LONDON GAZETTE, 17TH OCTOBER 1941

Stone, Cedric Pine, 754154, Sergeant, RAFVR

This airman has proved himself to be cool, keen and resourceful. Within the last two months, Sergeant Stone has carried out 28 sorties over Northern France. On one occasion, he became separated from his unit and was attacked by four Messerschmitt 109s. He succeeded in destroying at least one of the enemy aircraft without damage to his own. The following day Sergeant Stone destroyed another hostile aircraft. By his splendid example, often in difficult conditions, he has assisted in maintaining a high standard of morale in his unit.

---

unmolested. However, Flt Lt Kosinski (R7265), Plt Off Bishop (P8783) and Plt Off Rosser (AA749) managed to get bursts in against some Bf 109Fs, flying in line astern, which took rapid evasive action and fled. The sortie ended with no claims or losses, and the squadron scattered over a number of airfields as fuel shortage forced them to seek safe havens.

After a few days of uneventful patrols, the squadron was on the move again, returning to Gravesend on the 20th, and immediately they had settled in they recommenced convoy patrols. The following day the squadron had its first encounter with an aircraft which was to become the scourge of Fighter Command in the coming months – the Focke Wulf Fw 190. On an offensive sweep the Biggin Hill wing was acting as the rear support wing to cover the withdrawal of other wings also on offensive sweeps. Just off the French coast the ten Spitfires of 72 Sqn encountered several Bf 109s and took evasive action. Flt Lt Campbell (W3511) was then attacked by four enemy aircraft with radial engines and square-tipped wings which outclimbed him easily as he turned towards them. The squadron returned to Gravesend, having, luckily, suffered no losses from this encounter. The pilots of 72 Sqn and others of Fighter Command would not be so lucky in the months that followed, as the Spitfire Mk V was clearly outclassed by the Fw 190, and the *Luftwaffe*'s aces took great advantage of its capabilities.

The day's work was not over for the pilots, and eleven Spitfires took off in the afternoon to provide escort to four more aircraft, who in turn were giving cover to ASR launches searching in the Channel. During the escort Yellow Section was bounced by four Bf 109s which quickly took evasive action following their attack by climbing into the sun, where they were lost from view by the other sections giving chase. Luckily, Yellow Section escaped the attack without loss, and all of the Spitfires returned to Gravesend.

Bar to DFC Citation

LONDON GAZETTE, 21ST OCTOBER 1941

Acting Squadron Leader Desmond Frederick Burt Sheen

Since July 1941, Squadron Leader Sheen has led the squadron, and on occasions the wing, in 43 offensive operations over Northern France. He has carried out these missions with consistent skill and courage and, under his leadership, the squadron has attained a high standard of efficiency. On one occasion the squadron was menaced by a superior number of enemy fighters but, by his coolness and clever tactics, Squadron Leader Sheen saved his unit from suffering heavy casualties and succeeded in destroying at least 3 of the fighters. Squadron Leader Sheen has personally destroyed a number of enemy aircraft including 1 at night.

On 26th October the squadron took part in its first *Rodeo* operation. Unlike a *Circus*, which involved the escort of a small force of bombers to a target in the hope of enticing the *Luftwaffe* to come up and fight, the *Rodeo* was a pure fighter sweep with the same intention. Twelve Spitfires from the squadron took part, and the wing swept west of St Omer and west of Gravelines before setting course for home. Ten miles off Dover, at 16,000 ft, the 72 Sqn pilots sighted two Bf 109Fs, which did not attack, but a third sneaked in and bounced Sgt Stock, whose Spitfire (AB822) was seen to turn over onto its back and dive vertically, disappearing into cloud at 10,000 ft. Stock did not return. Plt Off Bocock (W3429) had become detached from the formation during the sweep, and descended to attack and damage a searchlight post before returning. A short while later the squadron was airborne on an ASR search for the missing pilot between Dover and the French coast, but had no success.

Rodeo was the order of the day on the 27th, and eleven Spitfires took off from Gravesend to rendezvous with the wing over Manston. They were to route to Nieuwport, turn right for Dunkirk and exit at Gravelines. When the wing was south of Dunkirk it was ordered to orbit Gravelines four or five time to allow any stragglers time to catch up. As they made the last orbit they were attacked from above, and the squadrons split into sections of four, each fighting its way out independently. At least two RAF aircraft were seen to go down over France; one of them was Sgt Falkiner (W3704) of 72 Sqn. Falkiner survived to become a POW. As the squadron was fighting this battle, a new CO was posted in, Sqn Ldr C.A. Masterman CBE, from No. 57 OTU. The days leading up to the end of the month were quiet, with only an uneventful patrol over Manston on the 31st.

Once Sqn Ldr Masterman had settled in, Sqn Ldr Sheen took his leave of the squadron on 4 November, posted to HQ No. 9 Group at Preston. The first week of the month was relatively quiet with few patrols, and the only excitement, brief as it was, was when Flt Lt Campbell brought his Spitfire in to land at Gravesend on return from a formation practice on the 6th. The port landing-wheel broke away, and he quickly lifted the Spitfire back into the air for another circuit. Using great skill and judgement, Campbell managed to land the crippled Spitfire with only slight damage.

Ops over the Continent resumed on the 7th with a wing-strength *Rodeo* covering Dunkirk, St Omer and Berck. As the eleven Spitfires of 72 Sqn departed Berck, Blue Section was bounced by Fw 190s from above and behind. As the Fw 190s dived away, Yellow Section, led by Flt Lt Campbell (W3430) and with Plt Off Rosser (AA864) close behind, followed them down. Campbell and Rosser opened fire on a fleeing fighter at extreme range, and Rosser saw pieces come away from it as it began to lose height rapidly. Rosser continued to close on the Fw 190 and continued to fire at it until he ran out of ammunition. Continuing to follow the fighter down, Rosser was forced to break off the chase by heavy flak as it passed through 4,000 ft off Boulogne. Yellow 3, Sgt Rutherford (AB818), reported seeing a Spitfire, believed to be one of Blue Section, going down between Berck and Boulogne. This turned out to be the Spitfire of the Canadian Plt Off Birkland (W3367). Birkland was captured and later took part in the famous 'Great Escape', and was one of those executed by the Gestapo.

During this period the attrition of Fighter Command's pilots was significant. On almost every operation where the *Luftwaffe* was encountered, pilots were shot down. Like Fighter Command in the Battle of Britain, the *Luftwaffe* was able to pick the time and place it would attack over its own ground, and usually

Sgt Stock in Spitfire 'Mohale's Hoek' at Biggin Hill in 1941.

only when it had a tactical advantage of numbers or height. Such a favourable day for the *Luftwaffe* was 8 November, and 72 Sqn was left counting the cost.

Eleven Spitfires left Gravesend to escort a formation of Hurricane fighter-bombers on a *Ramrod* to St Pol. The target was the distillery. Cloud negated use of the planned crossing-point south of Le Touquet, and the *Ramrod* crossed the coast at Berck, instead, and forged towards the target. As the Hurricanes made their dives, 72 Sqn circled Hesdin. Heading for home, the Spitfires flew to Le Touquet and orbited again, waiting for stragglers, and it was here that the *Luftwaffe* struck. Many formations of Bf 109s began to attack the top escort formations, and continued to do so until about eight miles out into the Channel. Engagements continued mid-Channel, and about nineteen miles off Dungeness Plt Off De Naeyer (R7265) probably destroyed a Bf 109E. Unfortunately this was little retribution for

Sqn Ldr Masterman on wing of Spitfire 'Moshesh'. (72 Sqn)

the losses inflicted on the squadron. Close to De Naeyer's engagement Sgt Dykes (AB893) baled out after his engine failed, and fortunately was picked up after 1½ hours in the water and landed at Dover. Plt Off Bishop (W3511) and Sgt White (AB855), shot down by a Bf 109, were not so lucky, failing to return. Both pilots were killed. The remaining Spitfires landed at Hawkinge, Lympne and Biggin Hill.

The survivors had little time to dwell upon the losses. The war went on, and that afternoon the squadron moved over to Biggin Hill to co-operate in an invasion exercise being held at Gravesend, returning the following day. A mix of patrols, sweeps and ASR cover operations filled the next few weeks, with little of note. Then, on the 22nd, twelve of the squadron Spitfires left Gravesend in company with Blue Section of 401 Sqn RCAF on a wing sweep. Flt Lt Hall (AD274) had difficulty keeping up with the formation, and elected to patrol between Le Touquet and Calais before returning to base. The rest of the squadron had more success. Australian Fraser 'Tiny' Falkiner was a pilot with the squadron at this time, and recalls Flt Lt Hall:

Flt Lt Hall had a very long chin and nose, and his oxygen mask would slip off his nose. On one sweep he was leading my section when he broke away from the formation (R/T Silence) and started climbing. We followed, he stalled, and spun. We followed him down until he came out of the spin and we went home…we were a bit disturbed by these unusual evasive tactics and were frantically searching for enemy aircraft, to no avail. On our return we found his manoeuvres were purely due to his lack of oxygen.

No. 72 (Basutoland) Squadron,
Royal Air Force,
Gravesend,
Kent.

Reference:-
72S/C.53/P.F.

28th October, 1941.

Dear Mr Falkiner,

I was extremely sorry to have to report that your son, Sergeant Fraser Falkiner failed to return from operations yesterday. He had been with us some considerable time and was most popular. He was a very good pilot and was doing very well and about to get his commission.

Sergeant Falkiner was missing after a scrap over France and after a mix up he was not seen again and we could not contact him. A search was made of the Channel but I'm afraid without result.

We all hope that he made a safe landing in France and that you will have received some news before this letter reaches you. The members of the Squadron and in particular the Australian members (including myself) would like to express our deepest sympathy to you and your family in this time of distress.

Yours sincerely

D. Sheen

Squadron leader,
Commanding No. 72 Squadron.

Mr R.S. Falkiner,
c/o Australian Club,
Melbourne,
Australia.

Sqn Ldr Masterman (AD183), Plt Off Rosser (AA864) and Sgt Ingham (W3430) shared one Bf 109E and an Fw 190 destroyed, while Sgt Thompson (AA749) and Sgt Enright (AD467) an Australian from Bruthen, Victoria, each damaged an Fw 190. The Fw 190s may have been superior to the Spitfire Mk V, but the pilots

Sgt J. Rutherford. (72 Sqn)

Sgt J. Rutherford relaxing with a book between sorties. (R. Gledhill via 72 Sqn)

were learning to counter them, even with their inferior equipment, and the Germans were not having it all their own way. Sgt Rutherford's Spitfire (AB818) was shot up during the engagement, but he managed to land it at Manston.

On the 24th twelve Spitfires took off to provide cover to the withdrawal of No. 9 Commando during a raid on the French coast. The pilots saw little, and eight of them landed at Shoreham and did not return to Gravesend until the 26th. The weather then took a hand, and little flying was done for the remainder of the month.

December 1941 opened with a period of bad weather which precluded operations until the 5th, when the squadron carried out a convoy patrol off Southend. Returning from this patrol, Plt Off Bates (R7265) crashed his Spitfire on landing, but escaped himself. That evening the squadron was called upon to provide four Spitfires for a 'Fighter Night', something they had not been asked to do since early 1940, to help counter the *Luftwaffe* night intruders.

On the 7th, the squadron had a slight change of routine when it had a day of practice flying, including squadron and section formation, cloud (instrument) flying and camera gun practice and a squadron scramble. One

POW photo of Flg Off Henry J. 'Hank' Birkland.

Plt Off De Naeyer in Spitfire 'Lijabatho'. (72 Sqn)

Rhodesian Sgt Thompson with Spitfire 'Qacha's Nek'. (72 Sqn)

of the highlights of the day was an interception of Curtiss Tomahawks from Gatwick. The day was marred, however, when Sgt Enright ran out of fuel and crashed his Spitfire just outside the airfield boundary. Enright survived the crash, but his luck was about to run out. On the following day the squadron escorted Hurricane bombers on a *Ramrod* to the alcohol distillery at Hesdin. Rhodesian pilot Sgt Thompson went missing, last heard of as they crossed the French coast on the way in; and as the squadron encountered several formations of Bf 109s a combat commenced, and Flt Lt Campbell and Sgt Enright became separated. Enright, an Australian, also failed to return. Thompson and Enright were both killed.

Attrition of the squadron's Spitfires continued on the 12th, when Sgt Smith belly-landed on the airfield, having broken the undercarriage in a previous landing attempt. The unfortunate Smith crashed again the following day while landing! A variation in the routine occurred on the 19th, when fog curtailed flying, and the squadron was given a lecture by Flt Lt Shore, who had managed to escape from Germany. The thick fog persisted for days, and flying did not resume until Christmas Eve. On Christmas Day the squadron received a visit from the Mayor and Mayoress of Gravesend and Christmas Dinner was held in Cobham Hall. The days following Christmas saw the squadron engaged in searchlight co-operation exercises, and on the 29th nine Spitfires went to Manston to take part in a *Smilax* operation. Following this operation, they attempted to return to Gravesend but were thwarted by fog and returned to Manston. By this time the fog had reached Manston, too, and the squadron could have been in dire straits had it not been for the coolness of Flt Lt Campbell, who made repeated circuits of the airfield, leading six other pilots in to safe landings. The only damage was to Sgt Jones's Spitfire when he made a heavy landing. The year 1941 ended with nine of the squadron's Spitfires fog-bound at Manston.

The new year of 1942 commenced with convoy patrol, and then on the 3rd the squadron began a series of anti-*Rhubarb* patrols. *Rhubarb* was the RAF codename for hit-and-run raids to the Continent by small sections, usually pairs, of fighters. Conversely, the anti-*Rhubarb* patrols were to counter the *Luftwaffe* also carrying out these hit-and-run raids on British coastal towns and ports. The first sorties occurred following the machine-gunning of several south-coast towns by a Bf 109.

On 8 January the squadron received a visit from Air Marshal Sir Sholto-Douglas, and in his talk to the pilots he stressed the importance of frequent gunnery training, both live and with cine-guns, as well as formation flying and practice sweeps. He also advocated the use of the Link Trainer for night-flying practice, and dispersal of aircraft in individual dispersal bays.

Flt Lt Campbell, who had taken part in numerous operations with the squadron, was posted to North Weald on the 12th to take command of 403 Sqn RCAF. The following days were filled with anti-*Rhubarb* and convoy patrols, interspersed by lectures from visiting experts on the Royal Navy, night-flying procedures,

Sgt F.E. Jones in the cockpit of 'The Darlington Spitfire'. (72 Sqn)

searchlight co-operation and the *Luftwaffe*. Practice sweeps were introduced to the training programme from the 24th, and on the 26th an uneventful sweep in support of Hurri-bombers was carried out.

February found the squadron snowbound for the first five days, after which there was a short period during which local flying was carried out before the snow closed in again. On the 8th the squadron took part in the No. 11 Group air firing competition at Shoreham, firing at drogues towed by Lysander target tugs. A change of command occurred on this day, when Sqn Ldr Masterman was promoted to wing commander and took command of the Biggin Hill Wing. Flt Lt Newton was also on the move, promoted to squadron leader and becoming commanding officer of 411 Sqn RCAF at Hornchurch. Masterman's replacement was Battle of Britain ace Sqn Ldr Brian Kingcome DFC & Bar.

Fog, lectures and convoy patrols filled the next few days, then on the 12th the squadron took part in one of the biggest air-sea battles to date. For some time the British forces had been watching closely the German warships *Scharnhorst*, *Gneisenau* and *Prinz Eugen* in case they made a break from port in Brest for the safe haven of German ports. The RAF and the Royal Navy had a co-ordinated plan to monitor the warships and to deal with them should they break out. The Royal Navy patrolled the Straits of Dover with numerous destroyers and motor-torpedo-boats, and the RAF sent out three Hudson aircraft equipped with ASV each night

> ### *DFM Citation*
>
> ### *LONDON GAZETTE, 6TH FEBRUARY 1942*
>
> ## Acting Squadron Leader Cyril Norman Stanley Campbell
>
> This officer has participated in operational flying since the war began. He took part in air operations in France from September 1939 to May 1940. Since his return to this country, Squadron Leader Campbell has performed excellent work both in operational flying and as an instructor. He has led the squadron on several sorties and his excellent leadership and initiative displayed on all occasions has contributed materially to the successes achieved. He has also performed valuable work in connection with rescuing pilots from the sea, often remaining on patrol in the vicinity despite the presence of enemy fighters. Squadron Leader Campbell has destroyed 1 enemy fighter and probably destroyed another.

Pilots at Gravesend in January 1942. L to R: Sgt Jemmett, Sgt Booth, Plt Off Bocock, Sgt Liby, Sqn Ldr Masterman, Sgt Warner, Sqn Ldr Sunderland Cooper, Plt Off De Naeyer, Sgt Jones, Sgt Garden, Plt Off Soga, Plt Off Bates, Flt Lt Campbell, Sgt Cammell. (72 Sqn)

Pilots playing 'Shove ha'penny' at Gravesend, January 1942. L to R: Flg Off White, Sgt Garden, Sgt Booth, Plt Off Soga, Sgt Jemmett, Flt Lt Campbell, Sgt Robertson. (72 Sqn)

to patrol the Channel in an effort to detect any movement by the warships and their escorts. The Fleet Air Arm had a squadron of Swordfish torpedo-aircraft on standby at Manston, led by Lt Cdr Esmonde, and Bomber Command had promised up to 300 bombers for the operation and Coastal Command would provide three squadrons of Beauforts, also equipped with torpedoes. The Beaufort squadrons, however, were scattered on airfields from Cornwall to Scotland and would take time to assemble, as would any Bomber Command response. Fighter Command's part in the planned operation would be three squadrons of Spitfires, Nos 72, 64 and 411, providing cover to the attacking Swordfish.

Plt Off Soga at Gravesend in 1942. (72 Sqn)

The preceding evening, at 2345 hrs, the German force slipped its moorings in Brest and set sail. As well as the large destroyer escort covering the *Scharnhorst*, *Gneisenau* and *Prinz Eugen*, they would also have a huge escort of *Luftwaffe* fighters by daylight. The three Coastal Command Hudsons on patrol that night failed to detect the departing force, two due to equipment failure and the third due to an early recall because of poor weather over England. As dawn broke, the weather was very poor, with a large amount of low cloud and mist masking the progress of the German ships.

In the morning Gp Capt Victor Beamish and Wg Cdr Findlay Boyd took off on a *Jim Crow* patrol from Kenley, and while over the Channel they encountered a formation of Messerschmitts. While diving to attack them Beamish was amazed to see the German fleet below. Realizing the importance of the sighting, but hampered by Fighter Command instructions to maintain radio silence at all times, they sped for Kenley and made their report. The fleet had been sighted at 1042 hrs, but they were unable to pass on the sighting report until 1109 hrs when they landed. Time was slipping away as the Germans steamed northwards, and the opportunities for attack slipped away with them. By 1130 hrs the Royal Navy was responding, and the first to go into action were the motor-torpedo-boats. Despite valiant efforts, the fighters and torpedo-boat escort fought off this small force. While this battle raged, Esmonde and his crew sat in their Swordfish at Manston waiting for the word to go and waiting for their fighter escort. With no sign of the escort and only a fifteen-minute window left in which to launch and attack the fleet, Esmonde left Manston with his pitifully antiquated force.

Unknown to Esmonde, the three fighter squadrons had already left their bases, 72 Sqn departing at 1218 hrs. The fighters had orders to rendezvous with Esmonde's force at 1230 hrs. Nos 411 and 64 Squadrons were intercepted by the *Luftwaffe* and failed to meet the Swordfish. The only unit to keep its rendezvous with the Swordfish was 72 Sqn, with eleven Spitfires.

Kingcome (AB150) and his men had their departure from Gravesend postponed three times before he received the order to 'Get to Manston to escort six Swordfish and intervene in a battle between German E-boats and British MTBs.' The German battlecruisers and their heavy fighter escort were not mentioned!

It was a brief meeting with the Swordfish, however, as the fighters descended through cloud and saw Esmonde's force beneath them. This was the last that any British force would see of the majority of Esmonde's force, which was destined for near-annihilation and glory. The sky was full of flak from the battlecruisers and their escorts, and thick with German fighters, which quickly pounced on 72 Sqn, and a huge air battle ensued.

Strapping in for another sortie in 1942. (72 Sqn)

Warner, Booth, Gregson, Stone and Liby, Gravesend 1942. (72 Sqn)

Warner and Liby at Gravesend in 1942. (72 Sqn)

As 72 Sqn wheeled around the sky battling against the German fighters, Esmonde made his attack. Unfortunately, all of the torpedoes missed the mark. The battlecruisers made their escape. In all, the air battle had involved some thirty-nine squadrons, comprising 423 from Fighter Command's 10, 11 and 12 Groups, as well as Esmonde's six Fleet Air Arm Swordfish. Coastal Command dispatched forty-two aircraft, and Bomber Command a further 242, of which only twenty-nine made attacks in the vain hope of stopping the fleet. Overall the British air losses were sixteen fighters and twenty bombers, and Esmonde's gallant little force. No. 11 Group made claims for fourteen aircraft destroyed, three probably destroyed and seventeen damaged, of which 72 Sqn's tally was three Fw 190s destroyed, one probably destroyed and three damaged. The claims were made by:

Plt Off Bocock (AA914)	1 Fw 190 destroyed and 2 Fw 190s damaged
Plt Off De Naeyer (AA867)	1 Fw 190 destroyed
Plt Off Ingham (AB848)	1 Fw 190 destroyed
Plt Off Rutherford (AB283)	1 Fw 190 probably destroyed
Sgt Garden (W3430)	1 Fw 190 damaged

No. 72 Sqn was the highest-scoring RAF squadron involved in the battle. As soon as the Spitfires landed at Gravesend they were rearmed and refuelled, and set off on a second sortie against the fleet. They were too late. The fleet was gone.

The days following the 'Channel Dash' were quieter, with the squadron carrying out convoy patrols and practice sweeps, interspersed with days without flying due to poor weather. On the 27th there was a break in the routine, with the pilots going to Biggin Hill to observe a series of tank manoeuvres.

On the 28th the squadron flew over to Biggin Hill to take part in a *Ramrod*. The target was the dry dock at Ostend, and the wing was providing cover to the six Blenheims taking part. No. 72 Sqn and the rest of the wing were the high cover at 22,000 ft, while the Kenley wing provided a diversion sweep to the east. As the squadron was withdrawing it sighted a formation of Bf 109s and Fw

Flt Sgt McCutchen at Gravesend in 1942. (72 Sqn)

190s at extreme range, and Plt Off Rosser (AA920) took a chance, firing a burst at an Fw 190, which he observed going straight down from 22,000 ft. He was unable to have his claim confirmed due to the great height, and in any case he was immediately attacked by another fighter, which put a cannon shell through his port wing, bursting his oxygen bottle and a tyre. Despite the burst tyre he managed to land safely at Biggin Hill. Sgt Jones (AA945) also got a burst in at a German fighter, but made no claim.

During the first week of March little flying was done apart from a quiet wing sweep on the 3rd. Operations were hampered initially by fog, followed by fresh falls of snow. Long-time squadron pilot Plt Off Bocock left the squadron during this period to become a flight commander with 602 Sqn at Kenley.

The 8th dawned fine and sunny, and the squadron took part in a wing practice sweep in the morning before getting airborne again in the afternoon for a *Circus* operation. By this period *Circus* operations had become relatively large scale, and the small force of six Boston light bombers had the Biggin Hill wing as close escort, 72 Sqn being the bottom squadron. Kenley wing provided the high cover, and a further two 10 Gp squadrons took part in the escort. The fighters rendezvoused with the bombers just south of Rye and escorted them to the target, the marshalling yards at Abbeville. No. 72 Sqn saw several aircraft fall out of formation and return to base with various problems, and luckily the *Luftwaffe* failed to respond, other than to put up copious amounts of flak. Such was the strength of Fighter Command now that a second *Circus* was taking place concurrently: six Bostons bombed Comines power station, escorted by Northolt, North Weald and Hornchurch wings, which destroyed one Bf 109 and one Fw 190 but lost three of its own. A third operation by the Tangmere wing escorting twelve Bostons to the Ford Lorry factory at Poissy was also flown, and the escort lost one Boston. The growing strength of these operations would appear at first sight to be encouraging, but there was growing opposition to the *Circus* operations. This was due to the high losses mounting in Fighter

Command in this battle of attrition with the *Luftwaffe*, whose losses were far lower, due mainly to its ability to choose to fight or not, depending on whether the conditions were favourable to itself.

The following day the squadron was once again supporting a *Circus*. The Biggin Hill wing was target support wing and Kenley wing was escort. In addition the six Bostons had two 10 Gp squadrons as escort cover, the Northolt wing as high cover and two 12 Gp squadrons as forward cover. The Bostons successfully bombed the Mazingarbe chemical works, and no opposition was met. The large number of escort fighters was unable to entice the *Luftwaffe* up.

As a postscript to the ill-fated attack on the *Scharnhorst*, several of the squadron pilots who took part made the journey to Chatham Naval Hospital to visit one of the survivors from the annihilated Swordfish squadron, Sub Lt Kingsmill, on the 11th. The following day the squadron was informed that it was to move back to Biggin Hill within the week, changing places with 401 Sqn RCAF.

On the 14th the Biggin Hill wing took part in *Circus* No. 114 to Hazebrouck marshalling yards. No. 72 Sqn was part of the forward support wing to eleven Bostons. Between Gris Nez and St Omer several combats commenced, and in total the escorts lost seven aircraft and six pilots, only Sqn Ldr Douglas, CO of 401 Sqn, coming down safely on English soil. No. 72 Sqn suffered one aircraft loss when 'Robbie' Robertson was forced to bale out of his Spitfire (RN-H) due to a glycol leak, which caused his engine to catch fire. Plt Off Rutherford (AB283) managed to destroy one Fw 190 and probably destroyed another.

For the next week the squadron flew numerous operations, but in the main these were unsuccessful due to lack of targets, or poor weather intervening. On the 19th fog descended and remained till the 23rd, forcing the squadron to make its move to Biggin Hill by road on the 22nd, being reunited with its aircraft on the 23rd when they were flown into Biggin Hill by the pilots of 401 Sqn.

Reunited with its aircraft, the squadron immediately recommenced operations, and on the 27th flew as part of the Biggin Hill wing providing high cover to *Ramrod 18*, twelve Bostons bombing Ostend power station. The Bostons were covered by twelve squadrons of fighters, which claimed one destroyed, three probably destroyed and ten damaged for the loss of one fighter. No. 72 Sqn engaged a number of Fw 190s, and Canadian Flt Sgt Jones (AD274) was able to claim one probably destroyed for no losses. This proved to be the final success of the month.

Operations continued on 1 April with a close escort to eleven Bostons bombing Boulogne harbour. The squadron was operating at 15,000 ft, and carried out the escort with no opposition, though Plt Off De Naeyer (AB848) did sight three pairs of enemy fighters skirting the formation at the same height on the way out, probably hoping to pick off any stragglers. One of the Bostons was hit by flak

A posed briefing of pilots with ground crew looking on for the benefit of press photographers. (72 Sqn)

over Boulogne, but managed to struggle to a point just short of Dover, where it ditched, with two of the crew being rescued by motor launches.

On the 2nd, a planned escort operation was cancelled due to high winds at the planned escorting level, and in the afternoon the pilots were able to take advantage of a visit by three Hurricanes and a Gladiator from an Army Co-operation Command unit based at Gatwick, and indulge in practice dogfighting. The operations record book commented, 'It makes a change from Spits.' The squadron lost another of its experienced pilots on this day when Plt Off Rosser was posted to 130 Sqn as a flight commander.

The North American Mustang, which was being used by Army Co-operation Command, had a close similarity to the Bf 109, and this had caused a number of friendly fire incidents. In order to reduce this possibility, Mustangs were sent to other fighter units so that the pilots could examine them and become familiar with their outline and differences from the Bf 109. One such Mustang arrived at Biggin Hill on the 3rd, and was examined with great interest by the assembled squadron pilots.

The 4th saw the squadron's first dogfights and serious losses for quite a while. The Biggin Hill wing was airborne early that morning to escort twelve Bostons to St Omer railway station, and just south of St Omer the *Luftwaffe* pounced to the squadron. Three or four Bf 109s attacked Blue Section, and Blue 1, Canadian Flt Lt Gillespie (BL721) and Australian Sgt Hake (AB258) from Haberfield, NSW, flying as Blue 2, were quickly shot down. Both became POWs. Blue 3, Plt

Off Kitchen (BL728), was also shot up during the attack, but managed to turn the tables by attacking one of the Bf 109s and damaging it. Diving away from the possibility of a further attack, Kitchen spotted an Fw 190 and manoeuvred into a firing position and gave it a burst. The Fw 190 emitted a stream of white smoke and fell into a vertical dive. Kitchen claimed it as probably destroyed. In the meantime others were embroiled with Fw 190s, and Canadian WO Robillard DFM (W3168) fired at one, damaging it, and later attacked another, shooting it down. Other pilots confirmed the kill, having seen the Fw 190 pilot bale out. Unfortunately Robillard's No. 2, Flt Sgt T Watson (BL935), was among those who failed to return. Watson was killed. Having completed their escort duties and returned to base, the squadron was quickly rearmed and refuelled, and within an hour of landing was airborne again to escort ASR launches close to the French coast in the hope of rescuing those missing. Several enemy fighters hung around the area, but did not engage, and the search proved fruitless. Sgt Hake ended up as a POW and later took part in the famous 'Great Escape', and was captured and executed by the Gestapo. Returning from the sortie, Sgt Garden (AA867) had to force-land, putting his Spitfire down on a farm near Maidstone and escaping with only a cut to his face.

At this stage of the conflict the *Luftwaffe* was winning the war of attrition. Despite numerical superiority, the escorts were still flying Spitfire Mk Vs against the superior Fw 190 and equally matched Bf 109F. On this day 11 Gp lost thirteen fighters, twelve of them on this single operation; whereas it claimed five destroyed, three probably destroyed and ten damaged (post-war revisions would greatly reduce this number). During this period the Biggin Hill wing was led by Wg Cdr Jamie Rankin, and he would often lead the squadron on these operations, usually flying Spitfire Mk V AA945. The station commander, Gp Capt 'Dickie' Barwell, would also fly with the squadron on occasion in his personal Spitfire coded YO-B.

From the 8th to the 11th the squadron took part in several wing sweeps and *Rodeos*, but the large numbers of RAF fighters in the sky discouraged any thought of engagement by the *Luftwaffe*. On the 12th twenty Spitfire sorties were flown to provide convoy cover, and during one escort Sgt Malan's oil pressure dropped and he had to make a hasty forced-landing two miles north of Eastchurch. He escaped the landing, which wrecked the Spitfire (BL875), with a few bruises.

The squadron took part in an uneventful sweep on the 13th – all, that is, except Sqn Ldr Kingcome (AB150) and his No. 2 (AB979), who collided while taxiing for the operation, and Flt Lt Armstrong (BM384), who had to belly-land at Gravesend on the way out. The 14th turned out to be a busy day, with a diversionary sweep with the Debden wing to assist other wings in 11 Gp. The squadron returned from this uneventful sweep to be met and inspected by King Haakon of Norway. In the evening the squadron was the middle squadron in the Biggin Hill wing (acting as middle wing) in a multi-wing sweep over the Pas de Calais. The *Luftwaffe* accepted the invitation to battle this time, the hornets'

POW photo of Flt Lt Albert H. Hake.

Flt Sgt L.W. Robillard DFM with Spitfire 'Basutoland Richards'. (72 Sqn)

Sgt T. Watson in Spitfire 'Lilahbato'. (72 Sqn)

nest having been stirred up by two earlier wing sweeps, and Plt Off Daniel (BM125), Sgt Roberston (W3406:RN-I) and Sgt Garden (AB848) all had combats, though no successes.

On the second sweep of the 15th, the squadron provided cover to eight Hurribombers attacking Desores airfield. Unusually the Hurribombers were bombing from a height of 15,000 ft rather than from low level, and the *Luftwaffe* came up to take part in this unusual event. Battle ensued, and Canadian Flg Off B.O. Parker (BL773) claimed one Fw 190 destroyed and another damaged, while the CO, Sqn Ldr Kingcome (AB150), also claimed an Fw 190 damaged. South African Sgt F. Malan (brother of the famous ace 'Sailor' Malan) was flying as Yellow 2, and recorded the action in his combat report:

I was flying Yellow 2, and just after the squadron had been warned of a 'jump' I saw 4–6 Fw 190s on the tail of Yellow Section. I warned Yellow 1, who went into a steep climbing turn, at the top of which he spun off, and had just taken evasive action myself when I recognized the yellow spinner and engine cowling of an Fw 190 which flashed past my nose. I immediately went into a turn, reducing my deflection to 60–45 degrees, and gave a 1-second burst with cannon and machine-guns, closing to 150 yards. Almost immediately I saw a puff of white smoke on the fuselage from between the wing root and the pilot's seat [port side].

At that moment another aircraft, which I had probably not seen due to a partial blackout in the turn, came into my sights immediately in front of me, partially obscuring my first Hun. Thinking this might be a Spitfire on the Hun's tail, I held my fire, then broke away to join a gaggle of Spitfires I saw leaving France.

Over the following days it became routine for the squadron to take part in large multi-wing sweeps and escorts, and although the *Luftwaffe* would come up for a look, in the main it steered clear of the superior numbers of Spitfires, looking only for the opportunity to pick off stragglers or strike quickly with hit-and-run dives.

On the 18th the squadron received the news that Sgt Hake was safe and well and a POW, and on the 23rd Plt Off Robillard DFM left the squadron, tour expired, to return to Canada.

The squadron got itself involved in a big fight on the 24th while on a diversionary sweep for twelve Bostons bombing the oil distillery and harbour at Flushing. Flying at 20,000 ft, the squadron had 124 Sqn below them and 401 Sqn above, with the Northolt wing higher still. South-east of Calais the squadron ran into a formation of 30+ Fw 190s, and in the fight lost the South African Sgt R.P.G. Reilly (BM125) and American volunteer Plt Off R.P. Frahm (AB375), both killed. On the credit side Sgt Roberston (BL334:RN-I) claimed an Fw 190 probably destroyed, and Plt Off De Naeyer (W3841) an Fw 190 damaged.

The following day the losses increased. In the afternoon the squadron was airborne on a target support operation for six Bostons bombing Abbeville marshalling yards. Hornchurch and Kenley wings were also providing support. Coming out of France at Le Touquet, the Biggin Hill wing was jumped by the *Luftwaffe*, and New Zealander Flt Sgt J.G. McCutchan (W3406) was lost. Plt Off De Naeyer (W3841) once again added to his score by claiming one Fw 190 probably destroyed.

Two sweeps on the 26th were quickly followed by two more on the 27th. On the last of these the target was Lille/Sequedin, during which the Biggin, Kenley and Northolt wings had a difficult job of keeping the Bf 109Fs and Fw 190s away from the twelve Boston bombers involved. Numerous attacks were made on the bombers, and luckily only one was lost, with two of the crew baling out, going down near Gravelines. The squadron was kept busy fending off the enemy, and the most successful were Australian Flt Lt H.T. Armstrong (W3168) with one Fw 190 damaged, and Plt Off Daniel (AB513) with one Fw 190 probably destroyed.

It was an early start for the squadron on the 28th, with the pilots up at 0430 hrs and airborne by 0550 hrs on a *Ramrod* covering eight Hurribombers to St Omer. The operation went off without incident and the squadron returned to prepare for a second sweep in the afternoon. It went back to St Omer, this time escorting six Bostons, and while the remainder of the escort stayed up at 25,000 ft, 72 Sqn descended to 15,000 ft and commenced a fight with some Fw 190s. Flt Lt E.N. Woods (BL773) and Sgt Robertson (BL334:RN-I) both damaged an Fw 190, and all returned safely.

On the 29th, operations were curtailed by high winds in the morning, and prior to the afternoon sweep the squadron was inspected by King George VI on a visit to Biggin Hill. The last day of the month saw two sweeps, and Flt Lt Armstrong (BM384) and Plt Off Colloredo-Mansfeld (AA924) came closest to scoring on the first, a sweep to Le Havre with Bostons, being the only ones to fire on intruding enemy fighters.

The squadron was airborne early on 1 May to make a rendezvous with eight Hurribombers intending to attack targets at Dunkirk. The operation was cancelled, however, due to cloud cover, and the Spitfires returned to base. They did not stay on the ground long, though, as the second operation of the day saw them airborne again at 1515 hrs. This was a wing *Rodeo* to Le Havre. The Germans responded to the incursion, and many combats took place, mostly at long range and inconclusively, before all of the squadron's Spitfires returned safely, some landing away from Biggin Hill. There was little time for rest, though, as the Spitfires were off again at 1845 hrs to provide a diversion sweep over Calais for a formation of Bostons bombing a silk factory. The *Luftwaffe* came up to counter the attack, but remained out of range, declining battle.

Operations on the 2nd and in the morning of the 3rd were cancelled due to poor weather, but the wing was able to get airborne in the afternoon of the 3rd. At 1520 hrs the wing was airborne for *Circus* 145, a repeat of the Boston attack on Dunkirk. This time the Biggin Hill wing was at 18,000–21,000 ft, with the Kenley wing below at 14,000–17,000 ft and Northolt wing above at 22,000–26,000 ft. The Biggin Hill wing was not engaged; however, Sgt Malan (AB283) of 72 Sqn was bounced by two Fw 190s on the way home. Fortunately, they were poor shots and he escaped to return to base.

Biggin Hill saw 124 Sqn depart that afternoon. They were replaced by 133 (Eagle) Squadron, made up of American volunteers. No. 72 Sqn watched them arrive and was then airborne itself at 1835 hrs for the second sweep of the day to the Dunkirk area. More than fifteen German fighters were seen over Abbeville, but they shied away from combat and the squadron returned to base without firing their guns.

Sgt 'Robbie' Robertson relaxing with a book at dispersal at Biggin Hill in 1942. (72 Sqn)

72 Sqn pilots with a very large dog! (72 Sqn)

Another shot of pilots with massive dog. (It is rumoured that the dog was a model).
(72 Sqn)

Plt Off Booth left the squadron on the 3rd to take up a post with an unusual
fighter unit, the Merchant Ship Fighting Unit. This unit flew Hawker Hurricanes
from catapult-equipped merchant ships on convoy escort. On sighting a German
patrol aircraft or bomber, the Hurricane would be catapulted off to attack it,
and the pilot would then bale out of the fighter and hopefully be picked up
by the naval escort to the convoy. An extremely risky venture, and all were
volunteers.

On 4 May there was a morning departure at 0945 hrs for the Spitfires
covering six Bostons attacking the power station at Le Havre. North Weald
wing provided escort cover, with Tangmere wing as close escort. *Circus*
153 was to be highly successful for the Biggin wing and for 72 Sqn, led by

the wing leader, Wg Cdr Jamie Rankin DSO, DFC & Bar. No. 72 Sqn's tally for the sweep was two Bf 109Fs destroyed by Australian Flt Lt Armstrong (W3429), one of them shared with New Zealander Plt Off Hardy (BL733), one Bf 109E destroyed by Plt Off Kitchen (AD513), and Plt Off Waters (BM384), another New Zealander, shared a Dornier Do 217 with the Biggin Hill station commander, Gp Capt Dickie Barwell (YO-B). Wg Cdr Rankin (AA945) also claimed one Bf 109F destroyed and another damaged. Adding to the wing's score, a sergeant pilot of 124 Sqn also destroyed an Fw 190. The day's tally brought the squadron's score to 101 aircraft destroyed, and gave rise to some celebration on return to Biggin Hill.

The squadron had recently had an influx of replacements, and in the morning of the 5th the opportunity was taken to put six new sergeant pilots through their paces with a sector recce. In the afternoon the Spitfires climbed away from Biggin Hill to join 124 and 401 Squadrons over Gravesend on a rear support wing sweep over Dunkirk, Cassel and Calais, while six Bostons and their escort went to a target at Lille. As the Bostons and escort came out of France, the *Luftwaffe* swept in to attack. No. 72 Sqn was involved in the mêlée, but none of the pilots were able to get into a firing position before the battle was over. All returned safely to base.

The squadron was roused from slumber early on the 6th. At 0500 hrs it was brought to readiness following a report of a large enemy shipping formation in the Channel. An hour later, a *Jim Crow* high-level recce sortie reported that the formation was in fact a single oil tanker, and the squadron was stood down. Not for long, though, as it was airborne at 1125 hrs to escort a formation of Bostons to Caen power station. By the time they reached the French coast the *Luftwaffe* was up in strength, and Sqn Ldr Duke Woolley, leading the wing, gave the order to withdraw. Red and Yellow Sections were able to turn away successfully, but Blue Section was repeatedly bounced by the aggressive German fighters. Blue 1 and 2, Flt Lt Armstrong (W3168) and Plt Off Kitchen (W3429), had a running battle with the Germans all the way to the English coast, while Blue 4, New Zealander Plt Off D.O. Waters (AB848), was badly shot up, suffering a large hole torn in his starboard wing and a piece shot off one propeller blade. He struggled back to the English coast, escorted by Flt Lt Balmforth of 124 Sqn, and was able to make a skilful belly-landing at Shoreham. Sgt Robertson (BL334:RN-I), Blue 3, had become separated and was returning on the deck when he was attacked by two Bf 109Fs. He had the satisfaction of seeing one of them fly into the sea in a tight turn while trying to engage him, and claimed it destroyed on his return.

The next few days were filled with training and uneventful sweeps, and then on the 9th the Biggin Hill wing was ordered off on a sweep of Gravelines, St Omer and Le Touquet. The sweep was uneventful until nearing Dungeness on the return leg. Red Section descended to investigate something on the surface of the sea, which turned out to be a life-raft. As they wheeled around it, Red 2,

'Robbie' Robertson with his ground crew and personal Spitfire 'Connie'. (R.D. Scrase)

Sgt 'Robbie' Robertson's Spitfire BM313:RN-H named 'Connie'. (R. Robertson)

Plt Off Daniel (AD513), saw Red 3, New Zealander Plt Off Waters (BM384), fly straight into the sea. The squadron had no time to dwell on the loss of Waters, as they were airborne again at 1645 hrs as high cover to six Bostons bombing the Bruges oil installations. On the way back, Canadian Flg Off B.O. Parker (AR347) was bounced by an Fw 190. He quickly turned the tables and had the satisfaction of seeing his bullets shoot it down into the sea near Ostend.

By the 10th the weather was beginning to make operations difficult, but the squadron managed to get in a sweep on *Rodeo* 29 in the afternoon with the Hornchurch wing. They covered Le Touquet, St Omer and Gravelines before being forced to turn back by the worsening weather. The poor weather continued till the 16th, when the Spitfires lifted from Biggin's runway at 1430 hrs on a wing sweep to Le Tréport, Abbeville and Dieppe. They sighted twelve enemy aircraft below them, but were not in a favourable position to engage them. Returning to base, they entertained the Secretary of State for Air, Sir Archibald Sinclair, who had come to visit.

Engine fitter Ben Hitt joined the squadron in mid-May, and recalls the hectic life of the squadron at this time:

> *Six of us were to join 72 Sqn at Biggin Hill in mid-May '42. It was operating Spitfire Mk Vbs at the time. Life was hectic, there was Double Summer Time and we were out of bed around 4.30 a.m. to warm up and do the engine testing for dawn readiness. Stand-down came at around 11.00 p.m. so it was a long day. Most of the activity was sweeps over the Channel and France. There were 'scrambles', the bell ringing in the crew room. We rushed out to start engines and strap in the pilots, multiple take-offs, from time to time the 'Victory Roll'. On reflection we were privileged.*

All four squadrons of the Biggin Hill wing were airborne in the morning of 17 May for a *Rodeo* operation during which Plt Off J.D. Daniel (AD513) claimed an Fw 190 damaged. During the afternoon the squadron was scrambled to provide an escort to two air-sea-rescue launches searching off Dungeness. The escort quickly turned into a free-for-all scrap with several Bf 109Es and Fs and Fw 190s. The squadron gave a good account of itself, with Flt Lt E.N. Woods (BM516) damaging an Fw 190, as did Australian Plt Off Ratten (BM256) and Rhodesian Sgt Wright (BL726), all for no loss.

On the 18th two pilots provided the escort for a Blenheim of No. 75 (Signals) Wing on a signals intelligence flight, and in the afternoon the Biggin Hill wing flew a repeat of the previous day's *Rodeo*. This time the Fw 190s were seen again, but declined to close with the wing, and no engagements took place.

The 19th saw a third attempt to draw up the enemy in a *Rodeo* to Dieppe. The squadron failed to find any suitable targets, but 133 Sqn was engaged, losing two pilots but claiming in return two destroyed, one probable and one damaged. Wg Cdr Rankin, leading the wing, also claimed one damaged.

On the 20th the squadron was visited by a BBC recording unit, and several of the squadron personnel were interviewed for an Empire Broadcast. As a diversion from the usual run of sweeps and *Rodeos*, the pilots of the squadron were able to test fly a Spitfire Mk VI, equipped with a Merlin 47 engine and a pressurized cabin.

The squadron's next operation was a wing sweep to Hardelot, St Omer and Gravelines on the 23rd, where two Fw 190s were seen and Wg Cdr Rankin (AA945) managed to get in a shot at them from extreme range before they sped away. The following day the squadron could only observe while flying top cover with 133 Sqn as 124 and 401 Squadrons below fought it out with a formation of enemy fighters between Hardelot, St Omer and Calais. Wg Cdr Rankin led the lower squadrons, and between them they claimed two destroyed and eight damaged. No. 72 Sqn's only consolation was the sighting of four Fw 190s which Flt Lt Armstrong (BM345) fired at from extreme range, with no result.

The weather interfered with operations for the next few days, but the squadron had a good day on the 27th. The wing flew a sweep from Dieppe to St Valery-en-Caux, and the squadron was positioned perfectly to bounce fourteen Bf 109Fs 3,000 ft below. Flt Lt H.T. Armstrong (BM345) shot the tailplane off one, and Sqn Ldr Kingcome DFC & Bar (AA945) claimed one as probably destroyed, for no loss to the wing.

The 28th saw a sad loss when Sgt Davies (AB152) was lost in a training accident. While local flying, he spun in from 300 ft and was killed instantly. He had only joined the squadron from OTU the previous day. The losses continued on the 29th during an early morning sweep from Ostend to Dunkirk. During a short engagement Sqn Ldr Kingcome (BM326) and Plt Off Kitchen (AD386) were the only pilots to fire their guns, with no result. On the way out of France and fifteen miles of Dunkirk, Flg Off Brady Parker's Spitfire (AB150) developed engine trouble and started down with smoke pouring from the engine. He was seen to bale out, but was not picked up by Air-Sea-Rescue. A fine pilot and popular on the squadron, he was sadly missed. That evening six aircraft of the squadron took off to search for him, but returned without success. Parker was killed.

The squadron's next success came on the last day of the month during a wing sweep in the Dieppe area. Plt Off J.R. Ratten (BM256) engaged an Fw 190 and claimed it destroyed, while Sgt 'Robbie' Robertson (BM313:RN-H) also shot one down and damaged another.

The early days of June 1942 were marked by inconclusive sweeps over France, during which the *Luftwaffe* declined to join in battle, and air-sea-rescue duties which gave a slight change in the routine by allowing the pilots to operate from Hawkinge on some days. On the 3rd, prior to a sweep escorting Bostons to Le Havre, the pilots were visited by HRH the Duke of Kent, during which he observed the briefing for the operation. The sweep was uneventful. Joe Dade recalls this and an earlier Royal visit to the squadron at Biggin Hill:

DFM Citation

LONDON GAZETTE, 29TH MAY 1942

Acting Flight Lieutenant Hugo Throssell Armstrong, Royal Australian Air Force

This officer has participated in 29 operational sorties over enemy territory. He has destroyed at least 5 enemy aircraft and damaged a further 2. Flight Lieutenant Armstrong has displayed courage and initiative and his judgement and skill as a leader have contributed largely to the success achieved by his flight.

Surprise, Surprise! A consignment of new Navy Blue boiler suits appears in the crew room! (The squadron veterans were unimpressed; they were proud of their blackened, oil-soaked tunics, with buttons worn smooth).

Nevertheless, we were to dress up like real technicians, for the King and Queen were coming!

The visit was still a few days off, so 'Chiefy' Hilton gave permission for nickname to be painted on the backs of our new livery (to save arguments over ownership of course!). Once again the 'signwriting department' went into action, and there appeared 'Hank', 'Taff', 'Paddy', etc.

Of course, there was little chance of Their Majesties' appearing at the 72 Sqn dispersal, as we were stuck out at South Camp, at the end of the new third runway (near the 'Black Horse').

Nevertheless, there was a great atmosphere on the day, as our pilots clambered into a truck, fully dressed in Mae Wests and flying boots for a wing aircrew inspection at main camp. This completed, it was back to where we were waiting with trolley accs plugged in ready for 'Chocks away!'

The Royal party, in two large Daimlers, then took up positions half way along the runway to watch a simulated wing scramble and one circuit. Then the squadrons resumed individual ops over France.

The next night some of us went to the local cinema. There in the newsreel, the name 'Joe' appeared for a few seconds on the back of my overalls as I marshalled our aircraft. Much cheering and jeering from the boys! (3 seconds of fame!)

Shortly after this we had a completely unannounced visit from Prince George, Duke of Kent, in Air Commodore's uniform. He chatted to the pilots by the crew hut before seeing them off on a sweep. How sad when, a couple of months later, we heard that the Duke had been flying in an RAF aircraft which had disappeared in mysterious circumstances.

On 4th June the squadron received some welcome news about two of its missing pilots. The news indicated that Flt Lt Gillespie was a POW in Germany, and a letter was received from Sgt Hake, who was shot down on the same day. He was able to tell his fellow pilots that he had a running fight with five Fw 190s, managing to shoot one of them down before being hit and set on fire at 1,000 ft. He baled out at 300 ft and amazingly escaped serious injury.

The squadron had a field day on the 5th. Detailed for a diversionary sweep to two boxes of six Bostons attacking Ostend and Le Havre, they flew across the Channel at low level in an attempt to surprise the German fighter base at Abbeville. The Spitfires flew below 500 ft until mid-Channel, then climbed quickly, completely surprising the *Luftwaffe* fighters as they climbed away from the airfield. With the advantage of speed and height over the Germans, the Spitfires tore into them. The squadron score was three Bf 109Fs destroyed by Flt Lt H.T. Armstrong (W3168), Flt Lt E.N. Woods (BL773) and Sgt E.S. Hughes (BM450), one probably destroyed by Plt Off F.F. Colloredo-Mansfeld (BM484), an American fighting with the RAF, and two damaged by New Zealanders Plt Off O.L. Hardy (BM265) and Sgt B.J. Oliver (BM327). Sgt Hughes had little time to enjoy his success, though. On the way back from France, having become separated in the fight, he was shot up from behind. His Spitfire was badly hit, losing all air pressure. The wings, fuselage and tail were riddled with bullets and several rounds smashed into the cockpit, destroying his artificial horizon and radio. One bullet tore through the earpiece of his helmet without touching him. Desperately trying to escape, he found the German pilot formating on him, apparently out of ammunition. The German looked across at him then turned away. Hughes concentrated on keeping his Spitfire in the air, and managed to land at Biggin Hill without flaps or brakes. The Spitfire ran the full length of the runway, over the perimeter track and onto a new runway extension, and was still going when that ran out. At that point Hughes pulled up his wheels and the Spitfire came to rest on its belly. Sgt Hughes was home. The American Plt Off Colloredo-Mansfeld recorded in his combat report:

I was Red 3. We were at 16,000 ft between the Somme estuary and Abbeville aerodrome when Red Leader dived to attack four Me 109Fs flying 5,000 ft below. They were flying line astern and we came down on them with considerable speed. I picked the front enemy aircraft and opened fire on the way down. Then he broke upwards and I followed and fired in a turn, allowing full deflection, from about 300 yards. After about one second I saw a burst of black smoke, which hung about in the air, and the aircraft turned very slowly onto its back, hung there for a second and then dived vertically downward. This was at about 6,000 ft, and I watched him for perhaps two seconds more while I turned away, and then I had to break quickly as another enemy aircraft was threatening me.

During the combat I saw several other Spitfires, one of which seemed to be firing at the same enemy aircraft as I. I claim this Me 109F as probably destroyed.

On 6th June the squadron took part in a diversionary sweep for a large *Circus* operation, and though the controller reported over 125 enemy plots to it, it found none of them. This was due to thick haze caused by the smoke of the fires burning in Cologne, which had been bombed four days previously. In the afternoon 'B' Flt was tasked with an air-sea-rescue search. It located a bomber dinghy with five men in it fifteen miles off Blankenberghe, and was able to vector a rescue launch to the survivors, having the satisfaction of seeing them picked up. A sequel to the rescue occurred on the 10th, when a letter arrived from the rescued bomber crew, containing a £1 note for the pilots to buy a drink, 'from all the crew of T for Tommy'. The letter explained that they were the survivors of a Stirling crew whose aircraft had been hit in the tail by a damaged Wellington, killing the rear gunner. The Stirling pilot had managed to keep the stricken bomber in the air till they were over the sea, where they ditched a few miles off the Belgian coast in the early hours of 6th June.

The performance of the Spitfire Mk V against the superb Fw 190 had been causing concern for some time, and during a visit on 7 June the AOC-in-C Fighter Command, AM Sholto Douglas, and the Minister of Aircraft Production, Col Llewellyn, promised the squadron pilots that they would have new Spitfire Mk IXs as soon as possible.

Joe Dade was the ground crew fitter responsible for Spitfire Mk Vb AR347:RN-C during the summer of 1942, and he recalls the Spitfire's return from a sortie over France on 8 June:

On a summer afternoon in 1942 the squadron all returned from an operation over France, except 'C-Charlie'. Minutes later, however, the noise of a rough-running engine was heard and the aircraft appeared in the airfield circuit with half its undercarriage down, but flapping about, not locked.

The pilot, a 19-year-old sergeant on his first mission, landed well down the runway. The undercarriage leg broke and he 'belly-flopped', continuing on into rough ground beyond the perimeter track. My colleague, engine fitter Jock McCreadie, and I raced around the perimeter on our RAF cycles just in time to see the pilot walk into an ambulance en route to the sick bay for a check-up.

I removed the pilot's leather helmet and headset, R/T cable and plug, oxygen mask, gloves, goggles and maps. Jock and I inspected the aircraft, and this is what we saw:

1. *Leather helmet grazed on left side by a bullet which had penetrated the artificial horizon on the dashboard.*
2. *A cannon shell crater in the centre of the windscreen (Triplex glass 1½ in. thick). This had, however, not penetrated the windscreen.*
3. *A dent in the armour plating covering the fuel tank in front of the cockpit.*
4. *Bullet holes in Perspex window behind the pilot. Holes in both sides.*
5. *All aerofoils (ailerons, rudder, and elevators) peppered with .303 in. holes.*

6. *Large areas of the main plane skin rolled back like 'Swiss Rolls', revealing unused cannon shells still in the ammunition belts.*

We had a drink with the pilot later the same evening in the Black Horse outside the camp, and this is what he told us:

The Me 109 pilot had attacked when our sergeant momentarily broke formation. He kept up his relentless attack, but our sergeant was only interested in returning to base as his fuel was running out. After a while the German pilot gave up, flew alongside for a minute, saluted and peeled off to return to base.

Joe Dade was also responsible for painting the many names added to the squadron's Spitfires during 1942:

Mr Campbell (flight commander) once tore me off a strip for sending him up with a dirty windscreen. I was not likely to forget it, but he did, and a good relationship was restored when, at his request, I painted his 'logo' on 'our' aircraft. This consisted of a 'Bobby's' helmet and truncheon (he had been a London policeman). I had only recently arrived from technical training at Kirkham, but it was soon 'leaked' that I was a signwriter by trade, because other requests followed. First, Sqn Ldr Masterman (CO) for his wife's name, 'Cynthia' and a little spanner – he carried one at all times. Then there was Flg Off Parker, from Texas. His emblem was the 5-pointed Texas star. Sadly 'Tex's' engine seized over the Channel while returning from a sortie and he was killed. My colleague, Jock McCreadie, and I kept our brightly painted chocks with Texas stars, and his name on the spacer bar, just to remember him by. Before this, however, the squadron received a request from the people of Basutoland for some pictures of their adopted squadron. It was then realised that several replaced aircraft had not been inscribed with Basuto names. I was duly commissioned to do this, with only a day or two to meet the deadline, when an Air Ministry photographer would arrive. Quthung was nicknamed 'Queer Thing'. A new experience was trying to make aircraft cellulose flow on a sable brush! Much thinners and a reduced brush life! Flg Off Parker would not agree to have an African name beside his Texas star, so I had to carefully do a 'Moshesh' in chalk and then rub it off after the photo was taken!

The patrols and sweeps in the middle of June were uneventful until the 18th, when the squadron was airborne on a practice flight which developed into a *Roadstead* anti-shipping sortie. Five small vessels were attacked and left sinking in the Dieppe area.

The following day shipping was again the target. This time Flt Lt Woods (BM516) led the squadron to the Le Havre area, where a 200-ton coaster was attacked about ten miles from the port. The squadron made two attacks on the vessel, using cannon and machine-guns, leaving it belching black smoke and

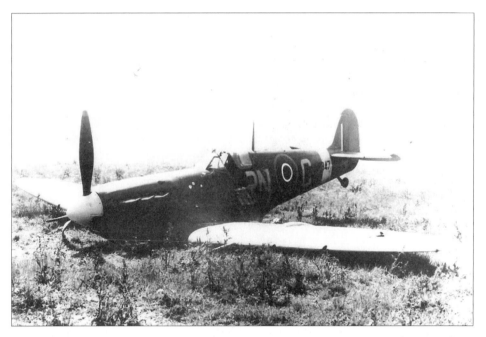

Spitfire Mk Vb AR347:RN-B force-landed at Gravesend on 8 June 1942. (Joe Dade)

sinking. The squadron discovered on its return that the wing leader, Wg Cdr Rankin, had just been awarded a bar to his DSO.

Shipping targets were becoming popular at Group, and 'A' Flt was airborne at first light for a sweep down the coast to Ostend at zero feet. It received intense flak from Gravelines and Dunkirk, and no shipping sightings for its trouble. Undeterred, 'B' Flt was off a short time later to the Boulogne area, where it sighted a large vessel escorted by six flak ships and twelve fighters. The Spitfires did not take on the superior force, but turned for home to report the sighting.

On the 20th the Biggin Hill wing flew a diversionary sweep in the St Omer area for *Circus* 193, twelve Bostons attacking Lille. The squadron was briefed that Typhoons would also be operating in the Dunkirk area at the same time. This information was important, as the Typhoon bore a marked resemblance to the Fw 190 from some angles, and mistakes could be made. The *Luftwaffe* responded to the incursions, but it was not till the squadron was on its way out of France that a brief skirmish ensued, during which Sqn Ldr Kingcome (BM326) and his wingman, Plt Off Robertson(BM313:RN-H), engaged three Fw 190s. Robertson claimed one damaged. No. 133 Sqn lost Plt Off Arends on this mission.

The 21st was a quiet day as the squadron prepared for a move to Martlesham Heath for a rest period. It left Biggin Hill on the 22nd, flying over Biggin Hill in squadron formation. On the 23rd the squadron began air firing practice at Martlesham, and several pilots were given leave. Suitably rested, the squadron

Flt Lt Campbell at Gravesend in 1942. (72 Sqn)

returned to Biggin Hill on the 29th. That same day two Spitfires were detailed to provide and escort to several aircraft of No. 1426 Enemy Aircraft Flight – an He 111, a Bf 109 and a Bf 110. These aircraft were used to tour fighter and bomber stations to familiarize crews with enemy aircraft, tactics and capabilities.

The squadron remained at Biggin only till the 30th, when it moved temporarily to Lympne, where it spent a hectic afternoon sorting out all the ammunition and equipment. While it was there, news came through of the award of the DFC

72 Sqn ground crew at Gravesend in 1942 with Spitfire Mk Vb W3380 'Basuto'. (R. Gledhill via 72 Sqn)

72 Sqn pilots with 'Basuto'. (R. Gledhill via 72 Sqn)

The squadron on parade at Gravesend in 1942, with Sqn Ldr Masterman in front of Spitfire AA845 'Cynthia'. (Joe Dade)

to Flt Lt Woods, and a suitable celebration was held in the officers' mess that evening. Fitter Cpl Jack Lancaster was involved in the road move to Lympne:

We moved back to Gravesend, where we stayed until March 1942. A short sojourn to Lympne to cover a landing at Dieppe by Canadian forces, which was cancelled, due it was said to the enemy being aware of what was afoot. On the way to Lympne I was detailed to go ahead with a fiver (£5) and 'Get 'em set up' at a large pub on the A20. I have never seen such a surprised look on the landlord's face. I seem to remember that beer was about 9d (4p) a pint then. We had the white stripes painted on the aircraft as there was going to be an awful lot of aircraft in the air over Dieppe. However, it didn't occur because I understand that the Germans were made aware of the situation before it took place.

The first three days at Lympne were filled with training sorties, and it was on 2 July that the squadron heard the sad news that Gp Capt Barwell, CO at Biggin Hill, who had flown many sorties with the squadron on wing sweeps, had been accidentally shot down off Beachy Head, while on a patrol with Sqn Ldr Oxspring. They had been patrolling in the hope of catching a German reconnaissance aircraft, which had been coming over each evening for the past fortnight, when they were bounced by two Spitfires from 129 Sqn from Tangmere, and Barwell was shot down.

Defensive patrols commenced on the 4th, but the pilots found the flying tedious. Things were not helped on the 5th, when the squadron was reduced to using only six of its twenty allocated Spitfires, as the remainder were painted with white stripes on the engine cowlings and tailplane and forbidden to be flown near the coast. Also on the 5th, the squadron was lucky not to lose a pilot and the squadron engineering officer. Plt Off Daniel was flying the engineering officer, Plt Off Tomlinson, over to Biggin Hill in the squadron Magister when they crashed near Sevenoaks. Daniel escaped with slight burns and Tomlinson with a bad shaking. The Magister, however, was burnt out. A replacement was delivered on the 7th.

The squadron pilots were baffled by the lack of activity during this period, and the compiler of the operation record book was moved to note on the 6th: 'WHY all this inactivity?' The squadron was sure something was afoot. On the 7th the pilots flew back to Biggin Hill, followed shortly after by the ground party, leaving behind a sense of disappointment at the lack of action at Lympne. The operation the squadron had moved to Lympne to take part in was Operation Rutter, a raid on Dieppe. Due to an unsuccessful exercise in preparation for the raid, and bad weather in early July, the operation was cancelled. The plan would be resurrected in late July and become reality with the large-scale raid on Dieppe in August – Operation Jubilee.

On the 8th two of the squadron pilots, Hugo Armstrong and 'Timber' Woods, had the opportunity to fly a new Spitfire Mk IX. Two days later they briefed the

Two photos of Desmond Sheen in the cockpit of 'Basuto'. (72 Sqn)

other pilots on its performance. They reported an indicated air speed at 25,000 ft in a shallow dive of 480 mph, or 715 mph true air speed. Needless to say, they were favourably impressed and the whole squadron was looking forward to re-equipment with the type. The station engineering officer promised deliveries of the new mark by the end of the month. Countering the news of new aircraft on the horizon was the news that the squadron was losing Sqn Ldr Kingcome, who was leaving to lead the Kenley wing.

Offensive operation recommenced on a small scale on the 12th, when the squadron left Biggin Hill in company with 133 (Eagle) Sqn to rendezvous with 401 (RCAF) Sqn overhead Gravesend. The three squadrons climbed steadily towards the Somme estuary, crossing the French coast at 17,500 ft before turning left and flying to Gris Nez. Here they reversed course and flew back to the Somme before turning for home. Six Fw 190s were sighted on the sweep, but they wisely declined to tackle three squadrons of Spitfires. The squadron returned to Biggin Hill to find the new CO, Sqn Ldr R.W. 'Bobby' Oxspring DFC, had arrived from 91 Sqn at Hawkinge.

A second sweep was flown later in the day. The wing leader, Wg Cdr Rankin (BM326), elected to fly with the squadron, and 401 Sqn flew over from Gravesend to attend the briefing for the three wing squadrons. The wing was to provide escort cover to twelve Bostons bombing Abbeville airfield. The Bostons flew in two boxes of six, and one box was made up of crews of the 15th Bombardment Sqn (Light) of the US 8th AF, flying borrowed RAF Bostons. The squadron pilots observed the Bostons' bombing runs and reported one stick of bombs landing on airfield buildings, while another hit the runway. The other sticks of bombs fell outside the airfield boundary. Despite the flak neither bombers nor escort suffered any losses, and all returned safely.

The following day produced another wing sweep in conjunction with the Kenley wing to provide a diversion for twelve Bostons attacking Abbeville airfield. Sqn Ldr Thomas DFC (133 Sqn) led the wing, while the wing leader, Wg Cdr Rankin (BM326), led 72 Sqn with the new CO, Sqn Ldr Oxspring (BM450), as his No. 2. Taking off and flying at low level to creep under the radar, the wing climbed quickly to 12,000 ft approaching Abbeville, where they encountered several pairs of Fw 190s. The squadron quickly engaged them, and five pilots managed to get into firing positions, although only one, Sgt Menzies (RAAF) (BM492), made a claim for a damaged Fw 190. During the fight Plt Off Robertson (BM313:RN-H) managed to overstress his wings during a steep dive and subsequent hard pull-out. He managed to fly the weakened Spitfire back to Biggin and landed safely. Two of 401 Sqn's aircraft were seen to collide during the engagement, and neither pilot baled out.

Cedric Stone, who arrived from 64 Sqn as a sergeant pilot with the squadron during 1941/2, recalled another incident which resulted in overstressed aircraft in early 1942:

Wg Cdr Robinson was our leader, followed by the squadron commander, Jamie Rankin, and I was No. 3. While at 30,000 ft, high on patrol over Dungeness, some E-boats were reported to be active below us. Our leader immediately put his nose down and we followed. I was at full throttle to maintain station, and the airspeed dials were soon on the second revolution of the dials. We vibrated and shuddered as if riding a bicycle over corrugated iron. The ASI was not readable. On our way down the aircraft was difficult to hold on station. The leader then fired his guns and an empty cartridge case hit the canopy of Jamie Rankin's aircraft and it burst. The canopy flew off but fortunately missed the tail. Then, with the air pressure building up in the empennage, the plates tore from the rivets and the handling of the aircraft became difficult. On return to base all three aircraft proved to be unserviceable. The wings of all three aircraft had a permanent distortion of seven to eight degrees, which of course affected stalling speed. We had passed through the sound barrier – probably for the first time in a Spitfire. We were lucky not to have lost a wing, but that was war.

For the next week or so the squadron flew sweeps, mass *Rhubarbs* and ASR sorties, all with little to show for the effort. On the 23rd four Spitfires were sent out on a *Rhubarb* during which they shot-up electricity pylons and a small utility truck in the Dieppe/St Valery area, forcing the truck to crash into a tree, and observing the driver jumping out. In the evening the stress of operations was relieved somewhat by a party and dance held in the Tea Pot in Biggin Hill village, at which seventy-two gallons of free beer were provided.

Three pairs of Spitfires took off on *Rhubarb* sorties on the 24th, with Plt Off Robertson (BM300:RN-E) and Plt Off Lowe (BM518) encountering the enemy. They were jumped by two Fw 190s in mid-Channel between Dungeness and Boulogne. Robertson and Lowe were at 22,000 ft when the Fw 190s dived on them from 26,000 ft but did not fire. One of the Fw 190s pulled up under Lowe's tail, positioning to open fire. Robertson saw this and manoeuvred to get on the enemy's tail, but had difficulty in closing the gap to closer than 800 yards. The Fw 190s saw him closing, however, and broke off, turning on their backs and diving away.

The 24th was also a day of celebration on the squadron as its long-awaited Spitfire Mk IXs arrived. Fifteen were delivered and a further three were

---

DFC Citation

LONDON GAZETTE, 14TH JULY 1942

Woods, F/L Eric Norman

This officer has participated in 74 sorties over enemy territory. He has led his flight, and occasionally the squadron, with courage, skill and judgement. Hs resourcefulness in difficult circumstances has helped to promote and maintain the high morale of the squadron. Flight Lieutenant Woods has destroyed one and damaged a further two enemy aircraft.

promised. The good news was countered, though, by a persistent rumour that the squadron was to be moved out of No. 11 Gp, and this caused some disgruntlement and unhappiness within the squadron. The rumours appeared to be confirmed on the 25th, when the squadron was told to hand over its Mk IXs to 401 Sqn at Gravesend. Fitter Cpl Jack Lancaster noted the arrival of the Spitfire Mk IX for the squadron:

Back at Biggin we changed our Spit Vbs for Mark IXs and the pilots were over the moon. A short spell at Martlesham Heath for air firing and then back to the 'Bump'. However, good things don't last for ever, and we learned that we were heading north again. We left our Spit IXs and took over some old Vbs again, much to the pilots' disgust.

On the 26th, 72, 133 and 401 combined for a highly successful *Rodeo* to St Omer. No. 72 Sqn was the top squadron for the sweep. The wing flew out at North Foreland via Gravesend at 500 ft, and after eight minutes at sea level climbed quickly. In addition to the Biggin Hill wing, Tangmere wing was sweeping to Abbeville and Northolt wing to Le Touquet and Gravelines. All was quiet for the wing until it turned back from St Omer and ran into twenty Fw 190s. Flt Lt H.T. Armstrong (BM271) and Plt Off R.C. Kitchen (BM513) both shot down an Fw 190 each, and Sqn Ldr R.W. Oxspring (BM326) added to his score with one probably destroyed, while Plt Off D.G.S.R. Cox (BM345) damaged another. Cox had previously served with 19 Sqn, where he shot down a Bf 109 before crash-landing his badly damaged Spitfire on the beach at Dungeness. He reported his victory over the Fw 190:

I was Blue 3. As the squadron was coming out of France to the east of Calais, we found we were being followed by three enemy aircraft with many more behind them. The squadron turned to meet these and Blue Section turned very sharply, and I became separated by some other Spitfires firing in front of us. Three or four Fw 190s nearby then made some half-hearted attacks on me, and after shaking off one of these, I saw a single Fw 190 coming head-on from the sea. When about 80 yards away he dived slightly and apparently he thought I had not recognized him for he began to pull out in an endeavour to get behind me, so I half-rolled on him and he continued to dive. We were both moving fast, and I closed the range to about 35 yards before opening fire. I gave him about two rings deflection, and after two seconds I saw a large white burst at the top of the engine cowling and well to the front. This was definitely not 'ha-ha' boost. It was too far forward on the engine for this. I then had to break away as there were three Fw 190s above me. I began to dive at about 10,000 ft and began to pull out at 4,000 ft.

Countering the victories was the loss of Sqn Ldr H.R. Tidd (BM484), who was killed. Sgt Fowler (BM265) was hit by cannon fire, which left a large hole in his

Flt Lt R.C. Kitchen DFC with Spitfire 'Basutoland Leribe'. (72 Sqn)

starboard wing. Fowler managed to keep control of the Spitfire and made a successful wheels-up landing at Manston.

After refuelling and rearming, eleven Spitfires took off to search for Sqn Ldr Tidd, but had no success, mainly due to the interference of cloud cover. In the evening the officers invited the sergeant pilots to the officers' mess for a party to celebrate the Biggin Hill Sector's 900th victory that day.

On the 28th, Flt Lt 'Timber' Woods was posted overseas, having been with the squadron since March 1942. As a flight commander he was sadly missed. The following day the squadron began preparations for a move to Morpeth in Northumberland on 2 August to take part in a major Army invasion exercise. No. 72 Sqn would provide air support to the 'enemy forces'. The month ended with an escort sweep to Abbeville, during which 133 Sqn lost three pilots, while 72 Sqn returned unscathed.

No. 72 Sqn flew its last sweep from Biggin Hill on 1 August; an uneventful escort to twelve bombers attacking Bruges. The advance ground party left for Morpeth the same day. The following day continuous rain and low cloud prevented the Spitfires from leaving for Morpeth till late in the afternoon. After an hour the pilots were forced to turn their Spitfires around, unable to reach their planned destination of Church Fenton, and landed at Duxford. The remaining ground crews were loaded into two Handley Page Harrow transports immediately the Spitfires left, and unlike their charges made it to Church Fenton and landed in very poor weather. The rear ground party travelled by train, and was the only group to actually arrive at Morpeth that night. By the end of the day the squadron was scattered over 200 miles and four bases – two sergeant pilots had taken off in the squadron Magister, but only managed to reach Grimsby before being forced to land by the weather. Ben Hitt remembers the move to Morpeth:

August '42 we were to leave Biggin Hill. Many ground crew members went by road with equipment, heading for Morpeth. An advance party went by air and the rest of us having seen off our Spits were also transported in ancient converted bombers, the Harrow or Bombay, which had a likeness to a dinosaur. There were no seats and we all had to sit on a metal floor. There were no parachutes and much to our relief no German fighter planes about. We made it and on reflection I don't think I would board such a plane today unless it was at gunpoint.

Morpeth was just being developed and the accommodation was somewhat utility, washing in cold water contained in large metal containers. The squadron engaged in low flying and some form of war games. The rumours were rife that we were going to the Azores, Iceland or maybe Timbuktu.

On the 3rd the ground crew air party managed to leave Church Fenton and arrived safely at Morpeth, where they immediately set to work to make the station habitable. Morpeth had opened as No. 4 Air Gunner School in April 1942, and the airfield, which saw its first occupants arrive in January 1942, had many teething troubles. Lighting was by paraffin lamp and the water supply was contaminated. Under the direction of the adjutant, Flg Off Le Petit, and the medical officer, Flg Off Griffin, the ground crew put in much hard work to improve the situation.

All was not well at Duxford, however. Fighter Command requisitioned the propellers fitted to the squadron's Spitfires, leaving the aircraft uselessly littering the airfield. However, twelve Spitfires from 71 Sqn at Debden were flown over and handed to 72 Sqn, allowing the pilots to complete the journey to Morpeth that evening.

While the squadron settled in at Morpeth the intelligence officer, Flg Off Orton, flew over to Dumfries to be briefed on the exercise and the squadron's part in it. The scenario for the exercise was that a British force comprising three brigades with air support, and capable of reinforcement, had invaded an imaginary coastline between Girvan and Edinburgh. The 'German' defence force comprised two brigades located at Dumfries and Lockerbie, and a third (Polish) brigade with additional tanks at Galashiels. Twelve squadrons of Fighter and Army Support Commands were held in support. The British had landed and forced a bridgehead between Ochiltree and Muirkirk and were advancing towards New Cumnock with the objective of capturing Dumfries. A second thrust down the Dalmellington road had been held up by the 'Germans' at this point, and they had turned towards New Cumnock. This was the situation in the evening of the 4th as 72 Sqn prepared to join the exercise the next day. They would play the part of 'German' fighters.

On the 5th one flight stood by at readiness for involvement in Exercise *Dryshod*, and at 1030 hrs it was scrambled to attack an armoured column moving south-east between Dalmellington and Carsphairn. The Spitfires took off but were unable to reach their objective due to low cloud, and returned to Morpeth. The weather improved in the afternoon, and four Spitfires took off to attack an armoured column on the road between Cumnock and New Cumnock. The column was quickly located, and ten tanks and a number of smaller vehicles, which made no attempt to disperse, were attacked and 'shot up'. Leaving the tanks, the pilots spotted an airborne Puss Moth and another in a field close to an Army camp, and attacked these, claiming them both 'destroyed'. They next turned their attention to escorting two friendly Bostons back to Dumfries before returning to Morpeth.

At 1640 hrs the squadron dispatched a further six Spitfires to attack the armoured column again. They found the column further down the road between Sanquhar and Entorkinfoot in a narrow defile, experiencing light flak, which in the umpire's opinion 'destroyed' two of the Spitfires. The final sortie of the day was to landing beaches west of the original 'British' bridgehead. Twelve Spitfires flew to the beaches, which were empty, but at least 500 troops were seen on the New Cumnock road in eight transport vehicles. Following this sortie the squadron was stood down for the remainder of the day, having completed over ten hours on readiness and four anti-invasion sorties.

On the very cold morning of 6th August one flight stood by on readiness from 0700 hrs, and six Spitfires were dispatched at 0814 hrs to attack an armoured column moving south towards Thornhill. The 'British' were closing on Dumfries, only fifteen miles away, and threatening the brigade HQ. Over fifty large tanks, bren-gun carriers, armoured cars and troops were spotted and surprised by the Spitfires as the troops ran to their guns. The umpire awarded the 'British' one aircraft slightly damaged.

A second sortie was launched at 0946 hrs to attack the same column near Glossburn, six miles from the brigade HQ in Dumfries, and 72 Sqn's pilots followed six other Spitfires into the attack, and in turn were followed by some Bostons. The umpires judged the main street of Thornhill to be blocked after the strafing and bombing of the heavy tanks and MT.

As soon as the flight had landed another was ordered off to attack another enemy column between Carsphairn and Loch Muck. During the sortie Plt Off Lowe (BM189) hit some high-tension cables south-east of Dalmellington, and force-landed. The Spitfire was wrecked but Lowe walked away unhurt. The pilots saw considerable numbers of bren-gun carriers and MT in the area. The third sortie of the day was to attack an armoured column, but this was well concealed and the pilots had to make do with 'shooting-up' light transport and staff cars on the side roads.

Control asked for a maximum effort for the final sortie of the day. The target was in the area that Plt Off Lowe had crashed in earlier in the day, and it was deemed advisable to send only eight Spitfires, which took off at 1733 hrs. The pilots found MT of all kinds, and many tanks, stretching from Patna to Carsfad Loch, and estimated that they put at least fifty MT vehicles 'out of action'.

On the 7th the weather stopped flying, and the squadron took the opportunity to visit its old stamping ground of Ashington, where a good time was had by all at a dance.

By the 9th the 'British' advance had reached a line from Lockerbie through Darmon to Ruthwell, cutting off the Wigtown–Kirkcudbrightshire peninsula and isolating the port of Stranraer. One of the main objectives of the exercise had been achieved, and a 'cease-fire' signal was received at 1030 hrs and the squadron was released.

On the 10th the squadron began preparations for a move to Ayr, and the following day the advance rail party boarded trains. The Spitfires took off for Ayr on the 12th, but were recalled, landing at Ouston. The main party also set off and reached Ayr. Once again the air and ground crews had become separated by the weather. It was at Ayr that the squadron discovered the reason for the move north, as Jack Lancaster recalls:

After a short stay at Morpeth we arrived at Ayr racecourse, where we were advised that we were for overseas and had to equip as a completely mobile squadron with our own transport, tents, cooks, etc. While at Ayr, Sqn Ldr Bobby Oxspring took some of the pilots, and collecting half of 222 Sqn at Drem, flew back to Biggin Hill to cover the Dieppe landing.

We lost a lot of friends at Ayr, being posted away, but we gained many more from the chaps being posted in. I was made sergeant and was joined by Bill Mann as Sgt Fitter IIA and Chiefy Landon i/c 'B' Flt. With Corporals Spencer and Fowler and a great bunch of mechanics and riggers, armourers, electricians, wireless mechanics, etc., what a great team we had. Jim the WO armourer was a great friend, with his first-class team, with Rio Wright, Alex McMillan and all whose names now escape me.

On the 13th Sqn Ldr Oxspring, Plt Off Orton and six sergeant pilots were detached to 222 Sqn at Drem, and Sqn Ldr Winskill of 165 Sqn, also at Ayr, took over command of 72 Sqn temporarily. The days which followed were filled with local flying and air firing. Sqn Ldr Oxspring and the detachment returned on the 22nd, and Sqn Ldr Winskill left the squadron to take command of 222 Sqn at Drem. Among the new arrivals on the squadron during this period was Jimmy Corbin, who had spent the previous twelve months as a flying instructor at an OTU:

The day of deliverance came and I was posted to 72 Squadron at Ayr on 20 August 1942, knowing that it was due for overseas. After a week of training and toughening up, and the usual 13 Group readiness, we moved to Ouston for hoped-

for embarkation leave. This was not to be, for with another of those uncanny moves one flight returned to Ayr for readiness duty and another to West Hartlepool.

American Dale Leaf joined the squadron in July, and almost left it on a low-flying sortie in Spitfire RN-S on 25 August. He noted in his logbook:

Local low flying. Glassy sea, very hazy, dipped prop in Irish Sea. Took off 2½ in. on each blade. Don't care to repeat.

Leaf left the squadron for the USAAC in September 1942, and went missing on 2 September flying with the US 4th FG.

On the 27th the station commander, Wg Cdr Bowling, and Flt Lt Evans escorted twenty-six USAAF P-38 Lightnings south, and had to divert into Squires Gate due to poor weather. On the same day four pilots were detached to Eglinton near Londonderry in Northern Ireland for convoy patrol work. One of the pilots was Plt Off Robertson ((RN- H), who hit a lorry on the perimeter track at Eglinton, but was not blamed for the accident.

On the 29th the squadron was informed that it would move to Ouston on 7 September, and preparations for the move commenced. The days at Ayr were filled with local flying, air firing and formation flying. Many of the experienced pilots, who had fought through the sweeps over France and Belgium through 1942, were posted away. In their place came new pilots such as WO Chas Charnock, Sgt Stoker, Flt Sgt J.W. Patterson and Sgt Piggott. Over the coming weeks many more new pilots would arrive.

On 4th September WO Charnock and Sgt Stoker escorted a Liberator into Ayr after it had become lost on an Atlantic crossing, and two days later Charnock was airborne again with Plt Off Cox to escort a Flying Fortress lost in similar circumstances. The move to Ouston was delayed indefinitely, and the squadron continued training its new pilots at Ayr. By mid-September they were flying cross-country practices and ZZ procedures, and on 26 September the squadron finally made its move to Ouston. Pilot Laurie Frampton was posted to the squadron at Ayr just prior to the move to Ouston, and recalls the preparations for the overseas move:

American volunteer pilot Dale Leaf flew with the squadron for about five weeks in 1942. (P. Bradley)

I joined 72 Squadron as a sprog sergeant pilot just out of OTU on 24 August 1942. The squadron was then based at Ayr and had been informed that it was to be sent overseas. Consequently we moved to Ouston where extra personnel, e.g. servicing echelon, catering, stores, transport, etc., together with their equipment, was added in order to make a fully self-sufficient, mobile unit.

All ranks had to suffer a 'Backers-Up' course, which included route-marching and weapons training with machine-guns, hand grenades, etc. to prepare us to defend ourselves against possible enemy attack. We were given refresher and additional injections, advice on health precautions for various climates and, finally, five days' embarkation leave.

Just a few days before the move, six pilots and Spitfires were detached to Ballyhalbert in Northern Ireland for convoy protection duties. The six returned to Ouston on 1 October, but were immediately detached again to Ayr. Three days after arriving at Ouston the squadron detached a further nine Spitfires to West Hartlepool. Training continued at all three stations, though it was limited by the poor weather in October. Sgt Lewis, a Canadian, and Sgt J.W. MacDonald from Brisbane, Australia, were commissioned and told they would stay with 72 Sqn, and further new arrivals bolstered the squadron, among them WO Alan Gear, who would become well known for his enormous handlebar moustache. Gear flew Hurricanes with 32 Sqn before taking up instructor duties at Upavon, Hullavington, Balado Bridge and Errol before joining 72 Sqn.

Further movements and commissions followed, with Sgt F. Malan, brother of the famous 'Sailor' Malan, being commissioned, and several changes occurred among the commissioned ground staff of the squadron. Engineering officer, Plt Off Tomlinson, was replaced by Plt Off R.H. Whipp, but when it was discovered that Whipp was unfit for service overseas he was replaced by Plt Off H.G. 'Greggs' Farish. Farish would become an indispensable member of the squadron. The intelligence officer, Plt Off Salkeld, was posted to 303 (Polish) Sqn and replaced by Flg Off Simm. It became clear to all on the squadron that

---

DFC Citation

LONDON GAZETTE, 18TH SEPTEMBER 1942

Acting Squadron Leader Robert Wardlow Oxspring DFC

This squadron commander has rendered much valuable service. His skill, whether in attacks on the enemy's ground targets and shipping or in air combat, has been of a high order. He has destroyed at least 7 enemy aircraft.

Laurie Frampton. (L. Frampton)　　　WO Alan Gear DFC.

an overseas move was planned when they commenced a ground training programme in mid-October, which included route marches, cross-country runs and physical training every day. Provision of equipment for the move overseas began at Ouston, and Jimmy Corbin recalls the hectic activity surrounding the preparations:

After ten days we were all recalled to Ouston, this being 11 October, where we were hastily equipped for overseas. A ruthless check of luggage followed. Half of us managed to scrounge five days' embarkation leave, but after four days that dreaded telegram arrived and we were recalled on 18 October. Before this date the whole squadron had been toughening up with PT and marches – a good thing, so we were told, but how painful. The 18th, a Sunday, a hurried check-up of kit, three inoculations and vaccine. We were told to our disappointment that there was to be a temporary split-up of the pilots, and the CO, Sqn Ldr Oxspring, and eight others were to proceed to Wilmslow on Monday morning. These eight were Flt Lt Ford, Flt Lt Krohn, Flg Off Cox, Flg Off Hardy, Plt Off Daniel, Plt Off Robertson, Plt Off Lowe and myself.

Packing of tools, instruments and equipment commenced, and on 20 October the first movements began, with Sqn Ldr Oxspring and eight pilots being attached to No. 2 Personnel Dispatch Centre at Wilmslow to await transport overseas. At Wilmslow further kitting and preparation was carried out, as Jimmy Corbin recorded:

Flt Lt D.N. Ford DFC. (72 Sqn)

At Wilmslow we had another inoculation, Yellow Jack, this causing much speculation as to where we were going. We had to leave our main kit behind and take only flying-kit, toilet stuff and a change of clothing, in fact only the stuff that could be packed into a fighter aircraft, which for the unwise is not very much, hence you can guess the crude cracks relating to BO. At lunchtime of Tuesday 20 October we were put into batches – 72 Sqn and 93 Sqn in one coach to be loaded into one ship, and 152 and 111 in another. We arrived at some canal near Liverpool where we waited in the rain for the arrival of our ships They arrived and we boarded about 5 p.m., sorted ourselves out and had food. The accommodation was not good but comfortable, and the food throughout was top hole. Our ship was a 4,500-ton cargo vessel. She was crammed with aircraft in crates.

Reinforcements for the squadron arrived at Ouston, and in the case of one new arrival, Darryl Briggs, it was 'out of the frying-pan and into the fire':

It was an inauspicious introduction to 72 Sqn. Just prior to departure I was languishing in the RAF Police cell at Ouston. I was going to phone my dad, but fizzing as the phone had been smashed. I reported it to the police, who accused me of the damage, despite my saying that if I had done it I wouldn't have reported it. However, I was missed (by the squadron), so I was reluctantly released.

Nine NCO pilots followed, moving to No. 1 PDC at West Kirby, and by the 21st the squadron had been taken off operational flying and preparations for the overseas move were almost complete. Ben Hitt recalled the move from Morpeth to Ayr and then Ouston, and the training the ground crew received in preparation for the move overseas:

After a while we moved to Ayr, and then to RAF Ouston near Newcastle. Before long there was a dramatic change. We changed our RAF blue uniforms for khaki battledress, which was not so much fitted but issued, and along with this we were also issued Sten guns and ammunition. We began to doubt if we were still in the RAF.

Sten gun practice shoots were held. We soon found that the best chance of hitting the target was to aim in another direction. We were confined to camp and not allowed to be seen in khaki. I had a reason to go to Newcastle for eyesight testing, and had to borrow a blue uniform. 'Go straight there and come straight back.' Finally the move started.

While the squadron continued its preparations for the overseas move, the pilots who had departed to West Kirby and Wilmslow at the end of October were transported to Gibraltar. Laurie Frampton recalls his departure from Ouston, and eventual arrival in a convoy at Gibraltar:

The pilots went to West Kirby PDC, whence we were dispersed in groups of four or five, each consisting of members of different squadrons. We went to Northern Ireland, and after spending the night at RAF Eglinton were taken the next morning to the RN docks at Londonderry, which was the base for convoy escorts. Each group was allocated to a ship, my group to join HMS Erne, a Black-Swan-class sloop of 2,000 tons, with a main armament of six 4 in. guns and four depth-charge launchers. Since she was moored four miles down Lough Foyle, we left port on another ship and transferred to Erne.

We sailed from the lough for Liverpool to collect orders, and while in port we pilots had to remain below decks. On leaving the Mersey we sailed north, collecting small groups of merchant ships, until we reached the convoy rendezvous somewhere in the region of Loch Linnhe. The convoy having assembled, we headed west into the Atlantic Ocean, whither –???

The NCO pilots were berthed in the chief petty officers' mess just below 'A' gun, a twin four-inch mounting. Our hosts made us most welcome even to the point of introducing us to Nelson's Blood (navy rum – neaters).

Three of the escorts were in the van of the convoy to ensure that no nasty visitors were waiting for us. Erne's station was on the starboard bow, so all we saw of the other ships was an occasional glimpse of a masthead on the horizon astern. The only exception to this was when we went into the convoy to refuel. One evening there was an extremely loud bang, and we all dashed up on deck to see that 'A' gun had fired a star shell, as the radar had picked up a blip, which fortunately turned out to be harmless.

The voyage continued in bright sunshine, with the ship rolling gently in the deep blue Atlantic swell, and early in November we were told of the 8th Army's success at Alamein and learned that we were headed for Algiers. Seventeen days after sailing we were told that Erne was to escort the convoy to Algiers, but we were to go to Gibraltar, therefore we had to transfer to another vessel. Somewhere in the Atlantic, while steering north-east towards Gib., we climbed down a rope ladder into a whaler to be rowed across to a corvette and climbed aboard. During the night we sailed through the straits, both shores being brilliantly lit, and the following morning returned to Gibraltar to disembark on 10 November, eighteen days after leaving Britain.

For the remainder the destination was, as yet, unknown. On 8 November the squadron left Ouston to join the MV *Staffordshire* in Liverpool. From there it sailed to the Clyde to join a convoy which left on the 14th. Ground crew members Harold Powell and Ted Mason were among those sent to Wilmslow, as Harold recalls:

The two of us sneaked off to Blackpool one weekend on forged passes with the SWO's stamp which we'd borrowed. We stayed with Ted's mother, who owned a hotel. The Army officers who were billeted there gave us some black looks when we sat down to breakfast in the dining-room, 'What were two 'Erks' doing here?' We returned to camp to find our group packed up, with full kit, ready to embark for the troopship SS Orontes at Glasgow!

Jack Lancaster also recalled the move from Ouston for overseas embarkation:

At Ouston we were finalizing, equipping, first time I'd seen one of the flight desks which were used for campaign-sort-of-style operations, which was more like a box which opened up. However, we got everything sorted out and boxed, and then we were told that we would be leaving from Newcastle, and we went by train to Liverpool and were most surprised that the train pulled up at the side of the SS Staffordshire, and we were told to go up the gangway and get on board. I think they weren't taking any chances about us deciding not to go. The embarkation officer was an RAF officer, and we were very fortunate because the SNCOs of the squadron were allocated cabins with just two bunks. This was ideal, but I went down to see what the boys were doing. They were very traumatized, I think, because they found themselves in the bottom of the ship in a hold, with hammocks or hard tables to sleep on. I don't think the Army took kindly to us sergeants especially, as we were in cabins with beds, and the only Army ranks who were allowed in cabins were sergeant-majors and above. The rest of the trip was quite uneventful except for one time when the whole fleet turned to the left, all except us, because our steering seemed to have broken down, and we were careering towards the middle of the Empress of Australia at a great rate of knots. However, they did manage to turn in time to avoid an accident, and we went sailing on. We landed at Algiers on the 21st. I remember that date well, as it was my 22nd birthday.

Darryl Briggs boarded the train for who knows where, and on sighting the ship they would board had some choice words to describe it:

We got our first glimpse of our cruise ship, and like the John Masefield poem it was 'a salt-encrusted relic of a glorious past': SS Staffordshire of the Bibby Line, with a single stack. What caused rumours as to our destination was a huge snowplough on her sharp end.

It was really packed: 'Brown Jobs' and RAF. Cook's package tours had really earned their cash! We were given a long table, but I can't recall if food was a 'free-for-all' or if someone at the table top was detailed. The menu card was missing. Owing to over-booking our cabins were missing; instead, eight hammocks for twelve men. Failing to get one, I was on the deck – away from the route to the toilets.

There was more consternation when we slipped our moorings on Friday 13th – for where? Norway? Russia? Some lads could even see their homes from the Clyde. My biggest shock was the toilets – for washing we were issued a bar of salt-water soap, no hot water. The toilet was communal, and the believed origin was ancient Rome. It consisted of a very long plank with holes along its length, suspended above a long torrent of rushing water.

The days so far were uneventful on calm seas, and we had acquired quite a big collection of ships: tankers, tramps and some lovely grey-painted liners. Nearest to us was a Canadian Pacific three-funnelled Empress class. Once we hit the Bay of Biscay life on board was more lively. Complexions turned from rosy to grey, vomit was everywhere, some spending long periods on the plank, which was extremely busy. If bacon was on for breakfast it caused a renewed rush to more contemplation of the torrent. We did lose one overboard, but the ship was not allowed to stop, so just guess as to his fate.

The weather and the sea got warmer and calmer. The torrent's clients got fewer. Our immediate escorts, a pair of dolphins. Occasionally depth charges were fired, accompanied by a great wall of water. Destroyers dashing up and down the convoy. I was detailed to break coal in the depth of the ship, which was not to my liking. Gradually we got our 'sea legs', and at night, sleeping on the deck, watching the graceful arc of the tip of the mast against the stars and looking at the phosphorescent wake was indeed the stuff of dreams.

Then one night the lights of Morocco on the right, and of Spain on the left, as we threaded the 'Pillars of Hercules' – a lovely target for U-boats. So, Algiers, Arabian nights, romance and magic beckoned us from a heavy sea and a grey day.

While the squadron had been training for its overseas deployment, the politicians and generals had been putting the final touches to the plan for the invasion of North Africa, Operation Torch. The plans were issued on 8 October. Two weeks later the Second Battle of El Alamein commenced, with Montgomery's troops pushing forward over a six-mile front, preceded by a 1,000-gun bombardment. Rommel returned to the battlefront from sick leave, but with the impending invasion would soon find his army caught like a nut in a nutcracker. The Germans would fight a strong rearguard action in the coming weeks, but their fate was sealed.

On the day the squadron left Ouston, Operation Torch commenced. Initially there was some resistance from the Vichy French forces, and the Germans countered the invasion by transporting troops to Tunisia, unopposed by the French. The Allied forces landing in Algeria and Morocco were led by Lt Gen Eisenhower, and while the landings were taking place Gen Montgomery's forces, advancing from the east, captured Mersa Matruh. The jaws of the vice were slowly beginning to squeeze the Axis forces in North Africa.

By 9 November US troops had advanced on both sides of Oran and captured 2,000 French prisoners, who had put up a stiff resistance. The Germans meanwhile had no intention of giving up the area without a fight, and quickly poured troops into Tunis, unopposed by the French Vichy forces. The following day the Americans captured Oran. Marshal Petain took control of all Vichy forces from France in an attempt to bolster resistance, and further British success in the east came with the capture of Sidi Barrani. By the 12th Montgomery was also in Sollum and Bardia, and Rommel was withdrawing toward Tripoli. By the 13th Tobruk had fallen to the 8th Army.

Ben Hitt embarked on the troopship for the voyage to North Africa:

A long troop train journey ending in Liverpool and then onto a troopship. Only those who have travelled on troopships will know the atmosphere, sleeping in three tiers – one row on the deck, one row on the mess table and another in hammocks, the smells being many and varied. We left Liverpool late afternoon – a last look at the Liver Building – would we see it again? By morning we were in the Clyde. A beautiful still morning – a vast armada of troopships. This was 8 November 1942.

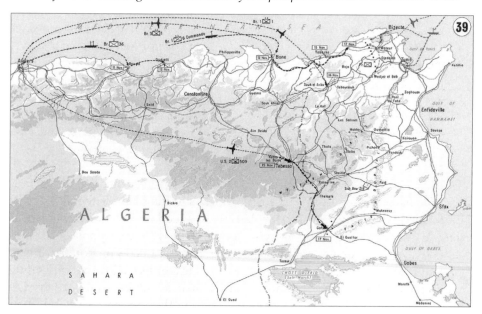

NW Africa Situation Map, 11–18 November 1942.

The news came through – 'Allied forces have landed in Algeria' – we knew where we were going. Our voyage took about fourteen days and it was very rough in the Bay of Biscay. There was much seasickness, which had the consolation that if the ship sinks you don't mind dying. In the main the voyage was uneventful and we had strong protection from naval destroyers. Occasionally in the distance they would go to and fro dropping depth charges. The weather improved and it got warmer. Sometimes in the distance we could see the lights of the distant coastline. After going through the Straits of Gibraltar, finally Algiers came into sight, and it looked beautiful in the sunlight.

The pilots waiting at Gibraltar were given an inkling of their destination on 11 November, as Jimmy Corbin recorded:

A lazy morning, not allowed out of camp. Lecture at 3 p.m. Wg Cdr Simpson with all the gen on campaign, maps, iron rations, escape packet and blood ticket. Algiers our port of call – call-signs of ships and Maison Blanche. High hopes Algiers in two or three days' time.

No. 72 Squadron had come to the end of its defensive period of the war, and was now ready to strike back with a new offensive far from home.

APPENDIX 1

Squadron Commanders, 1937–43

9 June 1937 to 14 January 1938   Sqn Ldr E.H.L. Hope
15 January 1938 to 13 December 1938   Sqn Ldr J.B.H. Rogers
14 December 1938 to 24 July 1940   Sqn Ldr R.B. Lees
25 July 1940 to 2 September 1940   Sqn Ldr A.R. Collins
2 September 1940 to 1 April 1941   Flt Lt (later Sqn Ldr) E. Graham
17 April 1941 to 27 October 1941   Sqn Ldr D.F.B. Sheen DFC
27 October 1941 – 8 February 1942   Sqn Ldr C.A. Masterman CBE
8 February 1942 – 12 July 1942   Sqn Ldr C.B..F Kingcome DFC & Bar
12 July 1942 – 13 August 1942   Sqn Ldr R.W. Oxspring DFC
13 August 1942 – 22 August 1942   Sqn Ldr A.L. Winskill DFC
22 August 1942 – 23 April 1943   Sqn Ldr R.W. Oxspring DFC

APPENDIX 2

Squadron Bases, 1937–42

United Kingdom

Tangmere	22 February 1937 to June 1937
Church Fenton	June 1937 to 15 October 1939
Leconfield	15 October 1939 to 1 November 1939
Drem	1 November 1939 to 20 December 1939
Leuchars	21 December 1939
Drem	21 December 1939 to 12 January 1940
Leconfield	12 January 1940 to 14 January 1940
Church Fenton	14 January 1940 to 3 March 1940
Acklington	3 March 1940 to 1 June 1940
Gravesend	1 June 1940 to 6 June 1940
Acklington	6 June 1940 to 31 August 1940
Biggin Hill	31 August 1940 to 1 September 1940
Croydon	1 September 1940 to 2 September 1940
Hawkinge	2 September 1940 to 4 September 1940
Croydon	4 September 1940 to14 September 1940
Biggin Hill	14 September 1940 to 14 October 1940
Leconfield	14 October 1940 to 20 October 1940
Coltishall	20 October 1940 to 30 October 1940
Matlaske	30 October 1940 to 2 November 1940
Coltishall	2 November 1940 to 29 November 1940
Leuchars	29 November 1940 to 19 December 1940
Acklington	19 December 1940 to 9 July 1941
Gravesend	9 July 1941 to 26 July 1941
Biggin Hill	26 July 1941 to 20 October 1941
Gravesend	20 October 1941 to 22 March 1942
Biggin Hill	22 March 1942 to 30 June 1942
Lympne	30 June 1942 to 7 July 1942
Biggin Hill	7 July 1942 to 1 August 1942
Duxford	2 August 1942 to 4 August 1942
Morpeth	4 August 1942 to 12 August 1942
Ouston	12 August 1942 to 13 August 1942
Ayr	13 August 1942 to 26 September 1942
Ouston	26 September 1942 to 8 November 1942

No. 72 Squadron Aircrew, September 1939

Rank	Name	Post
Sqn Ldr	R.B. 'Ronny' LEES	Commanding Officer
Flg Off	T.A.F. 'Jimmy' ELSDON	Adjutant
Flt Lt	F.M. 'Hiram' SMITH	OC 'A' Flt
Flt Lt	E. 'Ted' GRAHAM	OC 'B' Flt
Flg Off	L.F. 'Honstick' HENSTOCK	
Flg Off	D.F.B. 'Desmond' SHEEN	
Flg Off	R.A. 'Happy' THOMPSON	
Flg Off	J.B. 'Nic' NICOLSON	
Flg Off	J.A. 'Tommy' THOMSON	
Flg Off	D.B. 'Hobby' HOBSON	
Plt Off	O. 'Oswald' St J. PIGG	
Plt Off	R.D. 'Bob' WALKER	
Plt Off	E.J. 'Willy' WILCOX	
Plt Off	J.W. 'Pancho' VILLA	
Plt Off	N.C.H. 'Robby' ROBSON	
Plt Off	D.P. 'Dutch' HOLLAND	
Plt Off	R. 'Deacon' DEACON ELLIOT	
Flt Sgt	J. 'Jack' STEERE	
Sgt	M. 'Mabel' GRAY	
Sgt	R. 'Normy' NORFOLK	
Sgt	'Duffy' DOUTHWAITE	
Sgt	D.C. 'Snowy' WINTER	
Sgt	'Ronny' HAMBLYN	
Sgt	'Sam' STAPLES	
Sgt	M. 'Po' POCOCK	
Sgt	'Jack' ELSE	

APPENDIX 4

No. 13 Group Order of Battle, 0900 hrs 7 July 1940

13 Group HQ Newcastle

Sector	Squadron	Equipment	Base
Wick	3	Hurricane	Wick
	504	Hurricane	Castletown
Dyce	603 ('A' Flt)	Spitfire	Dyce
	603 ('B' Flt)	Spitfire	Montrose
Turnhouse	141	Defiant	Turnhouse
	245	Hurricane	Turnhouse (operational by day only)
	602	Spitfire	Drem
Usworth	152	Spitfire	Acklington
	72	Spitfire	Acklington
Catterick	41	Spitfire	Catterick
	219	Blenheim	Catterick
Church Fenton	249	Hurricane	Church Fenton (operational by day only)
	616	Spitfire	Leconfield

No. 13 Group Order of Battle, 0900 hrs 8 August 1940

13 Group HQ	Newcastle		
Sector	**Squadron**	**Equipment**	**Base**
Wick	3	Hurricane	Wick
	232	Hurricane	Sumburgh (one flight only)
	504	Hurricane	Castletown
Dyce	603 ('A' Flt)	Spitfire	Dyce
	603 ('B' Flt)	Spitfire	Montrose
Turnhouse	141	Defiant	Prestwick
	232	Hurricane	Turnhouse
	253	Hurricane	Turnhouse
	605	Hurricane	Drem
Usworth	72	Spitfire	Acklington
	79	Spitfire	Acklington (operational by day only)
	607	Hurricane	Usworth
Catterick	219	Blenheim	Catterick
Aldergrove	245	Hurricane	Aldergrove

APPENDIX 6

No. 11 Group Order of Battle, 0900 hrs 7 September 1940

11 Group HQ	Uxbridge		
Sector	**Squadron**	**Equipment**	**Base**
Debden	17	Hurricane	Debden
	25	Blenheim	Martlesham Heath
	73	Hurricane	Castle Camps
	257	Hurricane	Martlesham Heath ('B' Flt at North Weald)
North Weald	46	Hurricane	Stapleford Tawney
	249	Hurricane	North Weald
Hornchurch	41	Spitfire	Rochford
	222	Spitfire	Hornchurch
	600	Blenheim	Hornchurch
	603	Spitfire	Hornchurch
Biggin Hill	79	Spitfire	Biggin Hill
	501	Hurricane	Gravesend
Kenley	66	Spitfire	Kenley
	72	Spitfire	Croydon
	111	Hurricane	Croydon
	253	Hurricane	Kenley
Northolt	1	Hurricane	Heathrow
	1 (RCAF)	Hurricane	Northolt
	303 (Polish)	Hurricane	Northolt
	504	Hurricane	Northolt
Tangmere	43	Hurricane	Tangmere
	601	Hurricane	Tangmere
	602	Spitfire	Westhampnett

No. 11 Group Order of Battle, 0900 hrs 7 September 1940

11 Group HQ   Uxbridge

Sector	Squadron	Equipment	Base
Debden	17	Hurricane	Debden
	73	Hurricane	Castle Camps
	257	Hurricane	Castle Camps
North Weald	25	Blenheim	North Weald (one flight at Martlesham Heath in process of re-equipping with Beaufighters)
	46	Hurricane	Stapleford Tawney
	249	Hurricane	North Weald
Hornchurch	41	Spitfire	Hornchurch
	222	Spitfire	Rochford
	603	Spitfire	Hornchurch
Biggin Hill	66	Spitfire	Biggin Hill
	72	Spitfire	Biggin Hill
	92	Spitfire	Biggin Hill
Kenley	253	Hurricane	Kenley
	501	Hurricane	Kenley
	605	Hurricane	Croydon
Northolt	1 (RCAF)	Hurricane	Northolt
	229	Hurricane	Heathrow
	241	Defiant	Gatwick ('B' Flt)
	264	Defiant	Luton ('A' Flt)
	303 (Polish)	Hurricane	Northolt
Tangmere	23	Blenheim	Ford (one flight at Middle Wallop)
	213	Hurricane	Tangmere
	602	Spitfire	Westhampnett
	607	Hurricane	Tangmere

APPENDIX 8

Pilot Losses in the Battle of Britain

31 August 1940   Plt Off E.J. Wilcox
1 September 1940   Flg Off O. St J. Pigg
4 September 1940   Plt Off D.C. Winter
                       Sgt M. Gray
19 September 1940   Plt Off D.F. Holland
27 September 1940   Plt Off P.J. Davies-Cook
                       Plt Off E.E. Males
5 October 1940   Plt Off N. Sutton
12 October 1940   Plt Off H.R. Case

Aircraft Operated by No. 72 Squadron, 1937–43

Fairey Battle

K7676   To 72 Sqn March 1939.

Gloster Gladiator Mk I

K6130   From Manufacturer 22 February 1937. To 112 Sqn.

K6131   From Manufacturer 22 February 1937. Crashed and struck off charge 1 July 1938.

K6132   From Manufacturer 22 February 1937. To Ouston.

K6133:F   Crashed in bad weather near Barmby, Yorks, 23 July 1937.

K6134   To 112 Sqn.

K6135   To 72 Sqn 1936. To 112 Sqn.

K6136   To 72 Sqn 1936. To 112 Sqn.

K6137   Force landed but repaired August 1938. To 607 Sqn.

K6138   To 112 Sqn.

K6139   Collided with K6138 and crashed 29 June 1938.

K6140   To 72 Sqn 1936. To 112 Sqn.

K6141   To 112 Sqn.

K6142   To 72 Sqn 1936. To 112 Sqn.

K6143   From Manufacturer 12 February 1937. To 112 Sqn April 1939.

K6144   Abandoned in a spin and crashed at Monk Fryston, Yorks, 1 December 1938.

K7893   From 3 Sqn. To 80 Sqn.

K7897   From 3 Sqn. To 112 Sqn.

K7898   From 3 Sqn. To 607 Sqn.

K7922   To 72 Sqn. To 112 Sqn.

K7934   Hit high tension cables and crashed at Brough, 7 February 1938.

K7954   From 3 Sqn. To 112 Sqn.

K7963   From 3 Sqn. To 112 Sqn.

K7964   To 72 Sqn.

K7969	From 85 Sqn. To 112 Sqn.
K7974	From 87 Sqn. To 112 Sqn.
K7977	From 87 Sqn. To 112 Sqn.
K7978	From 87 Sqn. To 112 Sqn.
K7980	
K7981:RN-D	From 87 Sqn. To instructional airframe1597M, July 1939.
K7986	From 3 Sqn. To 112 Sqn.
K8004	To 72 Sqn. To 615 Sqn
K8018	To 33 Sqn.
K8019	To 33 Sqn.
K8020	
K8024	From 3 Sqn. To 112 Sqn.
K8027	
K9878	

Gloster Gladiator Mk II
All Mk IIs on brief loan from 152 Sqn.

N5547	152 Sqn. Built as Sea Gladiator.
N5630	152 Sqn.
N5640	152 Sqn.
N5644	152 Sqn.
N5645	152 Sqn.
N5647	152 Sqn.
N5677	152 Sqn.

Supermarine Spitfire Mk Ia

K9828	From 616 Sqn 7 October 1940. To 58 OTU 9 March 1941.
K9840	From 266 Sqn 25 August 1940. To 152 Sqn 23 September 1940.
K9841	From 616 Sqn 25 August 1940. Damaged by return fire from Do 17 and u/c collapsed in forced landing Little Hutchings Farm, Etchingham, Sussex, Plt Off Males safe, 10 September 1940. Struck off charge 10 September 1940.
K9847	To 72 Sqn 2 September 1940. Engine failed, force-landed Halstead 8 October 1940. To AST.
K9870	From 74 Sqn 7 October 1940. Shot down by Bf 109s near Deal, Kent, 11 October 1940. Plt Off Pool injured.
K9922	To 72 Sqn 11 October 1939. Crashed on landing during night training flight at Acklington 27 August 1940.
K9923	To 72 Sqn 21 April 1939. Wheels-up landing Church Fenton 13 July 1939.
K9924	To 72 Sqn 11 April 1939. To 6 MU 15 November 1940.
K9925:RN-C	To 72 Sqn 11 April 1939. Stalled on approach and u/c collapsed and cartwheeled at Woolsington 26 May 1940.

K9926:RN-B	To 72 Sqn 14 April 1939. To 603 Sqn.
K9928	To 72 Sqn 21 April 1939. To 74 Sqn 10 May 1940.
K9929	To 72 Sqn 14 April 1939. Damaged on ops 3 August 1940. To
Westland.	
K9932:SD-N	
K9933	To 72 Sqn 17 April 1939. To 602 Sqn 23 November 1939.
K9934:SD-K	To 72 Sqn 18 April 1939. To 2 SoTT 4 September 1939.
K9935	To 72 Sqn 19 April 1939. Damaged by Bf 109 over Channel. Flt Sgt Steere safe 5 October 1939. To 58 OTU 9 March 1941.
K9936	To 72 Sqn 21 April 1939. To 58 OTU 2 January 1941.
K9937:SD-B	To 72 Sqn 19 April 1939. Braked to avoid overshooting and tipped up Church Fenton 30 June 1939.
K9938:SD-H	To 72 Sqn 21 April 1939. Shot down by Bf 109 aircraft and abandoned, crashed near Herne Bay, Sgt Norfolk safe, 2 September 1940.
K9939	To 72 Sqn 21 April 1939. To AST 18 December 1939.
K9940:RN-Q	To 72 Sqn 24 April 1939. Damaged in air raid at Biggin Hill 6 October 1940. To 58 OTU 1 January 1941.
K9941	To 72 Sqn 24 April 1939. Control lost in cloud crashed Hooton Roberts, Yorks, 21 August 1939.
K9942	To 72 Sqn 24 April 1939. Belly-landed on return from patrol at Acklington 5 June 1940. To 7 OTU 17 August 1940.
K9943	To 72 Sqn 24 April 1939. To 7 OTU 17 June 1940.
K9959	To 72 Sqn 8 May 1939. To 1 CRU 30 August 1940.
K9960	From 610 Sqn 5 September 1940. Hit obstruction while taxiing at Croydon 7 September 1940. Damaged by Bf 109 over Ashford, aircraft abandoned and crashed at Orlestone. Sgt Bell-Walker safe 14 September 1940.
K9989	From 611 Sqn 9 September 1940. Collision with X4544 during scramble 0935 hrs, Plt Off Sutton killed, 5 October 1940.
L1007	From 603 Sqn. Prototype Mk Ib. Shot down Heinkel over Scotland January 1940? Landed on top of L1085 on landing Drem 15 May 1940.
L1056:RN-K	To 72 Sqn 24 July 1939. To Scottish Aviation 8 January 1940.
L1077	To 72 Sqn 15 August 1939. To 92 Sqn 28 August 1940.
L1078	To 72 Sqn 17 August 1939. Crash-landed on return from patrol at Acklington 6 August 1940.
L1083	From RAE 23 July 1940. To 222 Sqn 4 December 1940. To 72 Sqn 5 February 1941. To 58 OTU 21 August 1941.
L1092	From 20 MU 4 September 1939. To 3230M 9 SoTT 14 April 1941.
N3026	To 72 Sqn 11 September 1939. To 603 Sqn 21 February 1940.
N3068	From 602 Sqn 6 September 1940. Shot down by Bf 109 near Sevenoaks, Flg Off Davies-Cooke killed, 27 September 1940.

N3070	From 616 Sqn 2 September 1940. Shot down by Bf 109 near Maidstone, Plt Off Elliot abandoned aircraft, safe, 6 September 1940.
N3093	From 616 Sqn 2 September 1940. Shot down by Bf 109 over Tunbridge Wells, Sgt Gray killed, 5 September 1940.
N3094	From 266 Sqn 2 September 1940. To 57 OTU 23 August 1941.
N3113	To 72 Sqn 11 October 1940. To 92 Sqn 11 October 1940.
N3221	To 72 Sqn 1 April 1940. To Scottish Aviation 22 August 1940.
N3228	From 602 Sqn 13 October 1940. To GAL 18 October 1940.
N3229	From 603 Sqn 2 September 1940. To 92 Sqn 3 November 1940.
P9338	To 72 Sqn 6 June 1940. Left formation and crashed Capel-le-Ferne, nr Folkestone, Kent, Plt Off H.R. Case killed, 12 October 1940.
P9368	From 616 Sqn 2 September 1940. Damaged by Bf 109 near Gravesend, Plt Off Lloyd injured, 18 September 1940. To Scottish Aviation.
P9376	To 72 Sqn 3 September 1940. Damaged by Bf 109 near Maidstone. To AST.
P9424	From 266 Sqn 25 August 1940. Damaged 31 August 1940. To Scottish Aviation.
P9438	To 72 Sqn 12 May 1940. Damaged by Bf 109 near Dungeness, Flt Lt Smith abandoned aircraft, crashed New Romney, 31 August 1940.
P9439	To 72 Sqn 11 May 1940. To Scottish Aviation 26 June 1940. To 72 Sqn 2 September 1940. To 602 Sqn 14 December 1940.
P9443	To 222 Sqn.
P9444:RN-A	From RAE 4 June 1940. Airframe overstrained in dive after Plt Off Elliot passed out through lack of oxygen and crash-landed, 3 July 1940. To 1 CRU.
P9448	From ETPS 4 June 1940. Damaged by Bf 109 and force-landed, Flg Off Thompson injured, 1 September 1940. To AST.
P9457	To 72 Sqn 3 May 1940. Shot down by Bf 109 near Dungeness, Flg Off E.J. Wilcox killed, 31 August 1940.
P9458	To 72 Sqn 3 May 1940. Shot down by Bf 109 over Kent, Flg Off O. St J. Pigg killed, 1 September 1940.
P9460	To 72 Sqn 4 May 40. To 61 OTU 1 July 1941.
R6704	From 616 Sqn 2 September 1940. Shot down by Bf 109, Sgt Bell-Walker injured, 18 October 1940. To Scottish Aviation
R6710	From 266 Sqn 6 September 1940. Damaged by Bf 109, Plt Off Douthwaite injured, 11 September 1940. To Scottish Aviation.
R6721	From 603 Sqn. To 92 Sqn.
R6752	From 266 Sqn 27 March 1941. To 57 OTU 2 May 1941.
R6777	From 616 Sqn 2 September 1940. To 92 Sqn 3 November 1940.

R6881:RN-M	From 266 Sqn 6 September 1940. Shot down by Bf 109 near Canterbury, Plt Off Lindsay safe, 20 September 1940.
R6916	To 72 Sqn 22 July 1940.To GAL 11 August 1940.
R6928	To 72 Sqn 15 August 1940. Destroyed in air raid at Biggin Hill, 31 August 1940.
R6971	From 610 Sqn 19 August 1940. Shot down by Bf 110 near Hartfield, aircraft abandoned, Plt Off Males safe, 4 September 1940.
R6981	To 72 Sqn 24 July 1940. To 54 Sqn 9 August 1940.
R7022	From 266 Sqn 6 September 1940. Shot down by Bf 110, Sgt White safe, 7 September 1940.
R7069	
RN-O *Jason*	To 72 Sqn 30 March 1941. To 111 Sqn 26 April 1941.
R7265	From 91 Sqn. To 313 Sqn.
R7298	From 610 Sqn. To 309th FS USAAF.
X4013	From 610 Sqn. Shot down by Bf 109s, Elham, Kent, 5 September 1940
X4024	To 72 Sqn 11 October 1940. To 92 Sqn 11 October 1940.
X4034	To 72 Sqn 11 August 1940. Shot down by Bf 109 over Hawkinge, Kent, Flg Off Sheen abandoned aircraft, injured, 5 September 1940.
X4063	To 72 Sqn 9 September 1940. Shot down by Bf 109 near Gravesend, Plt Off B.W. Brown safe.
X4101	To 72 Sqn 8 December 1940. To 485 Sqn 11 May 41.
X4109	To 72 Sqn 13 August 1940. Damaged by Bf 109 and abandoned. Crashed at Court Lodge Farm, Ham Street, Kent, Flg Off Sheen safe, 1 September 1940.
X4167	From 74 Sqn 1 December 1940. To 57 OTU 2 May 1941.
X4239	From 602 Sqn 11 February 1941. To 303 Sqn 19 July 1941.
X4252	From 266 Sqn 6 September 1940. Swung on night take-off and ran onto soft ground and overturned at Acklington 16 January 1941.
X4254	From 266 Sqn 6 September 1940. Badly damaged by Bf 110 over Thames Estuary and crash-landed at Biggin Hill, Flg Off Elsdon injured, 7 September 1940.
X4262	To 72 Sqn 2 September 1940. Damaged by Bf 109 near Herne Bay and abandoned, Marden, Kent, 2 September 1940.
X4279	From 7 OTU 24 October 1940. Cannon equipped. To Rolls-Royce 6 February 1941.
X4337	To 72 Sqn 7 September 1940, damaged by a Bf 109 18 September 1940. To AST.
X4340	To 72 Sqn 9 September 1940. Shot down by Bf 109 near Sevenoaks, Plt Off E.E. Males killed, 27 September 1940.

X4410	To 72 Sqn 17 September 1940. Shot down by Bf 109 near Ashford, Kent, Plt Off Holland abandoned aircraft, killed, 20 September 1940.
X4413	To 72 Sqn 14 September 1940. To 57 OTU 2 May 1941.
X4416	To 72 Sqn 13 September 1940. To 222 Sqn 17 October 1940.
X4419	To 72 Sqn 16 September 1940. To 92 Sqn 20 October 1940.
X4478	To 72 Sqn 20 September 1940. To 66 Sqn 23 September 1940.
X4480	To 72 Sqn 20 September 1940. To 92 Sqn 22 September 1940.
X4481	To 72 Sqn 20 September 1940. To AST.
X4483	To 72 Sqn 23 September 1940. To 485 Sqn 29 April 1941.
X4486	To 72 Sqn 24 September 1940. To 122 Sqn 5 June 1941.
X4487	To 72 Sqn 24 September 1940. To 92 Sqn 24 September 1940.
X4488:RN-C	To 72 Sqn 24 September 1940. To GAL.
X4544	To 72 Sqn 27 September 1940. Collision with K9989 during scramble, Sgt Staples safe, 5 October 1940. To 123 Sqn 15 May 1941.
X4551 *Mimi I*	From 92 Sqn 28 September 1940. To 306 Sqn 6 November 1940.
X4595 *Tomiland*	To 72 Sqn 9 October 1940. To 57 OTU 2 May 1941.
X4596	To 72 Sqn 8 October 1940. To 123 Sqn 15 May 1941.
X4600 *Portsmouth & Southsea II*	To 72 Sqn 13 October 1940. To 57 OTU 2 May 1941.
X4601:RN-A *Argonaut*	To 72 Sqn 13 October 1940. To 485 Sqn 24 April 1941.
X4602:RN-B *Bahamas I*	To 72 Sqn 13 October 1940. To 485 Sqn 15 May 1941.
X4621 *Martin Evans Bevan*	To 72 Sqn 2 November 1940. To 485 Sqn 27 April 1941.
X4643:RN-F *Falkland Islands X*	To 72 Sqn 26 October 1940. To 485 Sqn 7 May 1941.
X4671:RN-G	
X4680	To 72 Sqn 17 January 1941. To Scottish Aviation.
X4766	From 61 OTU 26 November 1941. To 81 Sqn 15 December 1941.
X4855	To 72 Sqn February 1941.
X4857	To 72 Sqn 1 February 1941. To 57 OTU 2 May 1941.
X4918:RN-W *West Bromwich*	To 72 Sqn. To 123 Sqn 2 May 1941.
X4919	To 72 Sqn 2 March 1941. To FAR Defford 23 May 1942.
X4920 *Victor*	To 72 Sqn 3 March 1941. To 61 OTU 8 November 1941.
X4921 *Nix Over Six Primus*	To 72 Sqn 22 March 1941. To 57 OTU 2 May 1941.

Supermarine Spitfire Mk IIa

P7376	From 611 Sqn 23 April 1941. To 74 Sqn 9 July 1941
P7504	From 66 Sqn. To 74 Sqn.
P7551	To 74 Sqn.
P7751	To 72 Sqn 23 April 1941. To 74 Sqn 9 July 1941.
P7832:RN-P *Enniskillen*	To 72 Sqn 23 April 1941. To 74 Sqn 9 July 1941.
P7881:RN-G	
P7895:RN-N	From 65 Sqn 20 April 1941. To 74 Sqn 9 July 1941.
P7909:RN-N	
P7965	To 72 Sqn 24 April 1941. To 74 Sqn 9 July 1941.
P7968	To 72 Sqn 24 April 1941. To 74 Sqn 9 July 1941.
P8030	To 72 Sqn 6 May 1941. To 74 Sqn 9 July 1941.
P8042	To 72 Sqn 24 April 1941. To 74 Sqn 9 July 1941.
P8045 *City of Worcester*	To 72 Sqn 9 July 1941. Spun into ground Ouston, Northumberland, 2 August 1941.
P8091 *Miners of Durham II*	To 72 Sqn 6 May 41. To 74 Sqn 9 July 1941.
P8146 *Covent Garden*	To 72 Sqn 24 April 1941. To 74 Sqn 9 July 1941.
P8148:RN-Y *The Black Horse*	To 72 Sqn 3 May 1941. To 452 Sqn 7 July 1941.
P8149 *Lewis & Harris Fighter*	To 72 Sqn 6 May 1941. To 74 Sqn 9 July 1941.
P8164	From 65 Sqn 20 April 1941. To 19 Sqn 9 August 1941.
P8166	To 72 Sqn 3 May 1941. To 64 Sqn 20 August 1941.
P8174 *Baltic Exchange I*	From 65 Sqn 20 April 1941. To 122 Sqn 30 September 1941.
P8192	To 72 Sqn 24 April 1941. To 145 Sqn 30 July 1941.
P8200:RN-U *Winged Victory*	To 72 Sqn 24 April 1941. To 74 Sqn 9 July 1941.
P8231	To 72 Sqn 24 April 1941. Crashed in sea 4 miles north of Farne Islands. Believed shot down by return fire from Ju 88, 29 April 1941.
P8238 *Borneo*	To 72 Sqn 26 April 1941. To 74 Sqn 9 July 1941.
P8257	To 72 Sqn 23 April 1941. To 74 Sqn 9 July 1941.
P8322	To 72 Sqn 23 April 1941. To 74 Sqn 9 July 1941.
P8691	To 72 Sqn 9 July 1941. To 416 Sqn 14 January 1942.
P8750	To 401 Sqn.
P8751	To 416 Sqn.

Supermarine Spitfire Mk IIb

P8207	To 72 Sqn 23 April 1941. To 74 Sqn 9 July 1941.
P8252	To 72 Sqn 23 April 1941. To 74 Sqn 23 July 1941.
P8544 *Heart of England III*	To 72 Sqn. To 74 Sqn 5 July 1941.
P8631:RN-C *Ceredigion I*	To 72 Sqn.

Supermarine Spitfire Mk Va

P8706	To 72 Sqn 7 December 1941. To 154 Sqn 16 March 1942.
R6833	From 92 Sqn. To 312 Sqn.
R7293	*Rotherham & District* From 64 Sqn. To 72 Sqn. To 611 Sqn.
R7301	To 72 Sqn 28 March 1942. To RNDA Yeovilton 1 September 1942.

Supermarine Spitfire Mk Vb

P8541	To 64 Sqn
P8545	To 72 Sqn 30 April 1942. To 350 Sqn 20 May 1942.
P8560	From 74 Sqn 19 June 1941. To ASTH 14 August 1941.
P8600:RN-L *Lady Linlithgow*	Missing 10 July 1941.
P8604	Missing 10 July 1941.
P8609 *Heart of England II*	To 72 Sqn 27 July 1941. Ran out of fuel on return from sweep and abandoned 3 miles off Ramsgate, 27 August 1941.
P8700	To 72 Sqn 7 December 1941. To 154 Sqn 16 March 1942.
P8713	To 72 Sqn 27 July 1941. Missing escorting Blenheims to Hazebrouck, 29 August 1941.
P8741	
P8744 *Wonkers*	To 72 Sqn 21 November 1941. To Westland 11 January 1942.
P8749	To 72 Sqn 9 July 1941. To 610 Sqn 11 July 1941.
P8750	To 72 Sqn 9 July 1941. To Scottish Aviation 1 August 1941.
P8751	To 72 Sqn 10 July 1941. To Scottish Aviation 29 July 1941.
P8757:RN-Q *Quthung*	To 72 Sqn 14 July 1941. To 154 Sqn 13 June 1942.
P8783	To 72 Sqn 12 July 1941. To 401 Sqn 31 December 1941.
R7219 *Absque Labore Nihil*	From 74 Sqn. Shot down by fighters escorting Blenheims to Hazebrouck 14 July 1941.
R7228	From 74 Sqn 29 July 1941. Wheels prematurely raised on take-off, hit ground and crash-landed 1½ miles south-west of Valley, 26 August 1941.
R7265 *Grimsby I*	To 72 Sqn 30 September 1941. Engine failed take-off at Gravesend 5 December 1941. To Westland.

R7298	To 72 Sqn 28 October 1941. To ASTE 5 December 1941.
W3168	From 92 Sqn 24 October 1941. To 133 Sqn 15 June 1942.
W3170:RN-H *Henley on Thames*	From 74 Sqn 27 July 1941. Overturned on down-wind landing at Martlesham Heath, 5 April 1942.
W3178 *Thebe*	To 72 Sqn. To 401 Sqn 27 September 1941.
W3181 *City of Leeds I*	From 92 Sqn 9 July 1941. Ditched in English Channel while escorting Stirlings to Lille, 19 July 1941. Sgt R.F. Lewis killed.
W3229	To 72 Sqn 8 July 1941. To 306 Sqn 3 September 1941.
W3256	To 72 Sqn 8 July 1941. Missing escorting Blenheims to Mazingarbe 23 July 1941.
W3259	From 74 Sqn. To 74 Sqn.
W3316:RN-M *City of Salford*	To 72 Sqn 29 June 1941. Missing escorting Blenheims to Hazebrouck 24 July 1941.
W3321 *Elcardo The Thistle*	From 74 Sqn 19 August 1941. To 124 Sqn 29 June 1942.
W3367 *Lerumo*	From 74 Sqn 29 July 1941. Shot down by fighters on sweep to St Omer 7 November 1941. Plt Off H. Birkland (RCAF) POW.
W3380 *Basuto*	From 74 Sqn 27 July 1941. To ASTH 29 August 1941.
W3406:RN-I *Auckland II Mission Bay*	From 452 Sqn 13 February 1942. Shot down by Bf 109 escorting 6 Bostons to Abbeville marshalling yards 25 April 1942.
W3408 *Mr & Mrs Albert Ehrman*	To 72 Sqn 8 July 1941. Missing escorting Blenheims to Rotterdam 28 August 1941.
W3411	From 74 Sqn. Missing (Fruges) 10 July 1941.
W3429 *Mohale's Hoek/ Berea*	To 72 Sqn 20 July 1941. To 222 Sqn 15 February 1942.
W3430 *President Roosevelt I*	To 72 Sqn 20 July 1941. To 222 Sqn 14 May 1942.
W3431:RN-K *Kaapstad III*	To 72 Sqn 24 July 1941. To 403 Sqn 31 December 1941.
W3437:RN-L	
W3440 *Trengganu*	To 72 Sqn 10 July 1941. To 401 Sqn 8 December 1941.
W3441 *Alloway*	To 72 Sqn 10 July 1941. To 417 Sqn 24 April 1942.
W3446:RN-J *Jennifer/ Richards Basuto*	To 72 Sqn 1 May 1942. To 350 Sqn 20 May 1942.

W3511	To 72 Sqn 27 July 1941. Missing escorting Hurricanes to St Pol 8 November 1941. Plt Off N.E. Bishop killed.
W3513	To 72 Sqn 31 July 1941. To 54 Sqn 10 October 1941.
W3516	To 72 Sqn 27 July 1941. Missing on ground attack mission to Calais area 19 September 1941.
W3618	To 72 Sqn 30 August 1941. To 315 Sqn 1 September 1941.
W3624	To 72 Sqn 2 January 1942. To 504 Sqn 8 July 1942.
W3630 *Kuwait*	From 403 Sqn 20 October 1941. To 124 Sqn 17 November 1941.
W3648 *Wisbech*	From 609 Sqn 20 August 1941. To AST.
W3704 *Quacha's Nek*	To 72 Sqn 19 September 1941. Missing presumed shot down by Bf 109 near Dunkerque during sweep, 25 October 1941. Plt Off Falkiner missing.
W3771	To 72 Sqn 30 August 1941. To ASTH 9 September 1941.
W3841	To 72 Sqn 14 April 1942. To 121 Sqn 29 May 1942.
AA749 *Moshesh*	To 72 Sqn 3 October 1941. Missing from a ground-attack mission 8 December 1941.
AA841	From 412 Sqn 14 April 1942. To 121 Sqn 24 May 1942.
AA854	
AA864	To 72 Sqn 19 October 1941. Missing from sweep near Hesdin 8 December 1941.
AA867	To 72 Sqn 22 October 1941. To 222 Sqn 14 March 1942.
AA913	To 72 Sqn 12 November 1941. To 303 Sqn 8 April 1942.
AA914	To 72 Sqn 12 November 1941. Swung while taxiing in crosswind into an excavation at Biggin Hill 15 April 1942.
AA915	To 72 Sqn 12 November 1941. To 145 Sqn 15 November 1941.
AA920	To 72 Sqn 30 November 1941. To 124 Sqn 26 March 1942.
AA924	From 501 Sqn 26 April 1942. To 306 Sqn 18 May 1942.
AA945:RN-C	To 72 Sqn 11 December 1941. To 306 Sqn 22 August 1942.
AB150	To 72 Sqn 16 December 1941. Abandoned after engine cut 15 miles off Dunkerque 29 May 1942. Flg Off B.O. Parker (RCAF) killed.
AB152	From 124 Sqn. Spun into ground near Biggin Hill 28 May 1942.
AB194	To 72 Sqn 16 December 1941. To 111 Sqn 28 February 1942.
AB258	To 72 Sqn 28 December 1941. Missing presumed shot down near St Omer 4 April 1942.
AB260	From 611 Sqn 4 August 1942. To 504 Sqn 21 June 1943.
AB283:RN-F, RN-E	To 72 Sqn 2 January 1942. To ASTH.
AB324 *Mafeteng*	To 72 Sqn. To Middle East 3 May 1942.
AB375	From 124 Sqn. Shot down by Bf 109s near Calais 24 April 1942.
AB806	To 72 Sqn 22 August 1941. To 401 Sqn 21 October 1941. To 72 Sqn 23 March 1942. Shot down by Spitfire off Beachy Head 1 July 1942. Gp Capt P.R. Barwell DFC killed.

AB817 *Leribe*   To 72 Sqn 29 August 1941. To 452 Sqn 5 March 1942.

AB818 *Maseru*   To 72 Sqn 30 August 1941. To AST 7 December 1941.

AB822 *Harding* To 72 Sqn 30 August 1941. Shot down by Bf 109 10 miles off Dover 26 October 1941, Sgt L. Stock killed.

AB843   To 72 Sqn 28 July 1941. Missing from sweep to Mazingarbe, presumed shot down by Bf 109s near Mardyck, 27 September 1941. Sgt A.F. Binns killed.

AB848   To 72 Sqn 28 December 1941. To 332 Sqn 20 August 1942.

AB854   To 72 Sqn 27 July 1941. To AST 23 August 1941.

AB855   From 611 Sqn 24 October 1941. Missing near St Pol 8 November 1941, Sgt D.R. White killed.

AB864 *Makesi*   To 72 Sqn 30 September 1941. To AST 23 December 1941.

AB870   To 72 Sqn 18 November 1941. To 308 Sqn 24 August 1942.

AB879 *Hawkes Bay I Dannaevirke*   To 72 Sqn.

AB893 *Lilepe*   To 72 Sqn 20 August 1941. Abandoned after engine problems on return from sweep 19 miles east of Dungeness 8 November 1941.

AB922 *Liphamola*   To 72 Sqn 29 August 1941. To 401 Sqn 26 October 1941.

AB979   To 72 Sqn 4 April 1942. Collided with AB150 while taxiing at Biggin Hill 13 April 1942. To Westland

AD134   To 72 Sqn 30 August 1941. To 401 Sqn 17 March 1942.

AD183:RN-H   To 72 Sqn 30 September 1941. On return from Boston escort the pilot baled out over Brighton. Crashed near Ditchling, Sussex, 15 March 1942.

AD274 *Mokhotlong*   To 72 Sqn 11 October 1941. To ASTH.

AD324   To 72 Sqn 24 October 1941. To GAL.

AD347:RN-C   To 72 Sqn 2 May 1942. Damaged Cat B on ops 8 June 1942. To Westland.

AD375   To 72 Sqn 23 March 1942. Missing presumed shot down by Fw 190s south-east of Calais 12 April 1942.

AD386   To 72 Sqn 5 April 1942. To 133 Sqn 15 June 1942.

AD467   To 72 Sqn 28 October 1941. To ASTH 28 November 1941.

AD513   From 121 Sqn. To 340 Sqn.

AR347   To 167 Sqn

BL267   From 610 Sqn 29 July 1942. To 222 Sqn 15 August 1942.

BL318   To 72 Sqn 15 December 1941.

BL331   To 72 Sqn 8 January 1942. To 616 Sqn 8 January 1942.

BL334:RN-I   From 222 Sqn 26 April 1942. To 411 Sqn 18 May 1942.

BL338   To 72 Sqn 21 November 1941. To ASTH.

BL345	To 72 Sqn 8 January 1942. To 616 Sqn 8 January 1942.
BL418	From 611 Sqn 4 August 1942. To 71 Sqn 12 August 1942
BL496	To 72 Sqn 26 January 1942. To 65 Sqn 26 January 1942.
BL516	To 72 Sqn 13 May 42. To USAAF 6 September 1942.
BL636	From 611 Sqn 4 August 1942. To 71 Sqn 13 August 1942.
BL638 *Borough of Acton*	To 72 Sqn. To VASM 10 October 1942.
BL721 *Garut*	To 72 Sqn 22 February 1942. Escort Bostons to St Omer hit by flak and shot down 4 April 1942.
BL728	To 72 Sqn 15 March 1942. To 111S 16 May 1942.
BL733	To 72 Sqn 4 April 1942. To ASTH.
BL763	To 72 Sqn 26 April 1942. To 340 Sqn 18 May 1942.
BL773	To 72 Sqn 22 February 1942. To GAL 15 March 1942.
BL810	From 611 Sqn 4 August 1942. To 303 Sqn 1 June 1943.
BL857	To 72 Sqn 15 February 1942. Engine cut, force-landed 2 miles north of Eastchurch 12 April 1942.
BL864	To 72 Sqn 17 March 1942. SOC 13 April 1942.
BL935	To 72 Sqn 3 March 1942. Missing presumed shot down by fighters near St Omer, Flt Sgt T. Watson killed.
BL941	To 72 Sqn 13 April 1942. To 411 Sqn 18 May 1942.
BL979	From 401 Sqn 4 April 1942. To AST.
BM117	From 611 Sqn 4 August 1942. To AST 29 October 1942.
BM122	From 611 Sqn 4 August 1942. To Scottish Aviation.
BM125	To 72 Sqn 4 April 1942. Missing presumed shot down by Fw 190s south-east of Calais, 24 April 1942. Sgt R.P.G. Reilly killed.
BM143	From 611 Sqn 4 August 1942. To HAL 3 November 1942.
BM189	From 611 Sqn 4 August 1942. Hit h/t cables in mock attack and made a wheels-up landing at Dalmellington, Ayr, 6 August 1942. To Scottish Aviation.
BM192	From 611 Sqn 4 August 1942. To HAL 9 November 1942.
BM193	From 71 Sqn.
BM195	From 611 Sqn 29 July 1942. To 610 Sqn 27 December 1942.
BM210:RN-Z	
BM211	From 611 Sqn 4 August 1942. To 416 Sqn 29 March 1943.
BM253	From 501 Sqn 16 May 1942. To 65 Sqn 4 August 1942.
BM256:RN-F *Dorothy Mary*	From 501 Sqn 16 May 1942. To 65 Sqn 4 August 1942.
BM265:RN-T *The Pride of Newport*	From 331 Sqn 12 May 1942. To 243 Sqn 30 August 1942.
BM271 (LF Mk Vb) *Kenya Daisy*	From 133 Sqn 15 June 1942. To 65 Sqn 29 March 1943.

BM290	To 72 Sqn summer 1942.
BM291	To 72 Sqn.
BM300:RN-E	From 133 Sqn 15 June 1942. To 65 Sqn 4 August 1942.
BM313:RN-H	
Connie	From 331 Sqn 12 May 1942. To 234 Sqn 4 June 1942.
BM326	From 501 Sqn 14 May 1942. To 65 Sqn 4 August 1942.
BM327	To 72 Sqn 10 May 1942. To AST 16 July 1942.
BM345	From 331 Sqn 12 May 1942. To AST 16 May 1942.
BM361	From 41 Sqn 28 July 1942. To 71 Sqn 2 August 1942.
BM366	To 72 Sqn 29 July 1942. To 41 Sqn 2 August 1942.
BM384	To 72 Sqn 17 April 1942. Crashed into the sea while checking a raft off Dungeness 9 May 1942. Plt Off D.O. Waters (RNZAF) killed.
BM402	To 72 Sqn 15 May 1942. To RAE June 1942.
BM413	From 611 Sqn 4 August 1942. To 232 Sqn 23 September 1942.
BM418	From 133 Sqn 15 June 1942. To 65 Sqn 4 August 1942.
BM450	To 72 Sqn. Force-landed at Biggin Hill 5 June 42. To 65 Sqn.
BM470	From 133 Sqn 15 June 1942. To 52 OTU 5 February 1943.
BM484	To 72 Sqn 16 May 1942. Shot down by Fw 190s near Calais 26 July 1942. Sqn Ldr H.R. Tidd killed.
BM485	To 72 Sqn 16 May 1942. To 65 Sqn 14 August 1942.
BM490	From 132 Sqn 15 June 1942. To 322 Sqn 3 August 1942.
BM492	From 132 Sqn 15 June 1942. To VASM 18 August 1943.
BM495	To 72 Sqn.
BM515	From 133 Sqn 15 June 1942. To 65 Sqn 4 August 1942.
BM516	To 72 Sqn 10 May 1942. To 65 Sqn 14 August 1942.
BM518	From 133 Sqn 15 June 1942. To 65 Sqn 4 August 1942.
BM529	From 133 Sqn 14 June 1942. To 65 Sqn 4 August 1942.
BM591	To 72 Sqn 7 June 1942. To 133 Sqn 15 June 1942.
BM636	From 71 Sqn.
BM653	To 72 Sqn 12 July 1942. To 315 Sqn 4 September 1942.
EN793	From 121 Sqn 28 July 1942. To 306 Sqn 20 August 1942.
EP181	To 72 Sqn 10 September 1942. To 602 Sqn 18 December 1942.
EP183	From 302 Sqn 10 September 1942. To 610 Sqn 25 March 1943.
EP285	To 72 Sqn 28 July 1942. To 52 OTU 27 January 1943.
EP597	To 72 Sqn 30 August 1942. To VASM 21 June 1943.
EP904	To Gibraltar 14 September 1942. To 72 Sqn. Damaged Cat 2 5 January 1943.
EP911	To Gibraltar 1 November 1942. To 72 Sqn. SOC 31 December 1942.
EP914	To Gibraltar 1 November 1942. To 72 Sqn. To NW Africa 28 February 1943.
EP962	To Gibraltar 6 November 1942. To 72 Sqn. To NW Africa 28 February 1943.
EP981	To 72 Sqn 1 November 1942. To NW Africa 28 February 1943.
ER142	To Gibraltar 1 November 1942. To 72 Sqn. To Malta 1 July 1943.

ER257	To Gibraltar 1 November 1942. To 72 Sqn. SOC 31 January 1943.
ER307	To Gibraltar 9 November 1942. To 72 Sqn. To NW Africa.
ER490	To Gibraltar 6 November 1942. To 72 Sqn. To NW Africa 28 February 1943.
ER555	To Gibraltar 6 November 1942. To 72 Sqn. SOC 31 January 1943.
ER564	To Gibraltar 6 November 1942. To 72 Sqn. To NW Africa 28 February 1943.
ER586	To 72 Sqn. Belly-landed near Mateur 21 December 1942.
ER589	To 72 Sqn.
ER590	To Takoradi 27 December 1942. To 72 Sqn. To Middle East 18 January 1943.
ER598	To Gibraltar 6 November 1942. To 72 Sqn. To Middle East 23 December 1942.
ER603	To Gibraltar 6 November 1942. To 72 Sqn. SOC 31 December 1942.
ER615	To Gibraltar 6 November 1942. To 72 Sqn. To 111 Sqn.
ER620:RN-Z	To Gibraltar 6 November 1942. To 72 Sqn. Nosed over on landing Souk el Khemis, damaged Cat 2 17 December 1942.
ER635:RN-M	To Malta 1 July 1943. To 72 Sqn. SOC 26 April 1945.
ER656	To Gibraltar 6 November 1942. Crashed in forced landing 15 miles south of Souk-el-Khemis 8 February 1943.
ER660	To Gibraltar 9 November 1942. To 72 Sqn. To NW Africa 28 February 1943.
ER678	To 72 Sqn. Collided with ER589 and crashed west of Jefra 26 January 1943.
ER726	To 72 Sqn. FTR ops 2 January 1943.
ER732	To 72 Sqn. Damaged in air raid at Souk-el-Arba 31 December 1942.
ER808	To 72 Sqn. To Middle East 19 January 1943.
ER812	To 72 Sqn. Damaged Cat 3 on ops 17 January 1943.
ER878	To 72 Sqn. Hit by ER598 after landing at Souk-el-Khemis, 23 January 1943.
ER962	To 72 Sqn. Missing from ground attack mission 5 January 1943.
ER964	To 72 Sqn.

APPENDIX 10

No. 72 Squadron and the Great Escape

The two 72 Sqn pilots involved in the Great Escape were Al Hake and Hank Birkland. Al joined the squadron at Gravesend in February 1942, and flew fourteen sorties before being shot down on 4 April. He was subsequently held as a POW in *Stalag Luft III*.

Hank Birkland joined the squadron at Biggin Hill in September 1941, and flew his first sortie on 1 October, an offensive sweep led by Sqn Ldr Sheen. Flt Lt Kosinski (Polish) shot down a Bf 109E and probably destroyed another between Calais and Dover. Later the same day Birkland took part in an ASR search in the Channel for two pilots missing while escorting a rescue launch off Calais.

The following day Hank Birkland took part in *Circus* No. 104, an offensive sweep led once again by Sqn Ldr Sheen from Berck to Abbeville. The rendezvous with the bombers did not go as planned, and a diversionary sweep was flown instead, during which fifteen Bf 109s were seen and several dogfights ensued, during which Sqn Ldr Sheen probably destroyed one.

On 3 October Hank Birkland took part in *Circus* No. 105 to Ostend power station. Heavy flak was encountered, and several pilots reported seeing a Spitfire going down with its tail cut off. Birkland returned with undercarriage trouble but managed to land safely.

Hank Birkland's next sortie was on the 13th, *Circus* No. 108B to Mazingarbe power station. The wing crossed the coast east of Gravelines and encountered small formations of enemy fighters over the target. Returning from the target the squadron was attacked by Bf 109Es. There were several inconclusive tussles before the squadron returned, Birkland and three others landing at Manston short of fuel.

Hank Birkland did not fly again until the 21st, when an ASR sweep was flown by fifteen aircraft to provide cover for rescue launches. During this sweep Yellow Section was attacked by four Bf 109s, which quickly escaped before they could be engaged.

On 23 October Hank took part in a routine convoy patrol, and on the 26th an ASR sortie, with nothing seen. The following day it was a *Rodeo* operation, during which the wing had to orbit Gravelines several times to allow stragglers to catch up. During the last orbit the wing was attacked from above and the formation scattered. At least two aircraft were seen to go down over France, Sgt Falkiner being one of those who failed to return. Hank's last patrol of the month was on the 31st, with nothing seen.

Hank Birkland next flew on 3 November on a routine convoy patrol off Southend, and carried out another in the same area on the 7th. Later that day the squadron flew a *Rodeo*. As it was leaving the Berck area, Blue Section was attacked by Fw 190s from above and behind. Flt Lt Campbell and Plt Off Rosser of Yellow Section turned to meet the attack, and Rosser saw pieces come away from the Fw 190 he attacked. The Fw 190 began to lose height rapidly, and Rosser closed in firing till he ran out of ammunition. Sgt Rutherford reported that he thought he had seen one of Blue Section going down between Berck and Boulogne – it was Hank Birkland.

Al Hake had survived the dogfights of 4 April 1942 only to have a chance anti-aircraft shell smash his propeller and send his Spitfire out of control. Regaining control he set course for England, only to be bounced by a formation of Fw 190s. Al turned to fight and managed to down one of them. Losing height rapidly, his engine caught fire, and Al left the Spitfire with minor shrapnel wounds and burns, landing heavily close to a German troop depot. He was taken to a hospital to have his wounds dressed. During the fight his rank insignia had been burned off his battledress and the Germans assumed he was an officer, and planned to send him to an officers' POW camp. Al did nothing to disabuse them of this notion. A month after being shot down Al Hake was in East Compound of *Stalag Luft III*, where he would be joined later by Hank Birkland.

Stalag Luft III had been built as a result of the numerous escapes by RAF aircrew from other camps. Initially RAF aircrew had been held in *Stalag Luft I* at Barth on the Baltic coast, but following several escapes the *Luftwaffe* decided to split up the 'troublemakers', sending them to several camps. This only increased the 'escaping problem' by spreading the hard-line escapers all over Germany. Consequently, *Stalag Luft III* was constructed to hold all the 'bad boys' in one camp.

On his arrival Al Hake was looking forward to cultivating his own vegetable garden, but his skill in making gadgets was brought to the attention of Roger Bushell, 'Big X', by another POW, Johnny Travis, and Al was soon working on compass production for would-be escapers.

Originally three tunnels were begun – Tom, Dick and Harry. Tom was discovered by the Germans, but work continued on the others, with the plan to have at least 200 POWs escape simultaneously. The German guards were extremely alert, and it was decided to stop work on Harry on 15 September 1943, giving the workers a rest and at the same time concentrating effort on Dick.

Al Hake had just recovered from diphtheria, and he set up a compass factory in Block 103, his team working steadily throughout the winter producing compasses. Then, on the night of 24/25 March 1944, the escape was on. Among those to get out before the tunnel was discovered were Al Hake and Hank Birkland. On the night before the escape Hank Birkland wrote a last letter to his family, in which he said, 'I am not in a position to carry on a letter-for-letter correspondence for long.'

By the 27th many of the escapers had been recaptured, and among those arriving at Sagan jail was Hank Birkland. Hank had planned to do a solo run disguised as French workman. Initially travelling with Les Brodrick and Denys Street, Hank's journey took him over open ground covered in deep snow. Frequently back-tracking to avoid farms, they lay up in a hollow in a wood and were able to make some hot drinks. Their blankets were soaked through and they tried to doze, making the best of it. On the second night, trudging through hip-deep snow, they continued, lying up again the next morning. By now they were tired, cold and hungry, and annoyed by the inactivity of lying up they decided to carry on. By dark they entered another forest and struggled on for a few hundred yards before collapsing exhausted.

By now Hank was becoming affected by the damp and cold, and was showing signs of hypothermia, and so Denys and Les decided to find a place to hole up. They approached a farmhouse, and Denys, who spoke fluent German, spun a tale of being lost French workers on the way to a new job. Almost immediately things went wrong as four German soldiers rushed out of the farmhouse. Hank's escape was over. The small group was taken to the police station in Kalkbruch, and a few hours later transferred to Sagan police station.

Al Hake had managed to stay at large a little longer, but he too was captured, and on the afternoon of 29 March arrived at Sagan prison accompanied by Johnny Pohe. They had had a very rough time and Al Hake was suffering from frostbite. Later they were moved to Gorlitz prison, where the other POWs tried their best to ease Al's pain from the frostbite.

Many of the escapers had been returned to *Stalag Luft III*, and spent some time in the 'cooler' before being released into the camp, and it was not till 15 April that the full horror of the intervening days came to light. A list of forty-seven names was posted of those who had been shot allegedly attempting to escape.

The horror began on 30 March, when several prisoners were led out of their cells, among them Al Hake. They were seen to get into a covered truck, and it was hoped that Hake and Pohe were going to have treatment for the frostbite. Twenty-four hours later another group, including Hank Birkland, were pushed into a truck and taken away. Those remaining thought they were going to Sagan.

Al Hake and Johnny Pohe met their end in the woods outside Gorlitz, shot down along with Mike Casey, Ian Cross, Tom Leigh and George Wiley. Hank Birkland was murdered alongside Wally Valenta, Adam Kolanowski, Hunk Humphreys, Cyril Swain, Pat Langford, George McGill, Bob Stewart, Brian Evans and Chaz Hall, in a clearing outside Gorlitz. Chaz Hall had written jokingly on the cell wall, 'We who are about to die salute you.'

In July 1947 the war crimes trial in the *Stalag Luft III* case commenced, and when it ended fourteen of the first eighteen defendants were sentenced to hang for the murders of the escapers. One sentence was reduced later to life imprisonment, but the others were hanged in Hameln jail. It took until 1968 to track down and try all of the murderers, with the last, Franz Schmidt of the Kiel Gestapo, being tried and sentenced to two years for the deaths of four POWs.

The members of Breslau Gestapo involved in the executions were never found, believed to have died in the heavy fighting there, and the Soviets refused to hand over Wilhelm Scharpwinkel, who it was later claimed had died, though others believed he had merely exchanged one secret-police uniform for another.

Presentation Spitfires

No. 72 Squadron had re-equipped with Spitfires, and all of the World War II presentation aircraft that 72 Sqn flew were of this type, but of various marks. Basutoland donated seventeen Spitfires out of a total of seventy named aircraft that served with 72 Sqn.

The presentation Spitfires would not necessarily remain with the first allocated squadron, and would often be sent to an MU for repair and reallocated to another squadron. Spitfire Mk II P8149 LEWIS & HARRIS FIGHTER is a good example. It started life with 24 MU in March 1941, then was allocated to 72 Sqn in May before going to 74 Sqn in July 1941. After two visits to repair centres it went to 24 MU in October and then to 350 Sqn in December. In March 1942 it was on Northolt Station Flight and was struck off charge in July 1945 as beyond repair. The presentation aircraft used by the squadron included the following:

Spitfire Mk Ia R7069 JASON
One of four Spitfires presented with a donation of £20,000 by Sir Frederick Richmond and family of 91 Wimpole Street, London W1, with a name taken from Greek mythology, Mk Ia R7069 was taken on charge at No. 12 MU Kirkbride on 15 February 1941, the reason for the choice of name being unknown. From there the aircraft went to No. 72 (Basutoland) Sqn at Acklington on 30 March to take part in convoy patrols off the east coast. On 10 April Sgt Casey destroyed a Ju 88 near Alnmouth, one mile below low-water mark, off Boulmer. The aircraft was transferred to No. 111 Sqn at Dyce on 26 April.

Spitfire Mk Ia X4551 MIMI I
Donated by the Calcutta Swimming Club, X4551 was received from 92 Sqn on 28 September 1940 and passed to 306 Sqn on 6 November 1940.

Spitfire Mk Ia X4595 TOMILAND
Presented by the Madras Mail, X4595 was delivered to 72 Sqn on 9 October 1940 and passed on to 57 OTU on 2 May 1941.

Spitfire Mk Ia X4600 PORTSMOUTH & SOUTHSEA II
This Spitfire was donated with funds from Portsmouth and Southsea and delivered to 72 Sqn on 13 October 1940. It was passed on to 57 OTU on 2 May 1941.

Spitfire Mk Ia X4601:RN-A ARGONAUT
A Mk Ia, X4601 ARGONAUT was presented in August 1940 by the Hudson Steam Fishing Co. Ltd, trawler owners of St Andrew's Dock, Hull, with a

donation of £5,000, which was later included in the Hull Warplanes Fund total. It was taken on charge at No. 9 MU Cosford, on 7 October 1940, and six days later joined No. 72 (Basutoland) Sqn at Leconfield, flying sector and convoy patrols, and on the 25th Plt Off N.R. Chesters shot down a Bf 110 five miles east of Hornsey. It was sent to Scottish Aviation Ltd on 31 March 1941 for repairs, returning to No. 72 (Basutoland) Sqn on 9 April. The next owner was No. 485 (New Zealand) Sqn at Leconfield, coded OU-G, on 24 April 1941.

Spitfire Mk Ia X4602:RN-B BAHAMAS I
Purchased with donations from the Bahamas, this Spitfire was delivered to 72 Sqn on 13 October 1940. It later passed to 485 Sqn on 15 May 1941.

Spitfire Mk Ia X4621 MARTIN EVANS BEVAN
Donated by Martin Evans Bevan, X4621 was delivered to 72 Sqn on 2 November 1940. It was handed over to 485 Sqn on 27 April 1941.

Spitfire Mk Ia X4643:RN-F FALKLAND ISLANDS X
Funded by the Falkland Islanders, X4643 was delivered to 72 Sqn on 26 October 1940. It was later taken on charge by 485 Sqn on 7 May 1941.

Spitfire Mk Ia X4918:RN-W WEST BROMWICH
Funded and donated by the citizens of West Bromwich, X4918 was issued to 72 Sqn and later passed to 123 Sqn on 2 May 1941.

Spitfire Mk Ia X4920 VICTOR
Donated by Major James Kerr of Johannesburg, X4920 was issued to 72 Sqn on 3 March 1941 before serving with 61 OTU from 8 November 1941.

Spitfire Mk Ia X4921 NIX OVER SIX PRIMUS
Two Spitfires were presented with a donation of £10,000 by F.W. Woolworth & Co. Ltd, and given names which related to Woolies' pre-war policy of 'nothing over sixpence (2½p), PRIMUS indicating the first so named. Mk Ia X4921 was taken on charge at No. 12 MU Kirkbride on 12 January 1941 and allocated on 22 March to No. 72 (Basutoland) Sqn, flying North Sea patrols and sector reconnaissance from Acklington until joining No. 57 OTU at Hawarden on 2 May.

Spitfire Mk IIa P7832:RN-P ENNISKILLEN
Presented through the *Belfast Telegraph* Spitfire Shilling Fund, Mk IIa P7832 was taken on charge at No. 6 MU Brize Norton on 1 January 1941. On 12 January, while ferrying from Brize Norton to Tangmere, Flg Off W.C. Potter met deteriorating weather and had to make a forced landing at Farnborough, but overshot and hit an obstruction, causing Category C damage. The aircraft went on the 20th to No. 1 Civilian Repair Unit at Cowley for repairs, and then was flown to No. 12 MU Kirkbride on 7 April, to be allotted to No. 72 (Basutoland) Sqn at Acklington on 23 April, flying convoy patrols. On 9 July, Nos 72 and 74 Sqns exchanged aircraft and bases, and No. 74 (Trinidad) Sqn took over P7832 for convoy patrols.

Spitfire Mk IIa P8045 CITY OF WORCESTER
Donated by the people of Worcester, P8045 was delivered to 72 Sqn on 9 July 1941. The Spitfire spun into the ground at Ouston, Northumberland, on 2 August 1941.

Spitfire Mk IIa P8091 MINERS OF DURHAM II

Mk IIa P8091 was taken on charge at No. 24 MU Ternhill on 8 March 1941. The aircraft was allocated on 6 May to No. 72 (Basutoland) Sqn at Acklington, flying convoy and Kipper patrols. On 8 July the squadron flew down to Gravesend to exchange bases and aircraft with No. 74 (Trinidad) Sqn, which brought P8091 back to Acklington for more convoy patrols.

Spitfire Mk IIa P8146 COVENT GARDEN

Purchased by the people of Covent Garden, this Spitfire was delivered to 72 Sqn on 24 April 1941 before being passed to 74 Sqn on 9 July 1941.

Spitfire Mk IIa P8148:RN-Y THE BLACK HORSE

In August 1940 the directors and staff of Lloyds Bank Ltd donated sufficient in five days to pay for one and a half Spitfires It was hoped that there would be enough for three Spitfires when all contributions were in, but the final total was in fact £7,107. This was sufficient for one Spitfire, to be named BLACK HORSE. The 'Black Horse' sign had been handed down to Lloyds in 1677 by Barnett, Hoare & Co., who previously occupied the headquarters site. Mk IIa P8148 was delivered to 45 MU Kinloss on 15 March 1941, and allotted on 3 May to No. 72 (Basutoland) Sqn at Acklington for convoy patrols. Sgt E.W. Perkins carried out a perfect belly-landing at Acklington when the undercarriage failed to lower on 11 June. After being repaired the aircraft went on 7 July to No. 452 Sqn at Kirton-in-Lindsey.

Spitfire Mk IIa P8149 LEWIS & HARRIS FIGHTER

The 30,000 fishermen and crofters of the Islands of Lewis and Harris in the Outer Hebrides took just one week in September 1940 to collect £6,606 to donate Mk IIa P8149, which was taken on charge at No. 24 MU Ternhill on 6 March 1941, and later modified to Mk IIb. The aircraft was allocated on 6 May to No. 72 (Basutoland) Sqn at Acklington for convoy patrols and the occasional scramble. No. 72 Sqn moved on 8 July to Gravesend, where No. 74 (Trinidad) Sqn left its Mk Vbs and took P8149 back to Acklington.

Spitfire Mk IIa P8174 BALTIC EXCHANGE I

Purchased by the Baltic Mercantile Shipping and issued to 72 Sqn on 6 May 1941 before passing to 122 Sqn on 30 September 1941.

Spitfire Mk IIa P8200:RN-U WINGED VICTORY

The first of two Spitfires presented with donations of £5,000 each by Mr Frederick F.A. Pearson, an American multi-millionaire living at Sulby Hall, Rugby, Warwickshire, Mk IIa P8200 was taken on charge by No. 45 MU Kinloss on 19 March 1941. The aircraft was flown to No. 72 (Basutoland) Sqn at Acklington on 24 April for east coast convoy patrols. Sgt Harrison claimed a Do 17Z damaged south-east of Alnwick on 18 May. The squadron moved to Gravesend on 8 July to re-equip with Mk Vbs.

Spitfire Mk IIa P8238 BORNEO

Purchased by the people of the Netherlands, Borneo was issued to 72 Sqn on 26 April 1941. It passed to 74 Sqn on 9 July 1941.

Spitfire Mk IIb P8544 HEART OF ENGLAND III

Donated by the citizens of Leamington, Warwick and others. Passed to 74 Sqn on 5 July 1941.

Spitfire Mk IIb P8631:RN-C CEREDIGION
Purchased by the people of Aberystwyth and allocated to 72 Sqn.

Spitfire Mk Va R7293 ROTHERHAM & DISTRICT
Presented by the Rotherham Spitfire Fund, Yorkshire, with a donation in
November 1940 of £6,000, Mk Vb R7298 was taken on charge at No. 9 MU Cosford
on 5 April 1941 It was damaged in a flying accident on 22 June, being repaired
and delivered to No. 610 (County of Chester) Sqn at Westhampnett on 10 July to
fly sweeps, *Circus* and *Rhubarb* operations. The aircraft was damaged and sent to
Air Service Training Hamble on 14 August for repairs, awaited collection on 11
October and was sent to No. 8 MU Little Rissington three days later. From there
it was allocated to No. 72 (Basutoland) Sqn at Gravesend on 28 October, engaged
on similar duties until 27 November, when Sgt S. Croft hit a starter trolley and
the undercarriage collapsed, the aircraft being taken to Air Service Training at
Eastleigh on 5 December for major inspection and repairs. R7298 was awaiting
collection on 28 April 1942 and delivered to No. 38 MU Llandow on 9 May.

Spitfire Mk Vb P8600:RN-L LADY LINLITHGOW
Donated by the people of Scotland. Issued to 72 Sqn and went missing on 10
July 1941.

Spitfire Mk Vb P8609 HEART OF ENGLAND II
Purchased by donations from the Leamington and Warwick area and allocated
to 72 Sqn on 27 July 1941. The Spitfire ran out of fuel on return from a sweep and
was abandoned three miles off Ramsgate on 27 August 1941.

Spitfire Mk Vb P8744 WONKERS
Allocated to 72 Sqn on 21 November 1941 and passed to Westland for repair on
11 January 1942.

Spitfire Mk Vb P8757:RN-Q QUTHUNG
Purchased by donations from Basutoland and allocated to 72 Sqn on 14 July
1941. Passed to 154 Sqn on 13 June 1942.

Spitfire Mk Vb R7219 ABSQUE LABORE NIHIL
Purchased by the people of Darwen, Lancashire, and initially issued to 74
Sqn. Passing to 72 Sqn, it was shot down by fighters escorting Blenheims to
Hazebrouck on 14 July 1941.

Spitfire Mk Vb R7265 GRIMSBY I
GRIMSBY I and II were presented through the Grimsby Spitfire Fund by the
chairman, Mr Edwin Bacon, an 89-year-old trawler owner, with a cheque for
£9,436 1s. 4d. Mr Bacon, who had contributed to the fund himself, had already
loaned £45,000 free of interest to the Chancellor of the Exchequer, and was
persuaded by the mayor to make this fact public as an example to others.
Mk Vb R7265 GRIMSBY I was taken on charge at No. 6 MU Brize Norton on
29 March 1941, and allotted on 2 May to No. 91 (Nigeria) Sqn at Hawkinge,
engaged on sweeps, bomber escort and *Rhubarb* operations. Damage incurred
on operations on 13 June took the aircraft to Air Service Training for repairs on
17 June, emerging at No. 24 MU Ternhill on 22 July, to be allocated to No. 72
(Basutoland) Sqn on 30 September. Based at Biggin Hill, R7265 flew sweeps,
Circus and *Rhubarbs*, Plt Off P. De Naeyer claiming a Bf 109E probably destroyed
on 8 November. On 5 December the engine failed on take-off and the aircraft

overturned, injuring Plt Off R.G. Bates. R7265 was taken to Westland Aircraft at Ilchester for repairs on 12 December. When these were completed on 2 May 1942 it was handed over to No. 33 MU Lyneham on the 9th to be allocated to No. 313 (Czechoslovak) Sqn at Hornchurch on 25 July and returned to offensive operations.

Spitfire Mk Vb W3170:RN-H HENLEY-ON-THAMES
Donated by the citizens of Henley-on-Thames and allocated to 74 Sqn on 27 July 1941 before passing to 72 Sqn. This Spitfire overturned during a downwind landing at Martlesham Heath on 5 April 1942.

Spitfire Mk Vb W3178 THEBE
Presented by Basutoland and allocated to 72 Sqn before passing to 401 Sqn on 27 September 1941.

Spitfire Mk Vb W3181 CITY OF LEEDS I
One of four Spitfires donated by Mr W.E. Layland and the Leeds Spitfire Fund with a contribution of £20,000, Mk Vb W3181 was one of the three resulting from a donation of £15,000 in November 1940. Taken on charge at No. 6 MU Brize Norton on 17 May 1941, it was allotted on 11 June to No. 92 Sqn at Biggin Hill, and on 16 June the CO, Sqn Ldr J. Rankin, claimed a probable Bf 109F near Le Touquet. W3181 was damaged on operations on 28 June, and after repair passed to No. 72 (Basutoland) Sqn at Gravesend on 9 July, flying sweeps and bomber escort duties. On 19 July, engaged on *Circus* 51, it was shot down and ditched in the Channel while escorting Stirlings to Lille. Sgt Raymond Frederick Lewis 754684, aged 20, of Shirley, Southampton, is listed on Panel 47 of the Runnymede Memorial.

Spitfire Mk Vb W3316:RN-M CITY OF SALFORD
Purchased by the citizens of Salford and issued to 72 Sqn on 29 June 1941. Went missing escorting Blenheims to Hazebrouck on 24 July 1941.

Spitfire Mk Vb W3321 ELCARDO THE THISTLE
Donated by Lady Davidson, this Spitfire served with 74 Sqn from 19 August 1941 before serving with 72 Sqn and then being passed to 124 Sqn on 29 June 1942.

Spitfire Mk Vb W3367 LERUMO
Donated by Basutoland and issued to 74 Sqn on 29 July 1941. Passed to 72 Sqn and was shot down by fighters on a sweep to St Omer on 7 November 1941. Plt Off H. Birkland (RCAF) became a POW.

Spitfire Mk Vb W3380:RN-J BASUTO
Presented by Basutoland and named after the main tribe in that country, the name was put forward in October 1940, and in due course Spitfire Mk Vb W3380 was taken on charge at No. 33 MU Lyneham on 21 June 1941, and then allotted on 6 July to No. 74 (Trinidad) Sqn operating from Gravesend and Biggin Hill, flying sweeps and bomber escorts. No. 72 (Basutoland) Sqn moved to Gravesend on 8 July, and exchanged its Mk IIs for the Mk Vbs of No. 74 (Trinidad) Sqn, which then flew to Acklington the next day. Now coded RN-J, W3380 began an almost non-stop round of sweeps, *Rhubarb* and bomber escort operations. On 17 August, Sqn Ldr D.F.B. Sheen DFC, the squadron commander, claimed a Bf 109 damaged

five miles south-west of Cap Gris Nez, followed by a Bf 109E claimed damaged six miles east of Hazebrouck on 20 August, and another claimed as a probable at Abbeville on 2 October. On 6 November the undercarriage collapsed as Flt Lt C.N.S. Campbell landed, being repaired on site by 21 November. W3380 joined No. 412 (RCAF) Sqn at Wellingore on 26 January 1942. It flew with several other units, but then on 2 September 1944 W3380 was passed to No. 53 Operational Training Unit at Kirton-in-Lindsey, until sent to No. 33 MU Lyneham on 6 June 1945. On 10 September the aircraft was dispatched to Portsmouth Aviation for scrap and was struck off charge on 14 September 1945.

Spitfire Mk Vb W3406:RN-I AUCKLAND II MISSION BAY
Donated by New Zealand and first used by 452 Sqn from 13 February 1942, transferring to 72 Sqn, where it was shot down by a Bf 109 while escorting six Bostons to Abbeville marshalling yards on 25 April 1942.

Spitfire Mk Vb W3408 MR & MRS ALBERT EHRMAN
Purchased by Mr & Mrs Ehrman and allocated to 72 Sqn on 8 July 1941, this Spitfire went missing escorting Blenheims to Rotterdam on 28 August 1941.

Spitfire Mk Vb W3429 MOHALE'S HOEK/BEREA
Donated by Basutoland and allocated to 72 Sqn on 20 July 1941. Passed to 222 Sqn on 15 February 1942.

Spitfire Mk Vb W3430 PRESIDENT ROOSEVELT I
Purchased by the Warner Brothers Pictures Corporation and issued to 72 Sqn on 20 July 1941. Passed to 222 Sqn on 14 May 1942.

Spitfire Mk Vb W3431:RN-K KAAPSTAD III
Purchased by the citizens of Capetown, South Africa, and allocated to 72 Sqn on 24 July 1941 before passing to 403 Sqn on 31 December 1941.

Spitfire Mk Vb W3440 TRENGGANU
Purchased by Welsh donations and issued to 72 Sqn on 10 July 1941. Passed to 401 Sqn on 8 December 1941.

Spitfire Mk Vb W3441 ALLOWAY
Donated by Mr J.W. McConnell of Montreal, Canada, and issued to 72 Sqn on 10 July 1941. Passed to 417 Sqn on 24 April 1942.

Spitfire Mk Vb W3446:RN-J JENNIFER/RICHARDS BASUTO
Purchased by funds from Montreal, Canada and Basutoland, this Spitfire was allocated to 72 Sqn on 1 May 1942 before passing to 350 Sqn on 20 May 1942.

Spitfire Mk Vb W3630 KUWAIT
Purchased with contributions for forces in the Persian Gulf, and allocated to 403 Sqn on 20 October 1941 before passing to 72 Sqn which, in turn, passed it to 124 Sqn on 17 November 1941.

Spitfire Mk Vb W3648 WISBECH
Purchased with donations from Cambridgeshire, this Spitfire flew with 609 Sqn from 20 August 1941 before being taken on charge by 72 Sqn. It later moved to AST for repair.

Spitfire Mk VB W3704 QACHA'S NEK

One of many Spitfires presented by Basutoland, Mk Vb W3704 was named after a district in the south-western area of that country, the name having been put forward in October 1940. It was taken on charge on 28 August 1941 at No. 37 MU Burtonwood, to be allocated on 19 September to No. 72 (Basutoland) Sqn at Biggin Hill, engaged on sweeps and bomber escort operations. On 27 September Flt Lt R.M.D. Hall claimed a Bf 109 probably destroyed fifteen miles north of St Omer. On 27 October W3704 was reported missing from a *Rodeo* near Dunkirk, and was presumed to have been shot down by Bf 109s, Sgt F. Falkiner, Aus.400220 RAAF, being taken prisoner, to end the war as POW No. 39540 in *Stalag 9C* at Muhlhausen.

Spitfire Mk Vb AA749 MOSHESH

Purchased by Basutoland and allocated to 72 Sqn on 3 October 1941, it went missing on a ground attack mission on 8 December 1941.

Spitfire Mk Vb AB324 MAFETENG

Purchased by Basutoland and issued to 72 Sqn before going to the Middle East on 3 May 1942.

Spitfire Mk Vb AB817 LERIBE

Purchased by Basutoland and issued to 72 Sqn on 29 August 1941 before passing to 452 Sqn on 5 March 1942.

Spitfire Mk Vb AB818 MASERU

Purchased by Basutoland and allocated to 72 Sqn on 30 August 1941. Sent to AST on 7 December 1941.

Spitfire Mk Vb AB822 HARDING

Purchased by Basutoland and allocated to 72 Sqn on 30 August 1941. Shot down by a Bf 109 ten miles off Dover on 26 October 1941. Sgt L. Stock was killed.

Spitfire Mk Vb AB864 MAKESI

No. 72 (Basutoland) Sqn and No. 74 (Trinidad) Sqn exchanged aircraft on more than one occasion, and it is probably due to this that Mk Vb W3259 MAKESI, presented by Basutoland, is recorded as having served only with No. 74 (Trinidad) Sqn. The aircraft was one of five aircraft given the names of regiments of paramount chiefs, each of which bore the name of an important chief used in the 'Lithoko', or songs of praise. The name, which had been put forward in October 1940, also means 'swift hunting dog'.

Spitfire Mk Vb AB879 HAWKES BAY I DANNAEVIRKE

Purchased by donations from New Zealand and allocated to 72 Sqn.

Spitfire Mk Vb AB893 LILEPE

Purchased by Basutoland and allocated to 72 Sqn on 20 August 1941. Abandoned after engine problems on return from a sweep nineteen miles east of Dungeness on 8 November 1941.

Spitfire Mk Vb AB922 LIPHAMOLA

Purchased by Basutoland and issued to 72 Sqn on 29 August 1941. Passed to 401 Sqn on 26 October 1941.

Spitfire Mk Vb AD274 MOKHOTLONG
Purchased by Basutoland and issued to 72 Sqn on 11 October 1941, later passing to AST at Hamble.

Spitfire Mk Vb BL638 BOROUGH OF ACTON
Purchased by donations from London, this Spitfire was issued to 72 Sqn before going to VASM on 10 October 1942.

Spitfire Mk Vb BL721 GARUT
Purchased by the Netherlands and allocated to 72 Sqn on 22 February 1942. Shot down by flak while escorting Bostons to St Omer on 4 April 1942.

Spitfire Mk Vb BM256:RN-F DOROTHY MARY
Purchased by Canadian donations, this Spitfire was issued to 501 Sqn on 16 May 1942 and passed to 72 Sqn before moving to 65 Sqn on 4 August 1942.

Spitfire Mk Vb BM265:RN-T PRIDE OF NEWPORT
Purchased with Welsh donations, this Spitfire went to 331 Sqn on 12 May 1942 before reaching 72 Sqn, which then passed it to 243 Sqn on 30 August 1942.

Spitfire Mk Vb BM271 KENYA DAISY
Purchased by the pyrethrum growers of Kenya and issued to 133 Sqn on 15 June 1942 before passing to 72 Sqn and then on to 65 Sqn on 29 March 1943.

Spitfire Mk Vb BM313:RN-H CONNIE
Named by Sgt 'Robbie' Robertson, and received from 331 Sqn. Passed to 234 Sqn on 4 June 1942.

Spitfire Mk Vc JG806:RN-E PORT OF SUDAN KASSALA
Purchased by the Sudan Warplane Fund and issued to 72 Sqn in 1943.

Spitfire Mk Vc JK132:RN-B EL FASHER DARFUR PROVINCE
Purchased by the Sudan Warplane Fund and issued to 154 Sqn before passing to 72 Sqn and then on to 3 Sqn SAAF.

Spitfire Mk IX MA511 URUGUAY XI
Purchased with Uruguayan donations and issued to 72 Sqn in November 1943. Shot down by flak while chasing a Bf 109 four miles south of Ceccaro on 19 December 1943.

Spitfire Mk IX MA520:RN-B, RN-S SUNSHINE
Donated by Mrs F. Tucker and allocated to 72 Sqn, this Spitfire undershot on landing, hitting a tree, and the undercarriage collapsed at Falcone on 6 September 1943.

Spitfire Mk IX BETTY
Serial unidentified. Flown by Plt Off Des Gorham.

MOSHOESHOE
Presented by Basutoland. The name means 'the Shaver'. Not identified.

THABA BOSIU
Purchased by Basutoland. Serial and mark not identified.

WEBU
Purchased by Basutoland. Serial and mark not identified.

Bibliography and References

—, *The War Years 1939–1945, Eyewitness Accounts*, Marshall Cavendish Books, 1994

Bowyer, Chaz, *History of the RAF*, Bison Books Ltd, 1977

Bradford Telegraph & Argus articles – 22 March & 17 November 1943

Corbin, William James, and Mannings, Erik, Monograph: 'Memories of 72 Squadron', privately published, 2006

Elliot, Group Captain R. Deacon, OBE DFC RAF, *World War II December 1939–December 1940*, RAF Museum Ref. X002–5542

Frampton, Laurie and Mannings, Erik, Monograph: 'Into The Blue – With Seventy Two', privately published, 2007

Hooton, E.R., *Eagle in Flames, The Fall of the Luftwaffe*, Brockhampton Press, 1999

Lake, Alan, *Flying Units of the RAF*, Airlife Publishing Ltd, 1999

Lancaster, Jack, with Mannings, Erik, Monograph: 'All The Way With 72 Squadron', privately published, 2007

London Gazette, The

Mannings, Erik, Monograph: 'Sgt Allan James Casey 748049', privately published, 2007

No. 72 Squadron, from 540 Operations Record Book 1939–61

Ogley, Bob, *Biggin on the Bump*, Traplet Publications, 1990

Ogley, Bob, *Ghosts of Biggin Hill*, Froglet Publications, 2001

Rawlings, John, *Fighter Squadrons of the RAF and their Aircraft*, Crecy Books Ltd, 1993

Richards, Denis, and Saunders, Hilary St G., *Royal Air Force 1939–45, II The Fight Avails*, HMSO, 1954

Scrase, Rodney, and Mannings, Erik, Monograph: 'Spitfire Saga', privately published

Shaw, Michael, *No. 1 Squadron*, Ian Allan Ltd, 1986

Shores, Christopher and Williams, Clive, *Aces High*, Grub Street, 1994

Smith, David J., *Action Stations 7*, PSL, 1983

Wood, Derek, with Dempster, Derek, *The Narrow Margin*, Arrow Books, 1969

Useful websites:

The Wartime Memories Project: www.wartimememories.co.uk

North-East Diary: www.bpears.org.uk/ne-diary

RAF History: www.rafweb.org

Out of Service British Military Aircraft: www.demobbed.org.co.uk

Index